CATCHING
THE VISION

Working together
to create a millennial ward

CATCHING THE VISION

Working together to create a millennial ward

WILLIAM G. DYER

Bookcraft
Salt Lake City, Utah

Library of Congress Catalog Card Number: 93-73462
ISBN 0-88494-908-7

First Printing, 1993

Printed in the United States of America

Contents

Acknowledgments

This book has not been an easy one to write. Over a period of years, I have done major revisions four times. I owe a great debt to Hugh Nibley who, in *Approaching Zion,* a remarkable volume of speeches and essays (Salt Lake City: Deseret Book Company, 1989), has described eloquently the attitudes and behaviors necessary to establish the Lord's economic order so there will be no poor in Zion.

Bonnie has been an unfailing source of inspiration to me for our entire life together. I have watched her struggle with health problems and other adversities that would have devastated another being; she has considered them opportunities for spiritual maturing. Her good qualities have guided the progress of all of our children and grandchildren, and to live with them through eternity is my own greatest goal.

I gratefully acknowledge my debt to some of the people who have helped me understand some of those elements that must be present if people are to live together in complete faith and love: Reed Bradford, Jack Gibb, Bob Hamblin, Bob Dyer, Phil Daniels, Weldon Moffitt, Gene Dalton, Abc Maslow, Jerry Harvey, and Elder Neal Maxwell.

Introduction

Embedded deep in the doctrine of the restored Church is the belief that in the last days the Savior will come to earth in glory and will rule personally over the righteous for a thousand years. Both during his mortal mission among the Jews (see Matthew 24) and to Joseph Smith in our own period (see D&C 45:16–59), Christ identified the signs of the winding-up period that would precede his millennial reign.

Sign-watching is not a highly valued activity among us. Self-styled prophets in other denominations who have selected a given Tuesday morning upon which their white-clad followers will meet the Savior on a certain hill have always faced the fact that on Tuesday evening they have had to pull off the sheets and traipse back down the hill to the (admittedly relieved) jeers of their townspeople. Yet sign-watching is enjoined upon the believers: "He that feareth me shall be looking forth for the great day of the Lord to come, even for the signs of the coming of the Son of Man. And they shall see signs and wonders, for they shall be shown forth in the heavens above, and in the earth beneath." (D&C 45:39–40.) These individuals see in the catastrophic pattern of world events a signal that the coming of the Son of Man is nigh.

Others feel that sign-watching is a waste of time, even potentially dangerous to sound spirituality. They accept the position, also announced by Jesus, that "of that day and hour knoweth no man, no, not the angels of heaven, but my Father only" (Matthew 24:36). Like the ten wise virgins, they prefer to remain in constant readiness (Matthew 25:1–13). Both positions accept the doctrine that the Millennium will arrive and that the Lord will come to his people. I am aware of the dangers of sign-watching—of imposing a pattern that exists only in our minds on current events. Yet the dangers of complacency are even more lethal, dulling the awareness every Saint should have that the world we live in is not our true home.

Consider too this question, which also has profound implications: Can the Millennium begin if the Saints are not prepared to live a millennial law? Some feel that the fundamental issue is righteousness—if the wicked are all destroyed by the global devastations predicted as harbingers of the Millennium, then only the righteous will remain; their society, probably functioning under Church government, can be established to receive the Savior. (See D&C 65; 88:87–116.) They see a model in the Lord's first coming to the Nephites, who were winnowed by the whirlwinds and earthquakes until only the "more righteous" remnant remained. Still others see the necessity for first creating a society to receive the Savior, basing this conclusion on the Lord's instructions to Joseph Smith: "And Zion cannot be built up unless it is by the principles of the law of the celestial kingdom; otherwise, I cannot receive her unto myself" (D&C 105:5).

These scriptures encourage Saints in the direction of society-building; however, the record of Utopian societies leaves a great deal to be desired. From an organizational point of view they are, almost without exception, ineffectual, improperly conceptualized, and ineptly managed despite their inspiring goals. Furthermore, a significant few of such societies, in attempting to turn their backs on the world, have opened themselves to internal exploitation that has not stopped short of horrifying violence against their own members or outsiders.

But such discussions of the merit of each society miss the mark for me. I start from a different premise and raise a different question: How will members of the Church live during the Millennium? Our mode of life will certainly be different than the behavior that is currently typical in most wards and branches of the Church. In the scriptures we find two models, both described with frustrating brevity. The Nephites, during their golden age following the Savior's coming to them, had "no contentions and disputations." They "did deal justly one with another. And they had all things common among them; therefore there were not rich and poor, bond and free, but they were all made free, and partakers of the heavenly gift." (4 Nephi 1:2–3.) The people of Enoch "were of one heart and one mind, and dwelt in righteousness; and there was no poor among them." And they dwelled in "the City of Holiness, even Zion." (Moses 7:18–19.) We linger over these brief verses, with deep desire constructing vague images of perfect harmony, cooperation, and righteousness.

As a lifelong Latter-day Saint who has spent his entire professional career studying the challenges and successes of organizations, I am fascinated and absorbed by this question, not in terms of those two ancient agrarian societies but in terms of our own highly industrialized and technical society. Consider this question with me: What will our own wards and stakes look like and how will they function if we are seriously dealing with the question of being a prepared people?

First, for us to be a millennial people, each member will need to be seriously engaged in the process of becoming fully converted to the Savior. That is the ideal. The reality is that individuals vary markedly in their spiritual desires and capacities, although we believe that everyone has the potential to become fully mature in the testimony of Jesus. Our life as a religious community would simultaneously spring from this faith (which is in the process of growing into knowledge) and also be nurtured by it. We would take seriously the injunction of Paul to the Ephesians that the purpose of the organizational structure of the Church is "for the perfecting of the saints, for the work of the ministry, for the edifying of the body of Christ: till we all come in the unity of the faith, and of the knowledge of the Son of God, unto a perfect man, unto the measure of the stature of the fulness of Christ" (Ephesians 4:12–13).

The more modern New International Version casts this passage in perhaps more explicit terms: Church structure and organization exist "to prepare God's people for works of service, so that the body of Christ may be built up until we all reach unity in the faith and in the knowledge of the Son of God and become mature, attaining to the whole measure of the fullness of Christ." This translation continues:

> Then we will no longer be infants, tossed back and forth by the waves, and blown here and there by every wind of teaching, and by the cunning and craftiness of men in their deceitful scheming.

Instead, speaking the truth in love, we will in all things grow up into him who is the Head, that is, Christ.

From him the whole body, joined and held together by every supporting ligament, grows and builds itself up in love, as each part does its work. (NIV, Ephesians 4:12–16.)

Consider what a ward would be like in which "each part" did "its work . . . in love," prompted and fostered by a deep individual and collective faith in Christ! The shining principles behind our admittedly often lackluster programs would suddenly create new understandings. Suddenly? Perhaps not. But even slowly, the combination of work and love would be transformative.

Would presidencies have trouble staffing an organization? No, teachers would gratefully accept assignments, prepare with joy for the opportunity to testify regularly to the power of Christ in their lives, and thankfully see their assignments as an opportunity to nurture and serve the members of their classes.

Would inactivity be a problem? No, sacrament meetings would be filled to overflowing by members who, whether old or young, literally would rather be there than anywhere else because there they can feast on the Spirit. These meetings would be reverent celebrations of Christ's atonement, with each congregational hymn a collective prayer of gratitude and each talk an honest, inspired, and inspiring sharing of testimony.

Would officers need to nag about home teaching and visiting teaching? No, the desire to serve others would match a heightened sensitivity about others' needs. Statistics would become meaningless in a context of powerful prayers to know how to serve, the acknowledged privilege of being able to offer service, and the exquisite joy of doing "unto one of the least of these" the service so gladly offered to the Savior. The contributions of tithing, fast offerings, missionary funds, and other assignments would be willingly paid; and those with the ability to contribute more would find ways to secretly and generously relieve their needier neighbors.

What about personal spirituality? The scriptures would acquire a permanent fascination for young and old alike, with the refreshment of personal study being matched in enjoyment only by the deep pleasures of sharing insights and testimonies with family members, both in formal family home evenings and in quiet individual conversations with friends, with class members in auxiliary meetings, and with strangers.

Scrupulous honesty coupled with love would transform family and group life. People would abandon the petty pleasures of sarcasm, jealousy, gossip, and backbiting for the deep joy of strengthening and helping one another. The love within a family and within the community would become sacred, not to be blighted or tainted by deceit, cruelty, sexual sin, exploitation, or the exercise of unrighteous dominion. Even the few who maliciously rejoiced in sowing contention and giving offense would literally be unable to continue as those they injured honestly shared how it made them feel and freely forgave the perpetrators. Those committing unintentional offenses would be grief-stricken when they realized their mistakes, unable to rest until they had sought out their brother or sister and asked for forgiveness.

And radiating throughout such a community would be a consciousness of Christ—Christ the center of each heart and the center of the congregation. Whether voiced or silent, the implicit prayer of such individual and group life would be the prayer of John on the Isle of Patmos: "Even so, come, Lord Jesus" (Revelation 22:20).

I share with all members of the Church this longing for a Christ-centered community. I listen seriously to our prophets, seers, and revelators. I take seriously my personal responsibility to live a life worthy to stand in the presence of the Savior and am humbly aware of my inadequacies in doing so. And coupled with my longing for our future home is my sense of stewardship for the professional tools I have spent a lifetime acquiring, using, honing, and refining. These skills are also among the talents that I sincerely and humbly try to consecrate to the Lord. This book is a gift on the altar. I believe I have some potentially helpful insights to offer other men and women who also yearn quietly for the coming of the Savior and who are hungry to establish the righteousness of Zion and build a Christ-centered community.

My own deep interest in the approaching Millennium began when I was a child. Stories of the "last days" and the "great and dreadful day of the Lord," told in Sunday School and Primary, both fascinated and horrified me. I remember listening with wide-eyed awe and thorough fear to descriptions of how the elements of the earth would melt with fervent heat and the wicked would burn as stubble. Then World War II introduced me to evil and misery on a scale I had not imagined in Portland, Oregon, where I grew up. My heart ached, and I began to long for the coming of the Lord. I looked forward to it as a great day—not as a dreadful day.

It was probably the helplessness I felt in the face of human evil and its resulting burden of suffering that prompted my academic choices. I pursued a doctorate in the behavioral sciences and became interested in organizational and community development. I studied, did research, and worked as a consultant and change agent with a variety of organizations ranging from large companies like Exxon and AT&T to religious groups of many denominations, to government and school systems. I was strongly motivated to help people in these various human systems learn how to work together in an atmosphere of mutual trust and support, thereby reaping the rewards of creativity, high productivity, and—to put it simply—happiness.

Meanwhile, as Bonnie and I built our marriage and nurtured our four sons and our daughter, we found parenthood to be a severe test of my theories about how to create nurturing systems. Our home was the toughest and truest laboratory of these principles; and we learned lessons in integrity, unconditional love, and patience that we could not have approached in any other setting. I think we all sometimes tasted a kind of joy that gave us glimpses of what the Millennium might be like. I know that those moments kept us heart-hungry for more, while at the same time they temporarily satisfied our deepest longings.

As a professor at BYU, I started the Department of Organizational Behavior and began to prepare young graduate students, mostly Latter-day Saints, to follow a similar ideal in their professional lives. In 1956 I became bishop of the BYU Fourth Ward when the first stake was organized on a college campus. For the first time, I had the opportunity to try to create the kind of community with these young Church members that I had been trying to achieve in other organizations. It was a stimulating, stretching assignment. It was also frustrating. I struggled to keep my footing in the flood of programs that washed from Church headquarters. Most of my time went to administering these programs, and I struggled constantly to find spaces around them to build the kind of loving, trusting community that would truly nourish the spiritual hungers I knew these students had.

Almost thirty years later I was called to be a stake president in the same student stake where I had served as bishop. My idealism had only deepened, along with my commitment to helping people live together in effective, supportive relationships. My competencies had improved with experience and constant work, and I felt more confident in how I should behave. Also, the Church's posture had changed significantly. The General Authorities who came to counsel us told us that we were first to minister, second to administer. They told us that we should no longer expect all programs and instructions to come from Church headquarters; but within the general guidelines already established, we should use our own inspiration to shape activities that our people needed.

It was a wonderful four and a half years for me. I found the officers and members in my stake alive to this greater vision of themselves and eager to implement it. One of the bishops began each academic year by asking his young ward members to try to live like a Zion community. Many of them took that challenge seriously. Their freely offered love and selfless service was life-changing for many of them. I had many opportunities to reflect on the power of vision to change reality. I knew the desire these young, idealistic men and women experienced to create something better than what they currently knew, to give their all to a challenge worthy of their sacrifice. These experiences as their leader were crucial for me in conceptualizing millennial leadership.

I know that I am not the only individual, parent, or Church leader to ask myself, What would a leader need to do to help ward or family members begin to live at a higher level of righteousness? I strongly feel that every Church leader and teacher has been given the revealed principles for millennial living. We can help those for whom we have stewardship move to a higher level of spiritual effectiveness with the promptings of the Holy Ghost and with our willingness to let our faith in Christ empower our service.

This book is, in some sense, the fulfillment of an almost-life-long goal to combine my deep commitment to help build the Church and my understanding of the processes that bring about positive change in people. In 1972 I wrote a book about personal and organizational growth that stated the goal I still hold:

> I am by temperament, socialization, and inclination an idealist and a "helper." By profession I am an applied behavioral scientist, a professional consultant, and change agent.

My values and goals move me to keep trying to help people and organizations and society become better, somehow. Somewhere deep in me is the conviction that yearnings and striving for something finer in performance are characteristics of all men and women until and unless something or someone stunts those desires or causes them to die. An almost unpardonable sin, to me, is to be a "killer of dreams" in others.[1]

Leadership in a lay organization like the Church can be an ambiguous term. Because my interest lies in where we are, with our current organization, I use ward structure. This formal structure identifies leadership at the local level with a bishop or branch president, who acts under the direction of a stake or district president and who has been ordained and set apart to lead the congregation. This view inevitably overemphasizes the visibility of ordained priesthood leaders and underemphasizes the contributions of members, especially those of women. I hope that readers will be able to compensate for this imbalance from their own experiences.

It frequently happens that the sources of formal authority are not the same as the sources of moral and spiritual authority in a religious community. As a professional, I'm aware that leadership is shared. Every Church unit has a large number of men and women who are leaders—whether by virtue of their formal callings, by virtue of their individual spiritual authority, or—most happily—because of a combination of the two. No bishop's vision of millennial possibilities, no matter how inspiring, can function to change lives unless it is widely shared among the formal and informal leaders of his ward. Leadership motivates people to use their creative energies to accomplish important goals. Millennial leadership includes understanding the *principles* of Zion-like behavior and the *processes* necessary for their implementation. In a millennial community, the whole ward would be made up of leaders, both formal and informal. Both in and out of their callings, they would identify needs, love and serve others, and spontaneously do "many things of their own free will, and bring to pass much righteousness" (D&C 58:27).

Each chapter in this book is written in three parts: an explanation of a leadership principle, a story that illustrates the principle, and a discussion of the leadership principle and processes. The sto-

---

1. *The Sensitive Manipulator* (Provo, Utah: BYU Press, 1972), p. ix.

ries are examples, combinations of narratives and case studies drawn from the Plainville Second Ward, a mythical but fairly typical ward. George Pratt, the newly called bishop, seeks inspiration about his ward's needs and, rather than implementing new programs or beefing up old ones, is stirred by the possibilities of a Zion society. Writing fiction is not one of my gifts, although I enjoy reading it; but these narratives held the best promise, I felt, for dealing with realistic ward situations. In all cases, they are based on experiences that have happened to me personally, to my family, or to associates who have shared them with me and given me permission to adapt them for presentation here. I have not "invented" stories for two reasons: I wanted these accounts to have the ring of authenticity, and I felt I could hope more realistically for the accompanying witness of the Holy Ghost if I honored the real experiences of ordinary members of the Church.

I hope it is not presumptuous to say that I feel one of my personal contributions in this life may be to help people prepare to live in a millennial world. This book, a step in that direction, examines the principles and processes of leadership needed so that members of a ward can truly approach being of one heart and one mind, living righteously with one another, and growing together "in love, as each part does its work" (NIV, Ephesians 4:16). I hope it will encourage the same dream of preparing for Zion in others and that these dreams will someday be brought to complete fruition.

1

Vision and Personal Commitment

Behold, I will tell you in your mind and in your
heart, by the Holy Ghost, which shall come upon you
and which shall dwell in your heart (D&C 8:2).

The Principle

We can be called to a position of leadership, but that doesn't necessarily make us a leader except in the most formal sense. We become leaders, whether we act formally or informally, when we make a deep personal commitment to use our time and energy to accomplish the goals we identify, to minister to the needs of others, and to serve in a Christlike way. Some people occupy leadership positions but never function as leaders for the simple reason that they do not or cannot influence others to accomplish the mission or goals.

If we are committed to millennial leadership, then we must have a vision of our overall goals and be committed to taking action. In the Church, this commitment springs from a spiritual confirmation of the divinity of the Savior and of the Church's origins. All worthy action stems from this commitment, which can be confirmed to any member by the power of the Holy Ghost. Following this basic confirmed commitment is the vision of our leadership calling and a personal determination to fulfill it.

When Enoch was called by the Lord to become a leader and a prophet, he first resisted because he was focused on his inadequacies—his youth, his lack of popularity, and his lack of ability. He protested, "I . . . am but a lad and all the people hate me; for I am slow of speech; wherefore am I thy servant?" (Moses 6:31.) Many of us feel inadequate when we are called to a leadership position, but my experience and my testimony are that the Lord makes us equal to our callings. In Enoch's case, the Lord helped him first to gain a vision of what his mission was all about: "Anoint thine eyes with clay, and wash them, and thou shalt see" (Moses 6:35). What Enoch saw was a powerful vision of the earth from the beginning, all of "the spirits that God had created," and many "things not visible to the natural eye" (Moses 6:31–35). Few of us will receive such comprehensive visions, but Enoch's experience represents the process many of us must undergo. To overcome our feelings of inadequacy, we need to wash from our eyes any barriers to spiritual sight. Fortunately, the Holy Ghost is the power that helps people understand the spiritual reality of their personal situations and capabilities.

When we have a personal confirmation of the Savior and the Church, and a vision of our personal callings, we have entered the leadership path. Next, we need to take action—to share the vision, involve others, and begin to develop a plan for continuous activity. In the Doctrine and Covenants, the Lord instructs us first to obtain his "word" (his message, his vision) and then promises us his Spirit to declare his word by "the power of God unto the convincing of men" (D&C 11:21).

The Lord also rebuked some because they had a talent (or a testimony, or a vision) but would not open their mouths because of the fear of other human beings (see D&C 60:2).

In the following scene from the fictional Plainville Second Ward, the newly called bishop, George Pratt, enters this initial phase of leadership. He receives a personal confirmation of the vision of his calling, shares that vision with his united family, and then takes it to his file leader, the stake president.

Plainville Second Ward: Obtaining the Vision

At six o'clock, as Tuesday morning's sun began to scatter the light of early May between the trees, it found George Pratt on his knees in fervent prayer. He had tossed and turned much of the night, then had climbed silently out of bed at five o'clock so as not to awaken Phyllis, and sunk to his knees by the living room couch with a groan. Responsibility had pounded at him ever since he had been ordained and set apart as the new bishop of the newly created Plainville Second Ward in Plainville, Oregon, at ward conference in April. The first four weeks had been a merry-go-round of congratulations, of sorting out ward boundaries and records, of selecting his counselors and having them called, and of frantically staffing ward organizations. That part was over. He'd sat on the stand last Sunday, looking over the congregation and thinking, "There are just loose ends to tidy up now, so why do I feel so desperately that something of immense importance has been left undone?"

Was it just jitters, now that he had time to come to grips with the calling? George had struggled hard, trying to see himself as a bishop. He was not particularly well educated. He had graduated from high school, trained for two years at a technical college, and was now, at forty-two, production foreman in a local sheet-metal shop. Oregon had always been his home. Raised by a devout Mormon mother and a good father who had never joined the Church, George had never been deeply concerned about Mormonism's distinctive theological claims until he became the first missionary to serve from Plainville's little branch. The two years he spent in the New England Mission had literally changed his life. In all ways he had begun to blossom—his testimony, his self-confidence, his ability to speak and teach and even to lead others. Previously he had not thought of himself as a leader; but the years following his mission found him serving as a teachers quorum advisor, Scoutmaster, elders quorum counselor, elders quorum president, home teacher, and Sunday School teacher.

With gladness, George thought about Phyllis. "She is the best thing that ever happened to me," he marveled. They had met at a stake dance two years after his return from his mission—Phyllis was from a large ward in the stake and was home for the summer from Brigham Young University. During that first dance, George sensed that she was someone remarkable. Later when he called for a date, it pleased and surprised him that she accepted with such obvious pleasure. George knew he was in love after that first date. He spent as much time with her as he could, terrified by the speed with which the summer's end was approaching. When he haltingly expressed his love, he was literally speechless when Phyllis declared that she loved him, too.

They were married at Christmas, and their life together had been George's deepest happiness. Their four healthy and intelligent children were literal miracles to him. They had all the normal mischievousness, streaks of laziness, and fits of irritability of normal children, but George wholeheartedly credited Phyllis with how well adjusted and well rounded they were. Will was a cheerful and responsible sixteen-year-old, enjoying his newly earned driver's license. Susan was a quick-tongued and efficiency-minded thirteen-year-old with irresistible flights of imagination. Tommy, age nine, was a little shy and solemn outside the family but, within it, was generally thoughtful and sensitive. Ben, age five, was especially close to Will and effortlessly organized the neighborhood preschoolers in elaborate games of piracy, cowboys, and deep-sea divers that drew in the older children as well. George didn't see any of them as particularly spiritual, but they were good kids, decent and honest. For that matter, he didn't see himself as particularly spiritual.

Plainville's slow and steady growth had affected the Church as well. Seven years earlier, the branch had become a ward. Now the ward had been divided, and George was the new ward's first bishop. More than anything he could remember, George wanted to be a good bishop. Sure, he was prepared to work hard. He had determinedly read his way through the handbook already. He felt good about his counselors. They'd already had a preliminary meeting Sunday evening. But he was tormented by the sense that there was something else, something unusual about his calling that he had not yet seized. That uneasiness and sense of incompleteness had kept George awake and had brought him to his knees an hour earlier, pleading for guidance and direction from the Lord.

He sighed and rested his head on his hands. His ward. What did his ward need? He knew nearly everybody by name, though there were many he did not know well. Good people, trying hard. Decent people, salt of the earth, not particularly spiritual but . . . What did they need? The fragment of a scripture floated through his mind: "Of one heart, of one mind." He tensed, focusing on it. It was about Enoch's people, the City of Enoch. But wasn't that about living the United Order, something postponed until far in the future, while the law of tithes and offerings was the law for today? But what did money have to do with that scripture? "Of one heart," he thought with sudden intensity. "Of one mind. Be one. As I and the Father are one." Then a thought came with immense clarity into his mind—almost as though a voice were speaking to him. "Bring them to me as one. Live as though in my presence. Be a Zion people, a millennial ward."

George pushed himself to his feet, his mind locked on that extraordinary idea. His knees, stiffened by the hour of prayer, almost buckled, but he paid no attention. He paced slowly back and forth, repeating those three sentences over and over to himself. Being one. Being a millennial ward that could live with the Savior during the Millennium. Being a Zion people. And that sense of a burden for him: to *bring* them. He wondered, "Did I really get this message?" then dismissed the thought. He knew he had received his answer, and the challenge was clear and almost overwhelming. What would a millennial ward be like? Where would you start? How would you get the people to live in harmony like the people of the City of Enoch?

George opened his Pearl of Great Price, fumbling through Moses until he found the passage: "And the Lord called his people ZION, because they were of one heart and one mind, and dwelt in righteousness, and there was no poor among them" (Moses 7:18).

He shook his head and looked into the backyard, which was dappled and sunstreaked. He'd lived in Plainville most of his life. These members were good people, but they were far from being of one heart and mind. There were lots of differences among the Saints, and they did not dwell in righteousness. And there was that issue of money again. Some members were very affluent. Some were extremely poor. And both ends of the spectrum were likely to be pretty touchy about having it called to their attention. Why did economics seem to matter so much? How would he deal with all of these differences?

He looked at the cross-references. The last one listed "unity" in the Topical Guide. He read through the references, lingering over the last one in the Doctrine and Covenants ". . . and are not united according to the union required by the law of the celestial kingdom; and Zion cannot be built up unless it is by the principles of the law of the celestial kingdom; otherwise I cannot receive her unto myself." (D&C 104:4–5).

"That's at least a start," thought George. "I need to look for the principles revealed about the celestial kingdom and pattern the ward after those principles. I know the Millennium isn't the celestial world. Some principles like tithing are lesser laws. But I can start looking."

The household was waking up around him. Will was in the downstairs shower, and Susan was starting to practice the piano in the family room. Phyllis came quickly down the hall pulling her sweatshirt down, and he flashed her a grin as he went to shower and shave. She quirked an eyebrow questioningly, and he knew that she already could sense that he was concerned about something very important.

After supper that night, George dug into his pocket and said, "Will, if you think you can shepherd this bunch of wild Indians to the Baskin-Robbins, your mom and I will do the dishes."

"Reporting for duty, *sir*!" exclaimed Will happily, snapping him a crisp salute.

"Pistachio and choc'late almond fudge," chanted Tommy, hopping on one foot toward the door, while Susan scooped up Ben and followed him.

The hour that followed was a tender one. Phyllis listened comprehendingly as George related exactly what had happened and the challenge he felt he had received from the Spirit. His feelings almost overwhelmed him as he relived the moment, and she leaned tenderly against his shoulder, pausing in her swift drying of the silverware.

George picked up the scrubber and tackled the chicken pan ferociously. "I know I'm supposed to do it," he mumbled, "but I just don't see how I can. It's so—so lofty! And I'm not a college graduate. I'm not even such a great speaker. How is someone like me supposed to inspire people?"

He expected sympathy, or at most a noncommittal "Hmmm," but Phyllis surprised him. "George, your feelings remind me a lot of the answer Enoch gave the Lord when he was called. He wanted to reject his calling—said he was slow of speech and that the people hated him. You're better off than that. You aren't really slow of speech, and the members certainly don't hate you. But you've had a remarkable experience. How many new bishops get such clear direction? It just seems to me that you're going to have to get to work."

George looked at her in shock. She winked and slapped him

on the shoulder with her dishtowel. "I know you can do it, George," she said, "and you know I'll always help you."

George's self-pity vanished in a hurry, and Wednesday's dawn found him back in the dining room poring over the scriptures. At breakfast, George announced, "Will you please keep the evening free? I want to have a family council to discuss some important matters." He sounded a little awkward and pompous, even to himself, and Susan promptly asked, "What's up, Dad?"

"I don't have time to go into it now," George said, "but nobody's in trouble, if that's what you're worried about. Except maybe me."

"Oh," grunted Will comfortably. "Bishop stuff."

The children gathered willingly enough that evening. George lifted the phone off the hook and buried it under some cushions before he asked Phyllis to offer the prayer. Then, clearing his throat, he told the four children his experience Tuesday morning, adding: "This is really about living to come into the Savior's presence, maybe even living as if he's already here. I've never done it before. None of us have. I'm really serious about trying this, but I know I can't do it alone. It has to start here. I can't ask the ward members to do something that we're not doing. I feel we have to be of one heart and mind in our home, that we have to try to live as righteously as we can. You're good kids. I've always felt that you've been behind me and your mother, and we've always tried to support you. But I'm not sure we've ever tried to *go* anyplace before—in such a clear direction and with any kind of sense of urgency . . ." He paused, wondering if he had lost them.

Phyllis spoke up quietly. "I knew that your father would be a good bishop a long time before he received this calling. I knew I could be an adequate bishop's wife, too, although I certainly have never thought it's going to be a picnic. But I see that this isn't something just to slide through; and since your father told me about this yesterday, I've been thinking a lot. I really want to try this." Her voice rang with determination. "I want it with my whole heart. Everything we've ever tried to teach you kids about living the gospel and every reason that we've got for living the gospel ourselves comes down to exactly what Dad said: being united and being together, not just in this life but into the Millennium and into the celestial kingdom. Being with the Savior. I *want* this challenge. I'm grateful for it."

Susan, her eyes still resting on her mother's face, said softly: "Sure, Dad. I think about Jesus, but lots of times it's just really vague. Thinking about actually being with him. . . . Sure. I'll do anything I can."

"Me, too," offered Tommy. "I'll do everything we talk about in family home evening, too."

"Daddy, you can have all of the money in my piggy bank!" offered Ben eagerly.

George laughed, with a catch in his throat. "That won't be necessary right now, Ben. But it may come to a point where all of us will have to give all that we have."

Will said huskily: "I was real proud, Dad, when you were called. We talk a lot in priests' quorum about service and preparing for missions and stuff like that, but lots of times the Savior doesn't seem very real. This—I dunno—it makes him close, and I like the way it feels. I want to help. What do you think we need to do to live better?"

George heaved a deep sigh of mingled relief and pride. "Why don't we make a list of the things we think we could do better? We should think about two things: things we know that Jesus wants to happen and things the Church says are good things to do."

Phyllis observed dryly: "Well, first of all, it seems to me that the Church always says to put your family first; but how many bishops' families never see their father again except at church? Everybody else comes first because they only call if there are problems."

"Yeah," chimed in Will. "Tammy Roberts said that she knew the first week what her job was when her dad became bishop. She was not to cause problems and not to complain."

"Well, that would defeat the whole purpose of what we're trying to do," acknowledged George with a twinkle. "So how would you like to safeguard our time together?"

After forty-five minutes of brainstorming, they had a long list—some to do as a family, others to do as individual actions. They winnowed some out, consolidated others, and set some priorities that moved some items up the list and others off the list. The final list was ten items that they all agreed were very important and that they could do. Susan read it off in a clear treble:

"Number one. Make sure we read the scriptures and have

family prayer every morning after breakfast. This means we all have to be ready for breakfast fifteen minutes early." She stared meaningfully at Will.

"Hey, no sweat," shrugged Will.

"Number two. Dad will have a personal priesthood interview with each one of us kids every month. We'll put them on the schedule when we make up the calendar the last week of the previous month. And he and Mom will schedule their time together at the same time—date night, lunch, whatever—but that's supposed to be every week. Right?"

"Right," said George. Phyllis gave him the hint of a grin.

"Number three. We'll all have to do some extra chores because Dad won't be around so much. Mom will post family duties each week, and we'll all do our jobs without griping.

"Number four. Each one of us will think about one person our own age who needs a friend, and we'll try to be friendly to that person." Tommy looked a little anxious but nodded seriously.

"Number five," Susan continued. "Have a regular family night every Monday with everyone participating. The person who's in charge will give out assignments by Saturday, and we'll take turns helping Ben when it's his turn. And we start with Dad next Monday.

"Number six. Every day each family member will try to be as pleasant and kind to everyone as they possibly can be. Number seven, each one of us will try to obey all of the principles of the gospel that we can think of."

George interjected: "Boy, they sound a little heavy when we're just reading them off. Do you kids understand that you're not supposed to try to become perfect overnight and you're not supposed to try to do everything? I think it would be a good idea to talk over ideas you have about gospel principles—just so we can see that you're not trying to do something based on a misunderstanding. For instance, the Savior said, 'If thy right eye offend thee, pluck it out' (Matthew 5:29). Well, we don't want you to start looking for the forceps if you should happen to pick up a *Playboy* in the grocery store"—

Phyllis cleared her throat warningly. Will was staring at the carpet, his ears scarlet, and George hastily continued: "or happen to see something that you know you shouldn't be looking at. Is that clear?"

Susan nodded intently and continued, "Number eight. Every family member will write in his journal what he is doing and how he feels about his life. Ben can tell Mom, and she'll write down what he says."

"And this isn't supposed to be a righteousness checklist, either," added Phyllis. "You're not keeping score on yourself. *And*," she continued, "you're not keeping score on each other either, you understand? Same thing with Numbers six and seven. You don't get to tell other members of the family how they have failed to be kind and pleasant or how they should be living the gospel, okay?"

"Okay, okay. Number nine," Susan announced. "We will all accept Church assignments without complaining and will try to volunteer when we can see someone at church needs our help. And Number ten. If we see somebody with problems, like our neighbors or ward members, we'll talk about it and see if there's something we can do to help. There!" She beamed triumphantly around the room.

"I think it's a good list," said Will. He grinned mockingly at George, "We may actually see *more* of you now than before—if it works."

"To coin a phrase," said Phyllis, "it'll work if we do."

George had never been so proud of his family as he was when they closed that family council with prayer. As he knelt beside Tommy, hearing his earnest nine-year-old prayer, a strange feeling of intense love swelled in him, a momentary awareness of the essence of each personality, a sense of their infinite preciousness. Tears stung his closed lids. "Maybe this is already a taste of what it feels like," he thought humbly, "to be of one heart. Thank you, Father."

The next step was calling the stake president, who squeezed him in Thursday evening. George told John Stratford of his Tuesday morning revelation and his experience with his family. In a matter of two days much of his tentativeness had vanished. He was frankly eager for the next step, but he asked with real concern, "President, am I out of bounds? Is this within my jurisdiction as a bishop?"

President Stratford, who had listened absorbed and silent, weighed his words carefully. "Bishop, your dreams and goals are good. The General Authorities have told us that we are in the last time period of the earth's existence. At some point, all of us need to prepare ourselves to live in the Millennium. You have my permission—but just a word of caution. Don't impose your goals on your people. If you do, you'll destroy the very unity you're trying to accomplish."

"I know," George nodded. "'No power or influence can or ought to be maintained . . . only by persuasion . . . ,' right? I've thought about that a lot."

The president grinned. "You're not the kind to throw your weight around anyway, but that's right, Bishop. I think it's exciting. Give it all you've got. Keep in touch. If you run into difficulties, I'll be here to help."

George walked down the steps feeling invigorated and confident. He felt that what he was about to do was approved of by the Lord, his family, and his file leader in the Church. The next major challenge was how to explain his vision to the ward members so that the Holy Ghost would bear witness to them about it. At least I won't be tempted to rely on my own eloquence, he thought wryly. He breathed a prayer as he slipped his key into the ignition.

Discussion

George Pratt, a new bishop, has a pure desire to fulfill his calling perfectly, to be the best bishop he can be, and to provide the service to his people that the Lord would want. He has not accepted the calling because of its status or power. He recognizes the terrible possibility, identified by the Lord, that when a person gets "a little authority, as they suppose," the potential is always there for "unrighteous dominion" (D&C 121:39). Rather, George sees his calling as an opportunity for great service. Drawn by this selfless desire and also pushed by his own feelings of inadequacy, he fervently seeks the Spirit of the Lord, praying for direction.

This case could have involved any Church leader—a Primary officer, a Sunday School teacher, a home teacher, a quorum advisor—for the issue in any Church calling is the same. When we accept a calling, that is our stewardship; and we should fill that calling to the best of our ability as guided by the Spirit. A millennial spirit in a ward will come when every person in the ward accepts in the spirit of complete stewardship whatever calling he or she is given, pledging, "I will do everything I can to fulfill this calling to the best of my ability and live so I know that my actions are guided by the Spirit."

Phyllis reminds George to concentrate on faith in his strengths rather than fears about his inadequacies. The Lord has told us that every person is given a gift by the Spirit of God (see D&C 46:11). No one is left barren and giftless. Every person brings some gifts to any position. Part of our stewardship is to understand and magnify the gifts we have been given, to not envy the gifts of another.

George knows that he needs his family with him, not only because he needs their support but also because he can't behave like a phony with a public program that doesn't match his private life. We're all more effective in our callings if our homes are places where we can replenish our strength. And no test of a gospel principle in any other group can be as full and complete as the ongoing, twenty-four-hour-a-day challenges presented by the dailiness of family life. When a family is united in work and love, the resultant spiritual strength is enormous.

In the early days of the Church, the Lord chastised the early leaders, even Joseph Smith, telling them that their families were not in order and hence that they were not effective in their callings. The Lord rebuked Frederick G. Williams: "You have not taught your children light and truth, according to the commandments; and that wicked one hath power, as yet, over you, and this is the cause of your affliction. And now a commandment I give unto you—if you will be delivered you shall set in order your own house, for there are many things that are not right in your house."

Continuing the same revelation, the Lord told Sidney Rigdon "that in some things he [Sidney] hath not kept the commandments concerning his children; therefore, first set in order thy house."

And even to Joseph Smith, the Lord instructed: "You have not kept the commandments, and must needs stand rebuked before the Lord. Your family must needs repent and forsake some things, and give more earnest heed unto your sayings, or be removed out of their place." (D&C 93:41–48.)

This is not a mandate for harsh control but a mandate for loving leadership, as I read it—for a busy father to repent of neglect, for increased listening and understanding, for more "walking beside" and less "pushing from behind." Fathers are called to go back to their families and minister to their loved ones' spiritual needs rather than concentrating on the trappings of being efficient administrators.

With the same understanding, George shares his experience first with Phyllis, who willingly and intelligently supports him. Then he tells his children the desires of his heart and asks for their help. George's children are willing, even eager, to help. Together, they all work out a plan so they can feel that they are living righteously and George can, with integrity, ask for improved performance from ward members, knowing that as far as he can he has put his own house in order. Their family council shows the leadership ability of each family member. Phyllis not only supports George in the sense of believing his vision and being personally encouraging, but she also makes the goal of millennial family and ward life her own and identifies tasks she can accomplish that will actively support those goals. She is obviously a full partner with George in providing family leadership.

The children also feel a sense of partnership. At least part of their willingness stems from feeling their parents' affection and trust for each other and wanting to remain a part of that loving circle. In their respective ways, they also see George's vision and make it their own by identifying how they can help. In other words, understanding leads to commitment, which in turn leads to action. The vision is already stronger because George has been able to share it in a way that gives others ownership in it as well. It is no longer "my" goal but "our" goal. This is a service-oriented and Christ-centered view of leadership.

Thus, George found that the first steps on the millennial path were an abiding testimony of the Savior and his restored Church. Next, he received a specific answer to his plea for inspiration about direction and achieved the willing union of his family, then sought support from his file leader, the stake president. In the Church, all things must be done in order. Part of that order is to make sure that our personal visions about our callings are consistent with the vision of those who have watch care over us and to whom we are responsible.

While not everyone may receive so direct or comprehensive an answer from the Spirit as Bishop Pratt, we can all gain a vision of our own potential as families and our own callings in the Church if we follow the Lord's process. First we must have a deep commitment to the overall goal of the Church—to come and help others come unto Christ. We need to understand the three missions the prophets have currently defined that bring us to this goal: to preach the gospel, to redeem the dead, and to perfect the Saints.

Then we must understand how our personal calling or situation fits into the overall mission of the Church. This is done by reading relevant material, talking with knowledgeable people, and collecting others' experiences and suggestions. It is important not to make the same mistake as Oliver Cowdery did when he sought the gift to translate. The Lord told him, "Behold, you have not understood; you have supposed that I would give it unto you, when you took no thought save it was to ask me" (D&C 9:7). We cannot just ask the Lord to give us the insight and direction we need without doing our share, for he further counseled Oliver, "You must study it out in your mind; then you must ask me if it be right" (D&C 9:8).

Of course, praying during this part of the process is appropriate; but after we have done our part to capture the vision of our calling, we can pray with new purpose and power. It is my testimony that this is the stage at which the Lord confirms our understanding in our thoughts and feelings.

The Lord also expects all who have leadership callings to minister and serve others in his name and to exercise their own agency in implementing their plans. Our respect for the channels of authority and revelation should not suggest that we must wait to be told what to do. In one of the great revelations on stewardship, the Lord told the Saints that they should not have to be compelled in all things. Rather "men [and women] should be anxiously engaged in a good cause, and do many things of their own free will, and bring to pass much righteousness" (D&C 58:27). Such counsel honors the principle of free agency. There is little danger that we will be deceived into thinking a pet project is also the Lord's will—as long as we follow the procedural order of the Church by returning and reporting our inspiration and innovations to our file leader. This step is also part of being one and acting in harmony.

I freely acknowledge that the Pratt family is atypical. Only 19 percent of LDS households in the United States in 1981 were two-parent, temple-sealed couples with dependent children, and the divorce rates and economic pressures that have propelled women into the work force have only intensified in the last decade. I have chosen the Pratt family because it offers some advantages in creating this fictional ward. But I believe that because these principles of millennial leadership are true they will work under other circumstances: for part-member families, for two-career couples, for couples with rebellious children who choose not to support a family goal, for family members who have physical or mental limitations that severely limit their agency, and for spouses or extended family members who see the gospel in different ways. All of these families and individuals are equally precious to the Lord; and obviously, by the very nature of mortality, we know that the Lord does not expect us to be in perfect circumstances before we begin living the gospel.

Often, we think of consecrating only our strengths or of consecrating our time instead of our lack of time and our breathless, breakneck schedule. We think of consecrating talents like a wonderful singing voice instead of a limitation, like Moses' inability to speak fluently. We think of consecrating our physical strength instead of a chronic illness or even a terminal disease that will someday remove us from mortality. We think of consecrating our wealth instead of our limited means or even our poverty. The same is true of our family circumstances.

I insist on this point because there is a sometimes distressing tendency in the Church to say "the family" and mean just one kind of family—a temple-sealed couple with several children. Although this situation may be the ideal, the ideal, by definition, is not often the reality. Through my use of the Pratt family, I do not want to glorify the stereotype of the two-parent, traditional, active family, since it burdens everyone in other circumstances with an implied label of "inferior." I do not feel that way. Whatever your family circumstances or your Church calling, these principles are also relevant for you. I urge you to think of your circumstances as strengths to be offered freely on the altar.

If you are divorced, make your divorce something that you consecrate to the Lord. If family members are indifferent to the gospel or even hostile to your love for it, make those circumstances part of what you consecrate. If you are struggling with sorrow, with doubt, with feelings of resentment or despair, give them also to the Lord. Tell him: "This comes with my offering, Lord. If you can use it, it's yours." I can promise you that it will be the beginning of miracles. It is the same with other situations depicted in my fictional Plainville Ward. If your circumstances are different, rather than lamenting that the principle therefore cannot apply to you, consecrate those circumstances to the Lord and wait upon him in patience and faith.

2

Sharing the Vision

Where there is no vision, the people perish
(Proverbs 29:18).

The Principle

The history of the restored Church is a history of continual
revelation to us in these latter days. The Doctrine and Covenants
is an extended dialogue between the Savior and the Saints—a dialogue of comfort, of instruction, of reproof, of explanation, and of
yearning love. The Church is built upon the rock of revelation.
The spirit of revelation, not a manual or a handbook, is the mantle
of authority and the wellspring of creativity for every member acting in his or her calling. Revelations come in many forms—
dreams, promptings, strokes of insight, the whisperings of the
"still small voice"; a quiet sense of affirmation and direction for
ideas that are correct, an equally subtle turning away from ideas
and directions that are incorrect; manifestations, visitations, inspired utterances, and many more.

The Lord has promised that as we engage in the work of the
kingdom, every worthy person is entitled to receive this divine
guidance (D&C 76:5–7). This is a promise we may claim confidently—not apologetically, fearfully, or halfheartedly. After we receive this vision, it is important to frame it into a statement of purpose or vision so that all involved may clearly see the direction
that the inspiration is taking.

This reframing step is an essential act of translation. Joseph
Smith held the Book of Mormon in his mind when Moroni
showed him the golden plates under the stone on Cumorah, and

he held it in his hands when he picked up the plates; but until he translated the message into words that people of his time could understand, it had no power to speak to them in a way that created and confirmed faith. It is the same with our personal visions. Many times they come with a glory that words are incapable of capturing; but until we can frame them into words to bear that glory, we have no hope of transmitting their concepts to others.

Attributed to Solomon, the wise king, is the scriptural proverb, "Where there is no vision, the people perish." They perish from wandering to and fro, aimlessly wasting their energies. They perish from apathy and lack of motivation when they do things for which they do not understand the purpose. Again and again I have been impressed by the urgency with which current studies on leadership repeat the simple truth long ago revealed by the Lord: effective leaders have a clear vision of what they want to accomplish; by sharing this vision, they create new commitment in others to realize that vision. The model is the same in Church life, except that when a faithful person receives inspiration or personal revelation from the Lord, then the vision has a divine stamp of approval. However, the person receiving the vision still has the responsibility of communicating that vision to others.

The Plainville scene in this chapter shows George Pratt, strengthened by a clear vision of his stewardship, sharing that vision with those who must understand it if they are to help in the implementation.

Plainville Second Ward: Communicating the Vision

Plainville Second had drawn the afternoon block schedule. The morning seemed to drag, and George drove over to the meetinghouse at 11:15, half an hour before his first regularly scheduled priesthood executive committee meeting. At 11:30 his executive secretary, Jeff Burns, a fifty-year-old accountant at the local lumberyard, bustled in, looking down a list with an anxious look on his face. George tried to arrange the chairs so that he would not be enthroned behind the desk, but the office was too small; and when Blaine Hainesworth, the bluff and hearty first counselor, a rancher, came thundering down the hall, George gave it up as a bad job and went out to shake hands with him. Jim Butler, the second counselor, came in swiftly, ducking his head and displaying the infectious grin that endeared him to most of his high school students. Hot on his heels was Marv Lathrop, the ward clerk, a retired police officer. George had worked with him in the previous bishopric, since Marv had been the ward clerk before the division and had put in more than a few long nights making sure the transition went smoothly.

Coming in together were Jack Mueller, the high priests group leader, and Dean Suzuki, the elders quorum president. They had just finished their own leadership meetings and were now ready for the PEC. Jack, the owner of the local drugstore, was a strong personality and a real force for good. Dean Suzuki, a faithful Japanese convert originally from Hawaii, was a computer specialist for a Sears warehouse.

The final two to arrive were Sam Barnes, the Young Men president, a husky construction foreman, and John Emmett, the ward mission leader, who was now retired after a long career as a sales representative.

After their kneeling prayer, which Marv offered, George squeezed behind his desk feeling a great wave of appreciation for all of them. Good men all. Deliberately he asked himself the next question: Good men, sure. But millennial material? The question produced no turmoil. Instead, he felt only calmness.

Jeff had the agenda neatly typed: the day's meetings, the upcoming ward council, a welfare farm assignment, home teaching reports, and ward members with illnesses. As they finished the list forty-five minutes later, George glanced at his watch. 12:30. Fifteen good minutes before they should move out into the chapel and prepare for sacrament meeting at one.

Still feeling that unreal sense of calmness, George took a deep breath. "Brethren, I would like to talk with you about a sense of direction, a vision, if you will, for our ward. I feel strongly that our ward has the potential to be more spiritual, more loving, more committed to the gospel than we can even imagine. I would like to see the whole ward try to come together and be as one. I feel that we can build in the Plainville Second Ward a spirit of total unity, a feeling that we are truly a community of the Saints dedicated to each other and to the work of the Lord. I have a strong feeling that, if we can do this, we'll reap blessings unimaginable for all of us."

The others were listening respectfully but looked puzzled. Sam leaned forward. "Bishop, I need some help. I'm not clear how this direction you're talking about is different than what any ward is already expected to do. Aren't we all supposed to be living the gospel already?"

Blaine snorted. "Oh, come on, Sam! If we were already living the gospel, of course we wouldn't need anything more. But you're not gonna claim that we've got a ward that's totally committed to the full program of the Church, are you? What were those statistics the stake president told us about?"

Marv flipped over a page. "About 60 percent attendance at our meetings is tops. About the same for home teaching and visiting teaching. Less than 50 percent full-tithe payers, and it's murder to make people cough up more for missionary work or Scouting."

"The statistics don't tell the whole story, either," said George. "Some of you brethren are going to have the wonderful challenge of trying to find somebody who'll agree to be a den mother, the Scoutmaster, or the nursery leader. You were in the elders quorum presidency, Blaine. Who turned out for welfare assignments?"

Blaine snorted again and planted his ham-like hands on his knees. "Same eight men, and some of 'em were more trouble than they were worth after they got there."

Sam looked uneasy. "We're talking about living the gospel, Bishop, but we're discussing how to do that as though Church programs were the whole answer. I'm not sure leaning on people to do more things on the 'You, Too, Can Be Holy' checklist is going to improve gospel living."

"And even if it did," said Marv, "how would you do it? You know and I know how hard we worked in the last bishopric to get better participation, and we never got more than 70 percent in anything. There are some members who just aren't going to respond no matter what you do."

Jeff said with sudden enthusiasm: "If you can come up with some methods to light a fire under some of these people, the whole Church will be waiting for the answer, Bishop. What do you have in mind?"

George answered with deep humility: "Well, you've all put your finger exactly on the point. And I honestly am not sure exactly what to do, but I feel the Lord expects me to try. If you'll support me fully, that's all I can ask. We'll try to learn together."

"Bishop, you're the right man for this job," said Blaine with emphasis. "I don't know where you're going, but I'm with you."

The others nodded. John said, "Bishop, you have only to ask."

"Thanks," said George with a grin. "Any suggestions about the next steps we should take?"

Marv rubbed his hand thoughtfully over his chin. "I think you ought to talk to all the members of the ward council just the way you've talked to us. Let us know what you've got in mind. You haven't really said much. We've mostly told you why we think it won't work. But"—he was smiling a little—"I have a feeling that this isn't just a pretty paragraph out of the handbook that you recited to fill up the time. Our meeting this morning has made a difference to me. I think we need to get all of our ward leaders pulling together."

The others agreed. Ward council meeting would be held the next Sunday. Jeff said, "I'll call everybody and tell 'em to be sure to be present for a special meeting."

George nodded and smiled to himself as the accountant carefully made a note to himself. Progress already! Jeff was absolutely meticulous about carrying out any instructions George gave him, but this was the first time he'd volunteered. He felt a stirring of excitement, a glimmer of the possibilities if people could begin to see what was needed and then move on their own.

The ward council the next Sunday was a real test. Despite Jeff's calls, Nola Gardner, the Young Women president, wasn't there.

George Pratt had thought carefully how to approach this larger group. He wondered if he should tell them about his early-morning experience but decided not to. He wanted to focus on the specifics of the action rather than draw attention to his personal spirituality. In fact, as Phyllis had pointed out briskly, if he went around talking about hearing voices in the morning it was going to be hard for some members of the ward to take him seriously.

"I want us to be a better ward," was how George ended up. "I'm not interested in better statistics. The statistics will take care of themselves. What the Spirit is telling me is that our little ward can be a different kind of community—more united, more loving. I see us becoming stronger together, sharing the same goals and becoming more committed to them. I want us"—he paused and looked deliberately around the room—"I want us to be a Zion community."

He gestured. "Now it's your turn. I'm asking for your support, and I want to hear what you really think."

Jack Mueller, the outspoken high priests group leader, was first. "Bishop, I've thought a lot about this, but I can't help but feel this is far too ambitious for a ward as new and small as ours. How does a little ward like ours even try to become a Zion-type community of Saints? Of course we'll support you if that's what you want, but I'm wondering how. Take our temple attendance, for instance. You say you don't care about the statistics, but I'm telling you that if it weren't for Hy MacDougall we'd be in terrible shape. Since he's retired, he does about half of all the temple work done in our group."

Jack had opened the floodgates. The discussion continued from there: inactive families, rebellious teenagers, families that were on the edge financially, men and women with horrendous work schedules struggling to keep things together, people too caught up in material things, health problems, shaky marriages. Even as George listened attentively, he was glad that people were thinking of how this challenge affected their own callings. Jocelyn Smith, the Relief Society president and the nursing supervisor at the little county hospital, was one of the last to speak. When he looked at her invitingly, she spoke warmly. "Bishop, I'm sure the sisters in the ward would welcome the challenge to become more united with each other. There's already a wonderful spirit in our meetings. But there are problems in their homes. This ward has a lot of part-member and inactive families. Most of the active men in this ward are sitting in this room!" She grinned ruefully. "Well, it's not quite that bad; but I know many of the sisters feel worried, even depressed, because their husbands are just lukewarm about Church activity. How do the sisters go about supporting husbands who are not really committed?"

Into the silence, Jack spoke up again. "I said it before and I'll say it again, Bishop. It would be wonderful. I'll be glad to try it. But how do we begin? Where do we start?"

Lily Butler, the Primary president, surprised George by answering quickly. She was in her early thirties and had burst into tears when George had called her to be Primary president. Then she had explained, quenching her tears, that she and her husband had been struggling with infertility for a long time, and the chance to work with children was an answer to her prayers. "I think all the children in the ward—the Primary children and the teens—need to hear you describe your vision for the ward, Bishop. I suggest that we have a special time set apart at the beginning of our next testimony meeting. After you give your message and bear your testimony, then some of us can share our feelings."

They agreed this sounded good, but Jack Mueller pointed out: "That means Brother MacDougall and five of my high priests hear it. What about the other twelve?"

Jim cleared his throat. "Maybe if you wrote up your message, Bishop, then it could be the home teaching message for the month."

"And the visiting teaching message, too," put in Jocelyn Smith quickly.

"And I could mail it to everyone whose teachers didn't make contact," concluded Jeff.

George beamed. "Well, I think we've just taken the first step," he said.

Fast Sunday was two weeks away. In the interim George put in many hours on his address, praying hard, revising, and scratching out. Phyllis teased him: "I can always tell when you've been working on your message, George. You rub your hair into porcupine quills." Jim Butler turned out to be unexpectedly helpful in pinpointing ways to keep it organized, and George made sure that he consulted his counselors two or three times and everyone else on the ward council over the final draft, even the absent Young Women president. She'd sounded surprised but pleased to be asked for an opinion. The final message read:

Dear Members of Plainville Second Ward:

As your new bishop, I have been striving mightily to determine how the Lord wants me to fulfill my stewardship to you and to him. I've fasted and prayed over this goal, studied the scriptures, and talked to President Stratford. I feel strongly that we should set our sights on some extraordinary goals.

All of us are aware that we are living in the last days—the Saturday night of time, the eve of the Millennium. We've received much counsel about how to prepare—to have a year's supply of food and clothing, to have strong testimonies, to support missionary work so that the gospel can go to all nations, kindreds, tongues, and people. Temples are being built all over the world, and the doors of nations that have long denied the existence of God are opening.

All these things are supposed to prepare the world and the Church for the Millennium. But what do they have to do with Plainville Second Ward? I feel impressed that the Lord expects us in this ward to try to live the way we would during the Millennium, to be like the City of Enoch when the people were of one heart and one mind, had eliminated contentions, and had no poor among them. I want that to be our motto: "Of one heart" (Moses 7:18).

I have shared these feelings with my family, President Stratford, and all of the ward officers. There are a lot of problems, but we're all willing to try. It's not exactly clear how we should proceed, but we want to move ahead, try our hardest, and learn from our experience. I think there are things we can do as individuals, things we can do as families, and things we can do as ward members.

I'd like to suggest that all of us start with the following goals:

1. Have daily prayer individually and with as many family members as possible. In your prayers, please include something like this: "Dear Father, help me to be a blessing to everyone I meet today. Help me to understand who my neighbors are and how I can be a good neighbor to them."
2. Each person should read in the Book of Mormon every day. If possible, have family scripture study. Hold a family night every week with as many members of your family as you can.
3. Attend your meetings.
4. Try and do your very best in it if you have a calling or an assignment.
5. Live each commandment as completely as you can— tithing, Word of Wisdom, keeping the Sabbath Day holy, and the rest of the Ten Commandments.

This is a place to begin. I wish I could discuss it with each one of you, but please come to me if you have questions, see problems, or have concerns. We want input from all of you about how we can move ahead with this program.

Sincerely yours,
Bishop George Pratt

Before the meeting, Jeff efficiently ran off enough copies to paper the entire ward. He rubbed the end of his nose anxiously as he counted the neatly paper-clipped stacks twice, for the home teachers and the visiting teachers, but he smiled at George. "I think even the people who are here today are going to want copies, Bishop," he said, "so I made a few extra."

The older man's confidence buoyed George's spirits, and he went into the testimony meeting with renewed assurance. He spoke for about ten minutes, describing his goals for the ward, reading the letter, and closing with his testimony. "I am here to serve you," he concluded. "My deepest desire is to do whatever the Lord wants me to do, to serve you the way he would if he were here, and to increase the love in our ward."

Most of the members of the ward council also bore their testimonies. Lily Butler spoke thoughtfully about her feelings of what it meant to be "of one heart." Jim Butler drew a laugh from everyone when he started out: "Usually I don't feel like a servant over at school. I feel more like a prison guard or even Jiminy Cricket—but sometimes, rarely and beautifully, I've had the privilege of feeling like a servant." Then he went on to bear an unexpectedly moving testimony about how differently he had felt about his students on those occasions.

Mariah Dalton, a divorcee raising five children on an elementary schoolteacher's salary, expressed the feelings of many when she said: "For some time the kids and I have seemed to be drifting. We haven't had any real goals or purpose. Just surviving each day has seemed to take every ounce of energy we've got. My children are all good children, but I've felt lost and helpless when I've thought about how to give them the spiritual strength to do more than just survive. What Bishop Pratt has just said makes me feel that this is the direction we need to go as a family." She pressed her lips tightly together, then managed through a muffled sob: "If you will help me with my children, I'll help you with yours. This is the answer to many of my prayers."

The testimony meeting was personal and intense. The response of the ward members after the meeting left George Pratt with a feeling of buoyancy and confidence. He now felt optimistic that the ward could unite; if so, then surely they would find the way to move ahead. But he was realistic enough to know that this first step was not the journey and that many obstacles lay ahead.

Discussion

This episode from the Plainville Second Ward shows us both the power of a leader's personal vision and the process of communicating that vision to others so that they can deal with their misgivings about it and develop a personal commitment to the direction and objectives. The following points are crucial parts of this process:

1. Instead of just imposing his vision on the ward, the bishop shares his vision with those who work most closely with him. Most people see obstacles in their own situations and callings that would present stumbling blocks. They voice objections and concerns in an open discussion. The bishop understands that his job is to listen, not to criticize their concerns or override their hesitations. He listens carefully and patiently, returning when appropriate to the key point, or the vision. He thus uses his power and authority by "persuasion, by long suffering, by gentleness and meekness, and by love unfeigned; by kindness and pure knowledge" (D&C 121:41–42).

2. In both the PEC meeting and the ward council, the bishop functions in the role of teacher as described in the Doctrine and Covenants: "Appoint among yourselves a teacher, and let not all be spokesmen at once; but let one speak at a time and let all listen unto his sayings, that when all have spoken that all may be edified of all, and that every man [or woman] may have an equal privilege" (D&C 88:122).

3. As the discussion continues, members of the group begin to see the vision as larger than their own concern with the obstacles. They want to know more about the vision and then ask the key question, "What is the next step? How do we communicate this new direction to the rest of the ward?" The ward council now participates in planning, suggesting steps to follow. Although they did not articulate informing the full ward as the next step, it was clearly the most important value, for they made arrangements, even without George's input, to be sure that even those absent would be informed.

4. Capturing the vision in writing is a very important step. The written statement serves as a baseline document so that later developments and understandings can be appraised against it. Others can read and ponder its message. It also fulfills the requirement of the Lord for scripture, so that the dealings of the Lord with his people can be preserved.

5. The written vision statement includes specific actions as a place for individual members to begin. Obviously, there is no way to enforce or check up on full compliance; but if the vision statement has power to stir the soul and excite the imagination, it also needs to suggest specific steps for implementing that vision.

6. Finally, the whole ward (at least, those present) hears the vision and has an opportunity to express support. A full congregational discussion would be better but is often not practical. It is possible that the bishop heard only from people who agreed with him. But his invitation in the letter to come to him with questions or concerns at least opens the door for anyone who has real doubts about whether this proposal is a viable one. All ward members can read the statement and think about it at leisure. They can discuss it with family members, with home teachers, and with visiting teachers. The home and visiting teachers can report concerns back to their appropriate leaders.

There seems to be a heart-hunger in most Latter-day Saints to live with more commitment, to be more deeply wedded to significant goals, to accept ennobling challenges, and to seek more intense spiritual experiences. George Pratt has articulated this longing in words that his ward members can accept, has defined it as a potential reality that they can realize, and has moved the ward more or less together along a millennial path.

3

Stewardship: Duties, Expectations, and Accountability

Wherefore, now let every man learn his duty, and to act in the office in which he is appointed, in all diligence.

He that is slothful shall not be counted worthy to stand, and he that learns not his duty and shows himself not approved shall not be counted worthy to stand. (D&C 107:99–100.)

For it is required of the Lord, at the hand of every steward, to render an account of his stewardship, both in time and in eternity (D&C 72:3).

The Principle

Please read the above scriptures with feminine pronouns as well. It is a real mistake to think of all leadership and stewardship as being masculine. The first step for *everyone* with a calling is to capture the vision. The second is to share it with others who are involved. Third comes a more difficult but nevertheless essential procedure—developing a clear set of actions that define what the person will actually do in carrying out that goal. It is difficult, if not impossible, to *do* a goal. If one goal of a father is to help each child gain a testimony of the gospel, then he needs to see clearly what he must do, when he should do it, and how he must do it to achieve that goal. This action list determines to a large extent what an individual's stewardship is—what he or she can be expected to do in the position held. The stewardship, then, consists of the answer to two important questions: (1) What is my goal? and (2) What must I actually do to achieve it?

Who sets down the specifics of a leadership position? The person who is actually called to the position holds the primary responsibility—not a subordinate and not the hierarchical leader. Our supervisors can be sources of information and help to us, but it is our own responsibility to find out which duties are connected with the position to which we are called. This means reading the scriptures, Church handbooks, and other Church reference books; talking with our file leaders; and getting insights from others who may have held this position before.

In the Church (as in most organizations) we are accountable to someone for how well we do our job. Every leader in the Church has a file leader; and according to current Church procedures, part of this leader's stewardship is to help us understand our own callings and then hold a stewardship interview at regular intervals for review, encouragement, and help.

Our callings always involve other people. To adequately define our stewardships, we need to talk with all those who are connected with the position and get their ideas and expectations. The three questions recommended to every married couple seeking to build a better relationship are not a bad place for a leader to start:

1. What would make your job or role more satisfying?
2. What do you need from me that you're not getting?
3. What is one thing I could do to make our relationship better?

A Relief Society president, as a leader, is connected to the bishop, her counselors, the secretary, the chorister and organist, the teachers, the visiting teachers, the sisters in her ward, and the stake Relief Society president. As she creates her definition of her stewardship, discussions with the women holding the connecting positions clarify their expectations and needs. Of course, she will absorb administrative expectations and duties from the handbooks and manuals, plus any scriptures that may bear on her exact duties.

But administration constitutes just the planks in the floor. Far more important is the spiritual task of ministering to the needs of those with whom she associates. It is in ministering, rather than in administering, that the household of faith is constructed. Rather than drawing information only from other officers, everyone with a calling should also deliberately seek information from members as well.

Discussions with members not in the hierarchy have a way of providing unexpected illuminations for leaders. Rather sorrowfully, I've found that one of the most consistent responses is surprise at being asked to share perceptions. Members not in leadership positions are very used to being told what the organization needs from them; it is, alas, all too rare that anyone asks them what their needs are. I hope this will change as the spirit of ministering pervades the Church. I think most bishops would welcome more broadly shared participation and dialogue. In one ward where I lived, I became concerned about certain activities in the ward and asked the bishop if I could discuss my concern with him. He invited me to the next bishopric meeting where I described the situation as I saw it, discussed several aspects of the situation for a full hour, and received an invitation to come to a second meeting. I think this was a productive experience for all concerned, and I definitely feel we need to expand the opportunities in an average ward for open discussion.

We should be sure that these stewardship discussions are not a one-time event for new officers and teachers. Rather, they should be an avenue for ongoing discussions. Someone who may have been surprised by the initial discussion or solicitation of ideas on a certain topic should feel free to come to us later with additional ideas, responses, or suggestions.

Stewardship reviews generally are held every month or every three months, depending on the position or calling This is not designed to be a time of criticism or censure but rather an opportunity to affirm the relationship, to spiritually nurture the person with the calling, to honestly discuss the activities of the previous quarter, and to support him or her in developing new plans for improving performance in the next quarter. In the scene that follows, we see how Bishop Pratt built the definition of his own stewardship, then moved this process down through the ward.

Plainville Second Ward: Learning One's Duty

In his message, George had been sensitive to the circumstances of part-member or partially active families. He had wanted individuals to feel that they could accept the goal and make progress toward it even if they had to sometimes act alone. But the more he thought about it, the more he saw that it made sense for people to develop in three areas: personal growth, family development, and Church responsibilities. He felt that if he could get each person to have a personal plan, then get the families working for common goals, and then get committed service in each Church assignment, the results would become apparent almost at once.

He thought this through out loud to Phyllis while she was fixing supper. "Hmm," she said. "I'm sure you're right."

"But all this 'plan' stuff seems really vague, Daddy," said Susan, who was making cookies for family home evening.

"Yeah," chimed in Will, who was setting the table. "Why don't you have them brainstorm things they think they should be doing and things they think they can do, like you did with us? Even if we don't do everything all the time, we're at least doing something some of the time."

George paused in the act of snitching a cookie. "Look up Doctrine and Covenants 107, will you, Tommy?" he shouted into the family room. "My fingers are greasy."

Tommy pulled the triple combination off the television set and came in turning the pages. "Here it is, Daddy," he said.

"Thanks, son," said George, stuffing the last of the cookie into his mouth and wiping his hands on a paper towel. He read: "Verse 99. Wherefore now let every man learn his duty, and to act in the office in which he is appointed, in all diligence."

"Okay," said Phyllis. "So what are the duties? And how do you learn them?"

"The president," mumbled George. "This is a section about priesthood. So the president teaches the members their duties. Hey, tonight we could—"

"Not in my family home evening," said Susan. "Tonight we're talking about being honest."

George was up early the next morning, using the Topical Guide to make a list of scriptures about the duties of bishops. Then he reread the *Handbook of Instructions,* underlining passages and making notes as he read. He thought about bishops he had known and other bishops currently serving in the stake—what had impressed him and what had bothered him. Hands down, the unforgettable bishops in his life were those who had taken a personal interest in him and made him feel important. And oh, yes, there was Bishop— He frowned. He'd even forgotten his name. He'd been the one who always carped at the deacons on the welfare farm, no matter how hard they were working. No, he didn't want to be that kind of bishop.

"So stewardship includes what to do," he told Phyllis as she picked him up at work and they drove to the service station to get the pickup after its safety inspection. "But the how is pretty important too."

"I'll say," added Phyllis, deftly changing lanes. "The kids have been really good about helping with the new chores on the list; but honest to Pete, after Tommy and Will got through cleaning the downstairs bathroom, it looked worse than when they'd started."

"Did they know what they were supposed to do?"

"Oh yes," said Phyllis. "We'd specified scrubbing the fixtures, polishing the mirror, and mopping the floor. But I somehow forgot to mention that they should leave the towels straight and get most of the water off the floor. And another factor is *when*. They saved it until fifteen minutes before supper, so I couldn't make them do it over again."

George stared out the window and waved to Mariah Dalton, who was waiting to pull out of the grocery store parking lot. She smiled and waved back. "Sounds like home teaching," he sighed. "Jack Mueller was giving me the litany again last week: nobody says they *won't* do their home teaching, but so many just slop through it—think they've done the job if they show up. Or else they wait till the last day of the month and blitz through it. 'Nobody's stupid, Bishop,' he said. 'They know their home teachers don't care about them.' He's perfectly right, of course."

"Right," said Phyllis pulling into the service station. "And speaking of home teachers, who's Mariah Dalton's? Susan said that Amy said that Sarah doesn't want to go to the Daughter-Daddy party because all the other girls will have their fathers there."

George leaned over and kissed her on the cheek, then opened the car door. "You certainly have a way of getting the gospel down to specifics," he said.

George spent the next week drafting a list of what he thought he should do as a bishop—a Zion bishop—and how he should carry out those duties, as well as when they should be completed. He didn't try to include on the list everything from the handbook. In fact, after prayerful consideration, his list was concise enough to fit on a card in his shirt pocket:

General goal: To help in the spiritual growth and development of every ward member.

1. Know every person's name in the ward.
2. Visit every family in the first six months.
3. Train all home teachers and visiting teachers in how to do good teaching.
4. Have regular times for interviews each week.
5. Visit all those who are sick or in need.

He took the list to bishopric meeting with him—a total of five subgoals to help him achieve his main goal, with a second column for how he should carry them out and a third for when they should be completed. "Okay," he said, as he passed it out. "Here's where we get to test being of one heart and one mind. You've all seen eight or ten bishops in action. What would you add to this list? Or subtract? Or how would you change the priorities?"

He read the list out loud. When he got to item 2, "Visit every family in the first six months," Blaine interjected: "Who will go with you? And will you have some specific things that you want to find out about each family, or will it be just a general visit?"

"Good questions," said George. "Of course, I was visualizing some company. Jeff, maybe you can work out a schedule according to people's free evenings so we can spread it around a little? And let's brainstorm right now some things we'll want to include as part of the visit."

The discussion was lively and helpful. George jotted some notes to himself in the margin of his sheet, then added: "Now, there's one more question. You four all have your own jobs to do, but I know that how I do my job has an impact on how well you do your job. What could I be doing to make your job easier?"

Marv cleared his throat. "I don't know if you realize it, Bishop, but just scheduling your meetings at regular times and actually having them instead of cancelling them at the last minute has made a big difference so far. I can tell that it's not going to be a crisis getting the reports to the stake on time."

Jim said diffidently, "I don't think this is going to be a problem necessarily, but one of my concerns about being in the bishopric at all was that I'm not a particularly good team player. I like teaching because I'm on my own in my classes and have a lot of autonomy within the school structure. So if you see me getting cranky or starting to pull away . . ."

"I'll remember that," said George. "And don't think I want yes-men on my team. I get enough of that from the personnel office. I wanted you in this bishopric, Jim, and the Lord wants you in this bishopric—and that means with your autonomy and your own voice, speaking loud and clear." He smiled warmly at the relieved expression that flickered across Jim's face. "And that goes for all of you. Thanks for all your input. I'm going to consolidate these ideas and give each of you a copy. We'll review it one more time; and if we all agree, then it'll be my charter for what I'll try to do as a bishop."

"Will there be time to talk about our own charters next week?" said Jim. "I think I'd enjoy the experience of trying to get down in writing what I should be doing in my calling."

"I'm glad you said that, Jim," said George. "Obviously that's the next step. Yes, why don't you each see if you can bring a rough draft next week. And we'll start going over them."

Blaine seemed subdued. "I'm not much of a hand for writing," he said humbly, "but I can see how something like this really keeps things straight and clear."

"I really appreciate that, Blaine," said George. "Of course we can keep revising these things, too, until we get them the way we want them; but even while you're working on your own, could we also start spreading this practice down to every leader in the ward? I'll meet with Jocelyn Smith about the Relief Society, and then she can start talking to her own officers and teachers about their charters."

"I think now's a good time," said Marv contentedly. "We've got a lot of new officers and really a lot of new teachers. Many of them have taught before or had similar jobs, but this is just about right. They've had about six weeks to get an idea what they're doing, but it hasn't been long enough for them to get set in their ways." He laughed unexpectedly, "I'll be really interested to hear what you all have to say about *my* action list next week."

Over the next few weeks ward officers and teachers complied willingly enough, though some were pretty skeptical. In the ward council meeting, Lily Butler reported an interesting development that had occurred when the Primary officers and teachers had made their action lists at a preparation meeting.

Ada Shumway, who had been the Primary secretary in the previous ward as well, held up her paper and announced: "Well, that was easy. After all, all I do is to keep track of the attendance and send in the quarterly report."

Susan Chun, the Star-A teacher, quickly contradicted her. "Oh, no, Ada. You do much more than that. I count on you to let me know if any of my children have missed more than twice; and at Easter when I was so busy, you even called Marjean Suzuki to find out why Sybil had missed two weeks in a row."

Evelyn Pixton added: "And since we are looking at *how* we do things as well as what we do, one of the things I really appreciate about you, Ada, is that you're never critical or punishing if I haven't been as accurate in my class roll as I should. In my ward in California, we just hated to see the secretary headed toward us. We knew she was going to scold us for doing something wrong."

Lily Butler commented: "Well, Ada, it sounds as if some important parts of your job are to show teachers how to keep good records, advise them on absent children, help them check on absent children, and do all of this pleasantly. I've also appreciated how neat your work is and how you always get the reports done ahead of time. I'm just groping my way along here, and it was such a relief to have you hand me the report all ready to send off to the stake."

Ada was obviously pleased. "I wasn't aware that you sisters counted on me that much or that you noticed what I did. I'll do my best to keep it up."

The Aaronic Priesthood program was a different story. Blaine came to bishopric meeting shaking his head. Gordon Potter, the advisor and teacher for the teachers quorum, had balked at the assignment. "Gordon said he couldn't see what this would accomplish. It would take a lot of time, and it was already tough enough just to prepare the lessons and handle the activities. He also said that if we didn't think he was doing a good job, we could get someone else."

"Gordon's a holdover from the previous ward, right?" asked George. "What's your opinion, Blaine. *Is* he doing a good job?"

"Well, mostly," said Blaine dubiously. "But he cuts corners on quite a few things. For example, he never holds a presidency meeting to help the boys plan their activities. Usually he just tells 'em what he wants done. They don't squawk a whole lot because they usually like what he plans. They cleaned up four miles of the interstate before Roseville, you know, and then had a pizza party.

And they went waterskiing with the Mia Maids after they'd all written letters to the missionaries. But the boys aren't getting any experience in quorum leadership. My boy Ted is in his class, and he says that the lessons are usually well prepared, but Gordon never tries to tell any personal experiences or get the boys involved in a discussion. It's still pretty interesting—he talks about sports a lot, I gather—so they mostly listen quite well. I'd say he's far from perfect, but I'm not sure where you're going to find anybody better."

George thought for a moment. "Well, we're certainly not going to release him, but I think we can work with him on doing better. It seems to me that we need to start having regular personal priesthood interviews. That should help everyone who reports to the bishopric to review their assignments regularly, set goals for improvement, and get the help they need. The interview will let us know if people understand their assignments and are willing and able to carry them out."

He pulled his notepad to him. "Let's see, for me that would be all of you plus Jocelyn. Blaine and Jim, who's on your list?"

"Okay," said Blaine. "I've got the teachers quorum advisor, the Sunday School, the library, and the Young Women, right?"

"And I've got the deacons quorum advisor, the Boy Scouts, the Primary, the Activities Committee, and, oh boy! scheduling the building," said Jim.

All week long, George wondered, "What should I cover in these interviews?" He'd had stewardship reviews in the past, of course, but he'd never been very impressed. They were irregular, perfunctory, and pretty awkward. When he had been an elder, he knew that the elders quorum president was supposed to have an interview with him regularly about his home teaching, but more times than he cared to count, all he would get was a rushed phone call at the end of the month: "How many did you see? Any questions? Good. Call you next month."

People deserved more than that. Furthermore, George suspected, the quorum and the auxiliary presidents were going to interview their own people pretty much the way they got interviewed—and that meant his first interview with his counselors had better be an effective one. Of course, they'd just gone over their own action lists for their stewardships. That would be a good place to start. For the first interview, George decided to start this way:

1. How would you define your calling? What are your duties and responsibilities?
2. Right now, what has the highest priority?
3. What do you hope to accomplish in the next time period? (Write these goals down so we both have a copy.)
4. Outline your plans for achieving these goals.
5. What are your worries or concerns about this process?
6. What kind of help do you need and from whom?
7. Are there any personal matters or concerns I should know about that may influence your assignment?

Then the second interview would cover these points:

1. Let's review the goals you set last time. How do you feel about how things went? What did you learn about this job? About yourself?
2. Have your priorities changed, or the way you see your job?
3. What do you hope to accomplish in the coming months? (Write these goals down so we both have a copy.)
4. Outline your plans for achieving these goals.
5. What are your worries or concerns about this process?
6. What kind of help do you need and from whom?
7. Are there any personal matters or concerns I should know about that may influence your assignment?

He read the list to Phyllis. "It covers the territory, honey," she agreed. "I only see two possible hitches. This could really sound like an interrogation, and how are you going to get the copy? You can't have somebody sit in your office making a copy like a school assignment."

George brooded about the first point as he assigned Jeff to solve the second. Jeff's solution: several pads of paper with built-in carboned first sheets so that whatever you wrote on the top sheet would leave an impression on the next. He asked Jeff to schedule thirty-minute stewardship interviews within the next two weeks and then at the beginning of each quarter thereafter.

"Are you sure you want them all on top of each other, rather than doing them one per week throughout the quarter?" Jeff asked dubiously.

"I'm sure spacing them out would work, too," said George, "but this system fits my personality better. Doing them close together at the beginning will make them easy to remember and also give me a sense of a new beginning with each quarter."

Blaine, his first counselor, was the first interview, and they breezed quickly through his stewardship list.

Then George asked, "Blaine, how is Gordon Potter coming along with the teachers? You don't have a black eye, so he must have let you talk about writing out a description of his assignment, at least."

Blaine grinned. "It really worked out pretty good, George. In our first interview, when I asked him what his job entailed, I just scribbled down what he said. This gave us both a copy of his duties. When I asked him what he hoped to accomplish the next three months, he asked me if I had any suggestions."

"Did you dump that whole load on him?"

Blaine's grin broadened. "Nope. I'm an experienced cattle feeder, remember? I suggested that he might want to have the boys hold a weekly presidency meeting and let them plan the activities, with him just asking an occasional question if there was something they'd overlooked. He thought that sounded okay and agreed to try it." Blaine's grin faded. "You know, Bishop, I think his biggest resistance was not knowing how to write things out. He didn't know what we wanted from what I said. Can you believe it? I thought it would bother him worse if I took notes, but it didn't seem to. In fact, he seemed very pleased to get his copy. And relieved, like."

"Blaine," George said sincerely, "I think only you would have picked that up and solved the problem in a way that made Gordon feel good about it."

"Well, us cowboys can tell when a steer's actin' skittish," said Blaine gruffly.

George breathed a silent prayer of thanks. One hurdle crossed. No, two. Blaine's own uneasiness about stewardship interviews had dissolved in the experience of helping someone else. And there was a third thing. This interview hadn't felt like an interrogation at all. He'd been too busy feeling gratitude for that big weatherbeaten rancher. George wrote another line on both question pages: SAY thank you.

George had no illusions that teaching people a new set of leadership skills was going to be easy. He just knew it was going to be worth it. He was right.

It took about two months to get the new plan in place, and then the first quarterly stewardship interviews caused another predictable hitch. People naturally felt awkward doing something for the first time. But leader after leader reported that the time spent dealing with concerns in their areas was very well spent. They felt grateful to their own supervisors for their interest and concern, problems got solved, and people felt good about their stewardships.

At the July ward council meeting, George demonstrated a stewardship review with Jeff to the best of his ability; in the lively discussion that followed, he could see that the ward officers were trying on the role imaginatively, finding out where it fit and where they would need to adapt it to their personal styles.

George persistently encouraged all executives to keep the interviews going down through the organization, so that everyone felt linked more tightly, both in responsibility and in structure, to their stewardships. By autumn he was pleased and grateful. As far he could tell, every person in the ward had written a description of his or her duties and shared it with relevant others. And all of the ward executives were holding personal priesthood interviews or stewardship reviews with those for whom they were responsible. Morale seemed good.

Discussion

There are three key elements in understanding the leader's role in ensuring that everyone (including the leader) has a clear definition of each person's calling and responsibilities.

1. Developing a clear written statement of one's duties is a joint responsibility of the leader and the one accepting the calling. The leader's responsibility is to teach the person accepting the calling his or her duties to the extent that they have been defined (D&C 107:85–87). The person accepting the calling is to learn those duties and fulfill them. It was important that the bishop develop his own description of his stewardship before asking others to do the same; then he listened sincerely to their review of his list, understanding from their perspective how he impacted their own assignments.

   The person accepting the calling has a major responsibility to "learn his [or her] duty" by reading the relevant materials, talking with his leader, and gathering data from others who have held the position. Having this information, the person can then develop a list of duties for mutual discussion and agreement between him and the leader.

Agency is an important part of stewardship. This system is not designed to produce a ward in which all of the officers and teachers are little robot versions of the bishop. The genius of Church government is that, within the broad outlines of a calling's responsibilities, there is a great deal of room for personal style, individual preferences, and even downright idiosyncrasies. These factors give personality and individuality to callings, produce a level of quality simply not attainable with a mechanical carrying out of orders, and generate a delight and fulfillment that directly increase the level of happiness in members. A teacher who is truly expressing herself in a calling is affirmed in her personhood, as well as serving her class members by teaching them the gospel. It is an element that by-the-book leadership simply cannot duplicate, because true stewardship calls on elements to which a manual is blind.

Naturally, a leader can do a great deal to either encourage such creativity and genuine expression of self or to squelch it. Drawing on the full range of diversity in a ward will increase both the resource/talent pool and also the joy members feel in their callings. Squelching it may produce duty-driven, hardworking members—but not for long. The human need for freedom practically guarantees the onset of passive aggression, a show of compliance coupled with inward passivity that does not stop short of actual sabotage.

2. Since every position involves connections with other people, it is important to explore with these relevant others their expectations of the person accepting the calling. Virtually all conflicts and difficulties between people result from a violation of expectations. Consequently, it is extremely useful to find out what these expectations are. The simplest and most direct way is to ask, "Here are my expectations of you in this job. Are those fair and reasonable? What are your expectations of me?" If you need to broaden the discussion, ask questions like, "How does the way I do my job influence how you do your job?" "What

kind of help do you need from me?" and "How can I make our relationship better?"

Once inappropriate or unrealistic expectations are out on the table, in a vast majority of the cases just looking at them makes you realize where they are unreasonable. In the rest of the cases, you have the basis for a discussion based on facts ("It would really help me if all the teachers turned in their library requests a month in advance") instead of personalities ("You teachers never prepare. You're always running in at the last minute for things"). The bishop again set the pattern of gathering data from those who work closest to him to find out what they feel he should be doing in his position as bishop.

3. An important aspect of any leadership position is the willingness to both give and receive an effective stewardship review. Many leaders are uneasy about engaging in this process, for they feel uncomfortable talking with another person about that person's performance. The Lord has indicated that both now and in eternity, those with responsibilities in the kingdom must be accountable for their actions. A well-conducted stewardship review or performance review cannot be threatening or punishing, for it is focused on positives: the officer or teacher's vision of her position, her personal description of her duties, her concerns about individuals within her stewardship that need special ministering to, and the goals for the next time period that will grow naturally out of those concerns.

A stewardship interview is a wonderful time for the leader to minister to each officer and teacher, affirming the individual's vision, expressing appreciation, sharing larger visions of how her personal stewardship fits into his of the whole ward, praying together, offering a blessing when appropriate, and sharing personal feelings and experiences. It is a time to rejoice together and increase in love.

Although the "administrative" responsibility of the interview provides the framework, the content should be "ministration." In such an environment, instruction, coaching, or assistance are seen as they properly should be, as acts of love and concern rather than as "fixing" a malfunctioning part. Every interview should strengthen the personal relationship between leader and follower.

Again, Bishop Pratt set the example. He made sure that he saw everyone within his personal stewardship (and making time for someone is already a powerful expression of concern), affirmed their relationship, supported the ward leader in his or her own stewardship, and expressed appreciation. After going through an effective review meeting, the bishop then asked the others to conduct similar types of reviews with those reporting to them. Thus, the pattern was established at the top and leaders could begin a process they had actually experienced themselves.

4

Delegation

And Moses chose able men out of all Israel, and
made them heads over the people. . . .
   And they judged the people of all seasons: the
hard causes they brought unto Moses, but every
small matter they judged themselves. (Exodus
18:25–26.)

The Principle

Moses' experience with establishing secondary judges describes an important principle of leadership. At one point in the
wanderings of the children of Israel, Moses found that all of his
time was spent in adjudication because his people brought to him
personally every problem, dispute, and concern. Moses' father-in-
law, Jethro, saw that this burden was wearing Moses away and ad-
vised him to get other people to whom he could transfer some responsibilities. Moses followed this counsel and shared some of his
authority and responsibility with others. This process is called delegation.

A leader delegates work, responsibility, and authority to others
for two purposes: (1) to get needed help in the work that must be
done, and (2) to help others learn and grow as they participate in
new activities. The wise leader uses delegation to accomplish both
purposes. Thus, not only does the leader get needed assistance but
also people can tell that they are developing their own skills and
abilities as they carry out the delegated work. This means that the
leader must not simply delegate the routine and menial chores
while keeping all of the challenging and interesting activities for
himself.

The process of effective delegation calls for five steps from the leader:

1. Help the assigned person to clearly understand all the dimensions of the work to be done.
2. Spend time training or coaching the person so that she feels competent and confident that she can perform the activity.
3. Help the person receiving the assignment to understand clearly the degree of authority that goes with the responsibility. For example, in the Plainville Second Ward scene in this chapter, George delegates responsibility to the home teachers and visiting teachers consistent with the requirement laid out in the scriptures. It is important for a home teacher to know exactly what authority he has in working with his families. A home teacher who holds the Melchizedek Priesthood normally would receive authority to present a lesson, pray in the home, deal with family concerns, administer to the sick, and give ordinary, small-scale help and assistance to the family. The home teacher does not have the authority to issue a church calling, baptize a child, or perform other ordinances except by invitation of the family and by special authorization of the bishop.
4. Set up a time when the officer or teacher may account for his handling of the task delegated.
5. Give the officer or teacher the time, resources, and "space" or freedom to carry out the work. A leader is not effective who delegates to another and then constantly interferes, or hovers over, or overcontrols the person who is trying to carry out the actions delegated.

It should be obvious that these five steps of delegation will take time. The wise leader knows and accepts that the early steps of delegation will not necessarily save him time. Often it would quite literally be easier to do it himself. But leadership is a long-term investment—even an investment for eternity. Over time, the leader who delegates will have others who will share in the burden. They will be learning and growing, able to do even more in the future—even able to delegate to future leaders themselves.

Delegation is built into the structure of the Church. Even a master teacher cannot teach adults, youth, and children simultaneously. The teaching responsibility must be delegated among many teachers. And even if the bishop is a master teacher, his priorities mean that he can seldom handle a weekly classroom responsibility as well. In the same way, the bishop is responsible for the well-being of every member of his ward, but he cannot personally maintain the kind of close watch care needed to fulfill that responsibility. Hence, the Church structure provides home teachers and visiting teachers, a formal system to supplement family and neighborly care and concern. In the scene below, Bishop Pratt prepares the home and visiting teachers to do their job.

Plainville Second Ward: Delegating Home/Visiting Teaching Responsibilities

On the fifth Sunday in June, George Pratt held a special combined priesthood–Relief Society meeting that lasted an hour. All of the active adult men and women in the ward were there except for the Primary and Young Men/Young Women officers and teachers, who were needed to keep the auxiliaries staffed during this time. The president and one counselor from each of these auxiliaries had made arrangements to be present so that in their preparation meetings they could report on what happened.

George began the meeting by saying: "Brothers and sisters, I have been concerned about our home teaching and visiting teaching. Sister Smith"—he flashed a grin at the Relief Society president—"knows I have a lot to learn about visiting teaching, so let me concentrate on home teaching with the understanding that you sisters will be making mental modifications about what I say to make some of the same principles applicable to you."

Phyllis was smiling from the second row. Reassured, George added: "And of course, we're all here in two capacities. There are very few of you who don't have responsibilities as home teachers or visiting teachers, but every one of you is supposed to receive either home or visiting teachers."

Absorbed eyes met his as he began: "The Lord describes the duties of the home teacher in Doctrine and Covenants 20:51–55. Jocelyn, would you read those verses to us?"

The Relief Society president read in her low, clear voice: "And visit the house of each member, exhorting them to pray vocally and in secret and attend to all family duties. In all these duties the priest is to assist the elder if occasion requires. The teacher's duty is to watch over the church always, and be with and strengthen them; and see that there is no iniquity in the church, neither hardness with each other, neither lying, backbiting, nor evil speaking; and see that the church meet together often, and also see that all the members do their duty."

George explained: "What this says to me is that the Lord tells us to start by looking at what's going on in the home. Then we should move on to the relationship family members have to others in the Church, and finally we should examine the activity of the family in the Church. Too often we reverse the process. We get concerned if someone is not attending meetings and try to get them out, when we should concentrate on the family first. Let's just start with the first point. How many of you have home teachers who talk with you about family prayer or who pray with you? Or who ask if family members are doing their duties in the home?" Very few hands were raised. "Visiting teachers?" A sizeable number of women raised their hands.

"Even in 1830 when this revelation was given," George continued, "the Lord could see that parents would need someone from the outside giving them some support in getting kids to help around the house. And if it was needed then, think how much more it's needed now!"

Nola Gardner observed wryly: "It's not just the kids. Sometimes our husbands need to be reminded that we could use some help, too."

"We men probably have that coming," George admitted, grinning ruefully, while a ripple of laughter ran around the room. "Does focusing on family prayer seem like a pretty farfetched way to deal with a problem of getting family members to pull together?" He could see the nods.

Sharon Hainesworth commented: "I know it seems that way; but when Blaine and I are communicating with our Heavenly Father, we communicate better with each other and better with the children. I think part of it is that praying brings the Spirit into our home, but the rest of it is just good sense."

George agreed. "I don't think there's anything particularly mysterious or mystical about it. Taking the time for meaningful family prayer sends a signal about our priorities as parents; and if your kids are like our kids, they can pretty well figure out from there what our priorities are in other areas, too. So the question is, How can home teachers or visiting teachers do this? Lily, we've been talking about family prayer in the context of children, but what about people like you and Fred?"

Lily Butler nodded vigorously. "Family prayer isn't just for people with children. Fred and I think family prayer is important, but we get busy and let it slide. We'd appreciate reminders from our home teachers—but I'm not even sure who they are."

George saw Dean Suzuki, the elders quorum president, flip open a folder on his lap and start running his finger down a list. George smiled as he then called on Angela Martinez, the wife of the deacons quorum advisor. They had five children under age ten, thanks to a set of seven-year-old twins, and she frequently looked harried. "I think it would help if our home teachers would talk to us about what constitutes meaningful prayer on a level the children could understand. We tend to say the same prayers over and over again and not just for blessings on the food. I'm as bad as anyone."

As the discussion continued, it was clear that different families had different needs when it came to family prayer. George pointed this out and observed: "Sounds to me as if the best way home teachers could help with family prayer would be to talk with the whole family about what they feel they need. Then they could decide together what action to take. You visiting teachers go ahead and talk about personal prayer with the sisters that you visit. Maybe sharing experiences you've had will give each other ideas, too, about better family prayer."

Doug Pixton had been scowling at the floor uncomfortably. Now he raised his hand and said, fumbling for words, "Well, Bishop, I . . . I don't know quite how to say this, but . . . well, isn't it awfully nosy for me to sail in and start asking people about their family prayer? That's kind of personal, isn't it?"

Before George could respond, Chet Shumway gave an astonishing burst of laughter from two rows behind Doug. "My land, Doug, that's a funny thing for you to be saying," he roared. "You're the most tactful home teacher in the world. We've talked about a *lot* of personal things with you—some we've brought up and some you've brought up. And you always make us feel real good about it."

"How?" George pounced swiftly. "What does Doug do so that you feel comfortable sharing personal information with him?"

Chet shrugged helplessly, but Ada, his wife interjected briskly: "Why, he does it just by saying what he told you, Bishop. He says, 'I wanted to talk about something I noticed, but it's kind of personal, so if it's none of my business just tell me to butt out.' Well, three years ago it was because he'd seen our Dennis smoking out behind the Dairy Queen with some other sixteen-year-olds. We were real grateful. We knew he respected our privacy and that we had the right to tell him where the line was between what we wanted to share and what we didn't. Of course, he told us about Dennis in private."

George grinned at the surprise on Doug's face. "Did you know that you'd already found a way to solve your own problem? Folks, I think Doug is a great example to follow in case anybody else feels like he's barging in. Just ask permission and let the family know they get to draw the line. Now, what about that second point, carrying out home duties?"

A lively discussion erupted, and George nodded to Jim to start jotting ideas down on the blackboard as they popped up. At the end of ten minutes, Jim glanced at the bishop. "I think we've identified some principles here, Bishop, if you'd like me to pull things together." George nodded, pleased, and Jim quickly summarized: "We all agree that each family needs different jobs done, so there's no way we could generate a perfect list here. But for the parents and the children to feel good about home duties, everybody needs to feel some agreement in four areas." He summarized broadly as follows:

1. The parents need to identify the areas where they need help from the children—what kind of help, what level of performance, and how often. That way, the parents will feel good about the children.
2. The children need to agree that what the parents want is fair and appropriate. That way, they'll feel good about the parents.
3. The children need to identify what they need from their parents—not just in terms of help in doing their jobs, but what they need as individuals.
4. The parents need to identify what they need from each other.

"Obviously," Jim wound up with a flourish, "there's the basis for a lot of family and one-on-one discussions here. And I think the question Doug raised about privacy is an important one. Some parents and children would feel really uncomfortable discussing this with someone outside the family—and a lot of the actual jobs or arrangements are pretty trivial except to the family itself. So I'd say check first to be sure that the family is comfortable with the discussion, and then be as general or as specific as they want you to be."

Phyllis raised her hand. "The scripture says the home teachers should 'exhort' families to attend to their duties. There are lots of ways they can be encouraging without prying into personal family affairs, but there are plenty of times when the praise or notice of a friendly outsider means a lot to a youngster."

"Thanks," said George. "Now verse 53. 'The teacher's duty is to watch over the Church always'—meaning the members, and particularly the family you've been assigned to—'and be with and strengthen them.' What does it mean to be *with* someone? How do you go about strengthening them?"

The discussion that followed was a catalogue of neighborly services: sharing a family's distress in times of accident or illness; giving support when a family member is down or discouraged; providing physical assistance, food, child care, yard work, or help during a project; being available to give counsel or advice; and strengthening with praise rather than criticism. George glowed inwardly as several men and women shared appreciation for help received from visiting teachers and home teachers, including warm tributes to people now in the First Ward.

Jeff Burns made the point that George was hoping would come out: "I've had home teachers who have mostly come because it was their duty, and I was always glad to have them do their duty. But it was when there was something a little extra—that feeling of friendship and personal concern—that I felt I could actually ask for help if I needed it."

George glanced at his watch and saw they were going to have to pick up the pace. "Verse 54. 'And see that there is no iniquity in the Church, neither hardness with each other, neither lying, backbiting, nor evil speaking.'"

Dean Suzuki raised a practical question: "How can the home teacher know if anyone in the family is doing something wrong that would be considered iniquity, or if someone is lying or speaking evil about another person? Would the home teacher even know if there were any hard feelings in the family?"

Joan Butler responded quickly: "The home teacher wouldn't know, but the family members would. The home teacher could ask if there were any hard feelings in the family—ask each family member in turn, if need be, and get them to apologize and forgive each other. That would certainly help in our family. I'm not even sure that the home teacher would need to know what the exact problem was."

Mariah Dalton was frowning a little. "I think the home teacher might help in clarifying that there are tensions, but just making a child say 'I'm sorry' to a sibling doesn't necessarily make them *feel* sorry. And besides, that kind of discipline is my place as a parent—no one else's."

"I think I'd feel more comfortable," interjected Jim, "if the home teacher could present a lesson on what constitutes iniquity, lying, backbiting, or evil speaking. But I'd rather have a regular personal priesthood interview with each child than have the home teacher take over that responsibility."

Mariah rolled her eyes. "Priesthood again. Where does that leave me and my children?"

Dean Suzuki leaned forward, his dark eyes intent on Mariah's troubled face. "Is there some reason you couldn't have a personal mother's interview with each child in exactly the same way? Could the home teachers help by giving a lesson on how interviews work so the children and you would know what to expect?"

Mariah brightened. "Yes, that really *would* help. And I wouldn't feel as if I had both hands tied behind my back all the time."

George felt a warm glow even as he remembered Phyllis's question. Who *were* Mariah's home teachers? He cleared his throat. "We've got about three minutes for the third area," he announced. "Verse 55. 'And see that the church meet together often, and also that all the members do their duty.' Dean, how do you interpret this verse?"

Dean tapped his fingers on his knee. "Well, if home teachers and visiting teachers have been watching out for their families, they'll know if somebody's not at their meetings and can find out why right away. Did the dad stay home because one of the children was sick? Does the teenager have a Sunday job? Does someone not like a teacher? There's no need to get inquisitorial or to probe into someone's reason as if you don't believe him or her, but you can usually tell if you're getting the real reason or a polite excuse. I think it should be part of a general conversation—passing on an idea from the lessons, or announcements about upcoming events they might have missed. And for sure, as part of those ongoing conversations, you'd know what Church jobs your people have and how they feel about them. And maybe whether they need help."

George summarized: "Can you see what a different kind of visit and discussion would go on in the home if home teachers and visiting teachers were feeling the spirit of their callings that the Lord suggests? I get a whole different feeling about home teaching when I think that the Savior is my senior companion. That's basically why we have home teaching and visiting teaching—to carry the Savior's comfort and help to every home. I'm asking every home teacher to go into his assigned homes, read this section of the Doctrine and Covenants, and work out with your families what they'd like to talk about with you in the coming months. Jocelyn, what would you like to add as instructions for the visiting teachers?"

Jocelyn stood up and turned to face the group. "Bishop, we welcome the opportunity to be partners with the priesthood in bringing the healing spirit of the Savior into the homes in this ward. Sisters, please continue to pray as companions before your visits so that you'll be sensitive to the needs of each sister. The great difference—and it's a world of difference—is that many of our sisters have had to struggle alone if they were in less than ideal circumstances. Now I can see ways to approach some of these sisters' problems because the home teachers can be involved with their husbands and their children as well. Bring your sisters' needs to our attention along with your recommendations so that we as ward executives can talk about ways to help the whole family. Oh yes, if for some reason your own home teachers are hesitant to hold the kind of discussion with your family that the bishop has asked, then let's suggest to them that this is what we'd like to do as the basic activity during their visits."

As summer deepened, George could tell that the new perspective on home teaching and visiting teaching was producing a remarkable difference, but he never learned the details of one of the most powerful success stories.

Paul Sorenson, a relatively new member of the ward who was manager of the local hardware store, was assigned to visit Tom and Lori Reynolds, an inactive family, with fourteen-year-old Charlie Snow as his companion.

Dean Suzuki had been frank in making the assignment: "You know, Paul, nobody's really gotten through to Tom, and he usually doesn't even invite the home teachers in. He's been a member of the Church for about fifteen years—joined pretty soon after he and Lori were married. She was already a member but her own folks hadn't been too active. As I understand it, he stopped coming to Church almost immediately. He drives a truck for the feed store, but he's nearly always home on weekends, so that's not it. Lori comes to Relief Society work meetings every couple of months and always seems happy to see the visiting teachers, but she stiffens up whenever they mention coming to sacrament meeting. I don't know. She might be the problem. The children are nice kids as far as I know, but there's just a real wall there."

Charlie agreed. "Dixon, their oldest boy, is my age. He's okay. Everybody likes him at school, but you mention church to him and he's just not interested."

Paul had thought seriously about the bishop's meeting, and he talked with Becky, his wife, about possible ice-breakers. Becky observed: "If they don't usually let in the home teachers, then I don't think you and Charlie all dressed in suits and ties are going to be such a great hit if you appear on the doorstep with your scriptures in your hands. We could make some cookies for you to take over . . ."

"I don't know," mused Paul. "That seems a little too heavy-handed, too. I think I'll just take the bull by the horns and go introduce myself."

The next Sunday afternoon, Paul, dressed in a polo shirt and slacks, drove to the Reynolds house. A ten-year-old boy answered the door. "Hi," said Paul smiling. "I'm your new home teacher. Could I talk with your dad?"

The boy, unsmiling, disappeared and came back a few minutes later. "My dad said he's sick and can't come to the door."

Paul could hear someone in the kitchen; but if it was Lori, she obviously wasn't coming to his rescue. How can I be with and strengthen a family when I can't even get in the house? he wondered wildly. Then a thought came to him, "What's your name, young man?"

"Tim."

"Tim, go tell your dad that I'm here to see if he would like a priesthood blessing. If he's sick, then the best thing for him is to have a priesthood blessing."

Again the boy darted off. Another several minutes dragged by. Finally Tom, a husky man about forty years old, appeared and grudgingly said, "I guess I ain't so sick I need a blessing. Come in."

Paul shook hands with him and entered the home. Lori Reynolds was a pleasant-faced woman but shy. The two girls reluctantly turned off the television set, and Dixon, hearing a visitor's voice, emerged from his bedroom. Fortunately four-year-old Carrie broke the ice by coming over to stand at Paul's knee and stare at him thoughtfully.

Paul, thinking quickly, said, "Carrie, do you know that you have a magic ear?"

Dixon drifted to the arm of a chair, where he settled, grinning as his little sister shook her head solemnly. Paul took a nickel from his pocket, held it up before her, and said, "Now watch closely. Hocus pocus tiddely wocus," he intoned. Making an elaborate pass with one hand, he palmed the coin in the other, displayed the empty hand, and then pulled the nickel from Carrie's ear. She squealed with delight. "I think you'd better keep this," Paul said, dropping it into her hand.

"Me next!" shrieked seven-year-old Brittany.

"No, me!" insisted Tim.

"Children, calm down," said Lori ineffectually. Paul, elaborating the magician's persona, did the trick for both Brittany and Tim. By then Dixon was craning his neck, trying to figure it out. "Did you see how I did it?" Paul asked him grinning. When Dixon shook his head, Paul showed him the crucial moment of transfer, then flipped him the nickel. "Try it a few times. See how good you are."

Then he turned to Tom. "Brother Reynolds," he said, "Becky and I just moved into the ward about six weeks ago, and I've been assigned to be your home teacher."

Tom grunted: "They probably told you I'm inactive, didn't they? Well, I don't mind if Lori and the kids go, but usually we've got other things to do on Sunday. If I hadn't been feeling a little punk today we'd have been up at the lake, getting in a little fishing. I just don't feel much of a need to go to church, and that's the truth. I suppose the members are fine, but I don't feel any need to be around 'em."

With a flash of inspiration, Paul countered: "Brother Reynolds, you may not have much of a need to associate with people at church, but think of Becky and me. We're new here. We don't have many friends yet. This is one of the few homes I have been in since moving here. We need someone to show us around town, go to a movie with us, or get something to eat with us. So far, in five years of marriage, we haven't been able to have any children, and it would be fun for us to be around your kids. If you're not very interested in church, that's fine. But would you be willing to be our friends?"

Tom stared puzzled at the younger man. "Are you sure you want to be friends with us?"

Paul responded, "Yes. Very much." He held his breath. Tom glanced uncertainly at Lori, who seemed as confused as he. "Well, I guess we could show you a few things," he muttered. "We both grew up in Plainville, so we've seen a lot of changes over the years."

"That's great!" Paul enthused. He stood up. "We've got a van. What if we picked up you and your family next Saturday afternoon about two? You can show us around the town and maybe we'll even have time to drive up to the lake. You know, Becky and I haven't even been there yet."

Tom nodded, still bemused. Paul didn't give him time to change his mind. Shaking hands warmly all around, he left, waving and calling, "Saturday at two!"

Becky hugged him with glee when he told her how the visit had gone. "Pretty clever!" she enthused. "It's exactly twelve miles to the lake—as you very well know—so we can end up with a picnic supper out there. I'll call Lori on Tuesday and we'll iron out the details."

It worked. Tom and Lori both, once the initial shyness was gone, regaled Paul and Becky with dozens of stories about growing up in Plainville and with three generations' worth of folktales about its legendary eccentrics. Becky and Lori discovered a mutual fascination with historical fiction, and Becky, who worked in the children's room of the library, insisted that the children come in the next week and sign up for the summer reading program.

With a certain amount of formality, Paul set up the first "real" home teaching visit right after the Fourth of July to talk about family prayer. "So this is George Pratt's idea," said Tom. "He always was a go-getter, ever since grade school. He's a good man.

I've always liked him." Lori had even kept George's message to
the members, which had been mailed to the home because the
Reynoldses didn't have assigned home teachers then. It turned
out that the family had always had blessings on the food, and
there was surprisingly little awkwardness about extending these
prayers into more thorough-going family prayers.

Becky reported happily one night: "Alice MacDougall called.
She and Linda Potter are Lori's visiting teachers. She said they
went there this week and Lori is just as happy as can be. Couldn't
stop talking about you. Alice said she's always had the feeling that
Lori wanted to be active but just couldn't do it all by herself. Alice
said she wouldn't come to church, though, so she was calling me
to see if I had any suggestions."

Paul frowned in alarm. "I hope they haven't been putting
pressure on them. What did you tell her?"

"Just that," responded Becky. "That it's a good relationship
but it's a new one and needs space to grow—to give Lori lots of
support but not to make her feel guilty."

"I should have known you'd do the right thing," said Paul.
"Thanks, honey. And I'll call Dean Suzuki tonight and have him
tell Jocelyn Smith directly, too, so that we've got time to see what
develops."

As the summer swam past slowly, its high-heat days punctu-
ated with frequent, spectacular thunderstorms and its weekends
shared frequently with Saturday fishing trips, Paul found himself
pondering a mystery. Tom Reynolds was a good man. He didn't
smoke, didn't drink, worked hard, and was a contented family
man. Why did he shun Church activity? Was he afraid of its demands? Maybe he wasn't ambitious for himself and maybe he
liked his own convenience a little. But were those the real reasons
why he avoided church?

One September evening, Tom, Lori, and the children had
come over to watch a video at Paul and Becky's. Dixon and Charlie were off at the high-school grounds with a few other teenagers
playing softball. While Becky and Lori gathered up the root-beer
float glasses and popcorn bowls and the children dived into a box
of college-vintage clothes to play dress-ups, Paul rubbed a hand
over his jaw and took the plunge. "Tom, I hope I'm not being too
personal, but I just can't figure something out. Tell me if it's none
of my business, but it just doesn't make sense for you not to be
active in the Church. You've got a testimony. I know it. You feel

attached to the Church. You didn't just join the Church for Lori's sake. I can tell it from your stories. You live a good, clean life. I can think of a dozen reasons for you to be active and none to keep you away. What's the deal?"

Tom studied the floor, turning his glass around slowly in his hands, then looked up at the younger man and replied: "Paul, I've never told anyone the real reason why I don't go to church. I've always felt they'd laugh at me, I guess. But I know you wouldn't."

He took a deep breath. "I can't read, Paul. I just never figured it out when I was a kid. Teachers just passed me along until I got out of grade school. I dropped out of school as soon as I could and started work. There were always farmers who'd hire a husky kid, so I wasn't worried about making a living. And Lori was so anxious for me to join the Church. She attended all the missionary discussions with me and read the scriptures so I wouldn't have to, so the missionaries never knew. The bishop married us, you know. Well, the first time I went to church, right after my baptism, the Sunday School teacher took the lesson manual and passed it around the class and asked us all to read a paragraph. I thought I'd die. When it came to me, I just passed it to Lori, and when the teacher said, 'No, we want you to read,' I just mumbled that I wouldn't. The teacher thought I was mad at him. I felt bad about that, but I couldn't tell him the real reason. I was so embarrassed that I decided never to go back to church again because the same thing might happen again. Lori always reads anything I need to understand, and she helped me memorize the driver's test book before my license test. I don't think even the kids know." He looked up at Paul, his eyes haunted. "And that's the reason I don't go."

Paul was astonished. "But Tom, you drive a delivery truck. How can you deliver goods and not read the addresses?"

"That's not much of a problem," Tom said. "I grew up in this country. I know where everybody lives. And if I don't, I just ask and somebody'll point me in the right direction."

Paul looked at his new friend. "Tom," he said urgently and earnestly, "how would you like me to teach you to read? Just the two of us together. Nobody else needs to know, not even your family unless you want to tell them."

"Paul, that would be the greatest thing I could think of. But do you know how to teach someone my age to read?"

The home teacher responded: "You leave that to me. I'll need to tell Becky so she can help me get the materials. Is that all right? Then we'll start next week."

Becky knew exactly what resources the library had for teaching adults to read and had some ingenious ideas about children's books that would not be boring for an adult. Paul reviewed them carefully, and Becky role-played a few lessons with him. Three times a week, Tom would drop over to the Sorenson home and Paul took him systematically through the lessons, sending him home with flashcards or a phrase list as homework. When Tom read his whole first reader through from beginning to end with no mistakes, he grinned with satisfaction though his eyes were moist. He was a quick learner, and it wasn't too many weeks before he could go through the readers easily. They started next on the newspapers—the first time Tom had ever read a paper.

The ultimate test was reading through some lessons from the current Sunday School manual. As they finished the lesson, Paul said: "Tom, no one can ever embarrass you again. Are you ready to go back to church?"

Tom Reynolds only nodded, and the next Sunday, the Sunday before Thanksgiving, the whole Reynolds family went to church together for the first time, with Becky and Paul.

Dean Suzuki was one of those who welcomed them warmly, then quietly asked Paul later, "How did you do it?"

Paul smiled and shrugged. "Tom was just finally ready."

Discussion

This scene from Plainville Second Ward does not show all five steps of delegation but it identifies the connection between the clarity of the delegator's vision and the actions of the person who has committed himself to accept the delegated responsibility.

George Pratt derived that vision by thinking about what he felt an effective home teacher—and, by extension, a good visiting teacher—should do. First he went to the scriptures to find out what had been revealed on the subject. Then he prepared an out-line of suggested actions for the home teachers to carry out in the homes.

With this preparation complete, the bishop met with all of the potential home and visiting teachers, since he wanted all of them to understand his vision of home teaching. One of the people who did not speak in the meeting, Paul Sorenson, took seriously the charge to be with the Reynolds family and to strengthen them. He frankly appealed to their altruism in establishing a friendship, then sincerely worked at bonding the two families in genuine liking. When he found out the root cause of Tom Reynolds's inactivity, he understood how deeply wounded the man's self-esteem had been and instinctively took steps to safeguard his privacy as he offered his help in solving the problem. The solution required extra-mile effort, but it removed Tom's major reluctance to be active in the Church.

A full five-step analysis of the delegation process would also include the intermediate step in which the bishop meets with the ward priesthood and Relief Society leaders, recognizes their authority to organize and implement the home teaching and visiting teaching program in the ward, discusses the assignment with them, resolves any difficulties, and hears their plans for carrying out the goal. Another crucial step, of course, is the meeting in which they report their stewardship. In this particular example, Paul would report his success in removing an obstacle that had been keeping Tom from coming to church but would specifically state that an issue of confidentiality meant he could not discuss the details and that Tom should not be asked about it or be used publicly as a "success story."

Of course, one success story is not the end any more than one successful orientation meeting is the beginning. In effective delegation, the quorum and Relief Society leaders would make coaching to achieve high-quality home and visiting teaching an ongoing priority. They would also provide a clear opportunity for accounting at the personal interviews held by both the priesthood quorum and group leaders and the Relief Society presidency. Such reviews would also be opportunities to find out if problems in the family exceeded the resources of the home and visiting teachers.

Home and visiting teaching, like other areas of Church activity, prosper when the delegation process is understood and implemented effectively. That is why, as I have already mentioned, stewardship interviews must be opportunities for the leader to minister to the officer or teacher, meeting some of his or her individual spiritual needs and strengthening their relationship. A strictly administrative relationship that views the officer or teacher only as a tool to accomplish the leader's tasks can be emotionally barren and, in some cases, even spiritually abusive.

The importance of giving people a good role model to follow cannot be underestimated, and this is what George does by teaching his ward officers how to hold effective stewardship interviews. I recall hearing an LDS family therapist tell about getting a frantic call from a family friend in another part of the state. She was desperate, her marriage was in trouble, and her whole family was about to collapse. She had almost no money, and traveling for regular therapy sessions was out of the question, but she pleaded for help. In an act of personal leadership, the counselor and his wife invited her to come and live with their family for about two weeks so he could counsel with her in the evenings. At the end of that time, she went home and several weeks later wrote to the counselor: "My stay in your home has saved my life, my marriage, and my family. Everything is going much better. While I appreciated the counseling you gave me, I don't think that is what made the difference. For nearly two weeks I watched your wife manage an effective LDS home. It was a revelation to me. I had never seen how that was done—how to get children to help without a confrontation, how to organize things, how to plan and prioritize and get many things done in a day. I saw how to deal with differences without getting into conflicts. I have heard people talk about this in Relief Society and other places, but I never saw it in my parents' home. Until I watched Kathleen, I never really knew how all of this could be done."

This example has great application to many areas of Church activity. Often people are willing to accept the responsibility delegated to them, but without a good role model, they have only hazy ideas of how to take effective action. It is the leader's job to walk beside the person who has accepted the delegation until that person can stride forward confidently on his or her own.

5

Building the Team

I say unto you, be one; and if ye are not one ye
are not mine (D&C 38:27).

The Principle

One of the great tasks of nearly all leaders is to build a collection of individuals into a solid, collaborative, cohesive team. This is a challenge for every spouse, parent, stake president, bishop, quorum or group leader, auxiliary leader, and teacher. All must engage in a process that unites a set of individuals into a team where they are of one heart and mind, functioning together in a common purpose. Some teams are smaller or larger than others, and some will have individuals that are more difficult to unite; but unless the leader knows how to build a team and takes time to do it, the unity desired by the Lord will not emerge. Since all are leaders to some degree, the formal leader should know how to engage in a team-building process while the corresponding responsibility of members is to willingly participate in that process.

First, it is important to know what an effective team is like, whether it be the family, the Relief Society, an elders quorum, the Mia Maid class, or the whole ward. All such teams seem to share these eight characteristics:

1. The goals of the team are clear. Everyone understands and accepts them. Team members are goal oriented and result oriented. In gospel terms, the members of a millennial-minded team will be honestly striving to love the Lord with all their mind, might, and strength. Christ will be a

real presence in their lives, and they will be sensitive to and respectful of the influence of the Holy Ghost. The desire to love their neighbors as themselves will be powerful.

An understanding of goals often develops and deepens over time, but it will never happen if people start out with fuzzy ideas about goals and don't have a chance to express, sharpen, and refine those understandings with the whole group. This step seems easy to skip or shorten, but it is a crucial one.

2. People understand their assignments as team members and how their roles contribute to the work of the whole. As a professional consultant, I have seen executives send out memos saying, in effect: "All units will now start team-building. You have four months to accomplish this goal." Most employees will make "compliance moves," but real team-building doesn't occur until the team members—and especially the leader—make a real commitment, saying, in effect: "This is important to us. We need to become better at working together and supporting each other."

   The Lord's instruction to leaders and members is clear. Leaders are to teach members their duties, and members are to learn their duties. This is a joint process— leaders and members learning their duties together. (See D&C 107:88–100.)

3. Members basically trust and support each other. They accept their own limitations and imperfections but see beyond them to what they may become. Although not perfect, they will want to bear one another's burdens, mourn with those that mourn, and comfort those who stand in need of comfort (see Mosiah 18:8–9). I think trust is the hardest area to build; and from my professional experience, the roadblock is often that members don't trust the leader. They don't trust his motives. They may have had bad experiences with him in the past. They may see him as forcing them to do something that will not benefit them as much as it will him. Sometimes an outside person can be helpful—a high councilor, the stake Primary president, even someone with professional credentials to whom the group will listen. This person can talk with unit members, find out the reasons for the low trust, and then help the members and leaders take more appropriate action.

4. Communications are open. Opportunities to share all data relevant to the goals of the team are built into the functional structuring. Team members are rewarded, not punished, for open communication as long as it does not violate the group's trust. This means that the team needs to talk about how they will make decisions and how they will actively seek and take into account every person's ideas and feelings.

5. Team members participate in making decisions and influence the decision-making process. They make free, informed decisions based on data and personal commitment. The Lord has given some instructions about decisions that are made by a quorum (they are also applicable to any team), who must all be committed to implement those decisions:

And every decision made by either of these quorums must be by the unanimous voice of the same; that is, every member in each quorum must be agreed to its decision. . . .

The decisions of these quorums, or either of them, are to be made in all righteousness, in holiness, and lowliness of heart, meekness and long suffering, and in faith, and virtue, and knowledge, temperance, patience, godliness, brotherly kindness and charity;

Because the promise is, if these things abound in them they shall not be unfruitful in the knowledge of the Lord. (D&C 107:27, 30–31.)

The Lord has made it clear that in certain matters, such as disciplinary councils, the stake president or bishop will make the decision, listening to input from and being sustained by the relevant counselors (D&C 102:19). But even in these cases, there should be open lines of communication so that the final decision-maker will have access to all relevant information.

However, when the total team is involved, then in a spirit of meekness, brotherly or sisterly kindness, long-suffering, patience, and knowledge, the group will come to unanimous decisions—that is, every member agrees to the decision. We know that there are times when people have publicly agreed to a decision despite private disagreements, but the Lord clearly intends that these unanimous decisions in his kingdom are to be fully agreed upon both publicly and privately, both in word and in deed.

There is an interesting blessing attached to the Church team that makes decisions according to this method: "They shall not be unfruitful in the knowledge of the Lord." I take this to mean that the group will know what the Lord wants the decision to be, their knowledge of the Lord and how he works will increase, and they will feel simultaneously closer to each other and to the Lord.

6. Everyone implements the decisions with commitment.
7. Leaders support team members and have high personal performance standards. This means that the leader should have high standards for himself or herself, leading by example. It is a simple fact of leadership that members are motivated less by advice and high standards than by the example of the leader. For the Christlike leader, this means a serious effort at living all the principles of the gospel perfectly.
8. Differences and conflicts get discussed, respected, and recognized. They are not ignored or brushed over lightly. (See the discussion on conflict management below.)

Imagine the comparative ease of building a team if all of the members willingly went the extra mile, turned the other cheek, forgave those who trespassed against them, loved their enemies, and did good to those who treated them with malice and spite. Perhaps in the Millennium all Church members will possess such qualities; however, as we prepare for the Millennium in the world we now inhabit, teamwork is not an automatic skill, and the leader who wants to prepare for the coming of Zion will need to work at building Church members into more effective teams.

Many leaders, both inside the Church and out, do not know how to build a team and spend virtually no time in team development. Families should be a closely knit team; but too many families, even those headed by fathers who take their priesthood responsibilities seriously, do not build the kind of oneness the Lord desires.

Team-building starts with mutually shared agreement about goals. Most parents have some common goals—to see that the children develop a good self-concept, develop self-discipline and sound work habits, get a decent education, go on missions, get married in the temple, and become useful and productive citizens. In the normal course of events, children adopt these goals, consciously or unconsciously, as their own—or rebel against them. When parents have the explicit goal of also becoming a unified family team, then they do not simply assume that the children will absorb that goal. Instead, they talk explicitly about the process of becoming one, listen to how children at various ages interpret what it means to "get a decent education," explore feelings about missions and marriage, model and praise good work habits, and encourage the children's input into that process. Here's a list of questions that may be helpful in identifying some assumptions parents are making and allowing explicit exploration of family goals:

- On a scale of one to ten, how effective are we as a family team?
- What are our strengths as a family?
- What do we need to do better if we are to be a more effective family?
- What are our duties?
- Where do you feel a need to do better?
- What do we need from each other if we are to be the kind of united family we want to be?

Of course, these questions can be adapted to any kind of team—a high council, bishopric, quorum presidency, Primary presidency, and so forth. Be prepared to be patient when you start to deal with team issues. Members are often hesitant and reluctant to express themselves honestly. Part of this is just human nature and how organizations work. But for Latter-day Saints, part of it is a natural outcome of Church structure. The respect for priesthood authority and the orderliness created by Church hierarchy are real positives, but they come with some disadvantages, too. Members may see their job as simply finding out what the leader wants (listening to instructions) and doing it to the best of their ability and/or interest. Often, the only question that seems to be asked is, "Who's in charge here?" rather than "What does the task need?"

If you are the team leader, it's important that you set the stage, talk about the importance of trust, set an example of listening and trying to understand each other, and come to common agreements together.

Another way for a team to begin to build itself into a more cohesive unit is for each team member to have a turn to describe how he or she sees his or her role and then ask the group as a whole, "What does each of you need from me if I am to be more effective as a member of this team?" Obviously, for this process to really work, you need to plan time to allow it to happen—a retreat, an evening meeting where this topic is the only one on the agenda, or a sacrosanct part of regularly scheduled meetings over a considerable period of time. If team members can talk with each other about what they need from each other, they have a good chance of agreeing about duties and responsibilities. The process of talking will simultaneously develop enough trust that they feel they can count on other team members to meet their needs. And in the process of defining what needs to happen administratively, the empathic listening and honest sharing will minister to the spiritual and emotional needs of the people present.

What kinds of major obstacles block Church leaders from building effective teams?

1. People love each other but lack trust. It is interesting to note that the scriptures seem to differentiate between love and trust. Not only are we to love the Lord, but we are also told, "If you will turn to the Lord with full purpose of heart, and put your trust in him, and serve him with all diligence of mind . . . he will . . . deliver you out of bondage" (Mosiah 7:33). Nephi declared, "O Lord, I have trusted in thee, and I will trust in thee forever" (2 Nephi 4:34). Trust is defined as a sense of confidence that we can put ourselves in the care or keeping of another without any fear or misgiving. Love is a gift, the seal of a relationship. We love our parents, our children, our friends. But trust has to be earned. We trust others with our problems, our fears, our weaknesses, our confidences, and our emotions when we have confidence that they will deal with these matters in a way that will not be damaging to us. Many groups in the Church that should be teams lack trust that they can honestly say what they think and feel without being rebuffed, ridiculed, or rejected. We trust in the Lord but are not sure we can trust those around us.

2. A second major block is time. Too many leaders feel they do not have the time to try and build a quorum or unit into a team. The leader is worried about finding time for a lesson or is so busy giving instructions or trying to get members to accept an assignment that he or she has no time to build the conditions that might save time in the future.

3. A serious obstacle to team development is the fear of taking a risk. The leader hasn't done this before and is afraid of failing. He will "feel dumb" trying something so different. He doesn't trust the group members to come with him, but rather expects resistance and antagonism from them. Thus he goes into the experience defensively. The Lord warns that he is not pleased when some refuse to use their talents "because of the fear of man" (D&C 60:2). If the leader is afraid to try to deal with problems in the team because of fear of what someone might say, then fear stops all progress. It's been my experience, too, that a defensive approach, based on the assumption that you'll encounter resistance, practically guarantees that there *will* be resistance.

4. Another obstacle emerges when leaders are uncomfortable with open discussion where differences may emerge. (See "Conflict Management" below.) Some leaders fear trying to improve their team because they worry that there may be differences of opinion, and they do not know how to deal with differences. They do not know how to get people to discuss, listen, work out differences, and come to agreements in which everyone feels they can support the decisions made.

    Some years ago an elders quorum president asked me, "How do I deal with my quorum on home teaching? The members just aren't doing their work well." I suggested he might take some time and collect information from them, asking why they found it difficult to do home teaching. He said, "I couldn't do that!" "Why not?" I asked. "Because they'd just tell me the reasons, and I'd have to tell them they still had to do home teaching." He was seeing himself as an administrator, rather than as someone who ministered. He did not know how to get negative feelings out in the open and use the information to solve the problem.

5. Some leaders balk at building a team because they are more comfortable with a more authoritarian style. If the leader finds it easier just to tell people what he wants rather than discussing the matter with them, then team-work with its standard of open communication and real consensus in decision-making is difficult to pursue. If this is your situation, let me invite you to prayerfully consider the description of leadership in Doctrine and Covenants 121:34–46.

Conflict Management

What if someone takes seriously the invitation to speak openly with results that you think are irresponsible, critical, or even angry? Respectful listening is *especially* important if the comments seem divergent, divisive, and off-the-wall. Even if someone seems to be difficult on purpose, other team members will readily notice whether you respect and reward only thinking that already agrees with yours. If this is what they see happening, they will quite properly interpret your team-building encouragement as "just rhetoric" and patiently wait until you tell them what you really want.

How do you manage conflict or other divergent feelings? I think it's important to sense the person's motivation in creating the difficulty. I'm not talking about someone who has trouble staying on the subject or someone who just enjoys talking because he is charmed with the sound of his own voice. I'm assuming that you already know how to use redirecting comments like: "Let's refocus on the problem, which I see as being. . . ." or "I'm going to recap what you've just said, Henry. You feel that. . . . Is that more or less right? Then we need to hear from the others now."

Nor am I talking about a situation in which people genuinely see things differently but express their differences reasonably and logically. I'm assuming you know how to listen carefully, summarize the points of differences accurately, and lead the group through these questions:

- "Do you agree, Harvey and Mitch, with the summary of the differences I've just made?" (If they don't, have them restate their positions, summarize them again to Harvey and Mitch's satisfaction, then ask, "Does everyone in the group understand these differences?"

- "Can these differences be resolved? Or can we find a position that we can all support and implement, even if it isn't exactly what each personally wants?"

    — If the answer is yes, then ask: "Can someone see a way to phrase a compromise that will be acceptable to both positions and that will still meet our goal?"
    — If the answer is no, then ask: "In light of our goal and based on your own understanding of the people we're supposed to serve, which position do you think should take precedence?"

Team decisions are often based on compromise. The decision is not exactly what any individual may personally want, but it takes into account all of the diverse points of view and is something all can feel good implementing. The critical issue is that everyone must be willing to implement the decision. If they are not, or if the compromise requires such dilution of the goal as to make the goal meaningless, then the answer to the second question should obviously have been no instead of yes.

Let's discuss two situations of potential conflict that are different from the two situations above: (1) emotional intensity that seems excessive for the situation under discussion or even irrelevant to the discussion, and (2) malicious trouble-making for its own sake.

In the first situation, what do you do when a question about goals, values, or procedures unleashes a surprisingly intense reaction from someone, whether it is focused on the topic directly or whether it seems tangential to the subject? I suggest that you consider whether something else is the real problem or target. It is sad but true that open discussion is not often encouraged in the Church, and many people have feelings for which no legitimate forum exists in which to express them. If you are getting what appears to be an excessive reaction or even anger, especially if it is accompanied by what seems to be personal pain, recognize that you may be hearing what the individual wishes she had told an insensitive home teacher twenty years earlier, or a father's frustration at damage done to a child a decade earlier. Even though you can tell that the topic will not help you deal better with the task at hand, remember that you cannot manage the task *at all* without good team relationships. Attending to the needs of the one communicates powerfully to the ninety and nine.

If the topic seems to be so personal that you feel it should not be discussed in a group, ask respectfully, "We want to hear what you're saying, Elizabeth. Do you want to share it with all of us or would you rather have a more private setting?" Unless the experience involves someone else in the ward who *should* be present to tell his or her side, let Elizabeth continue if she wishes.

Help her articulate what she means with open-ended questions like:

- Can you please tell us more about that?
- How do you feel/think about that? Why?
- What do you mean when you say that . . . ?
- Do you see that as being positive or negative? Why?
- Is there anything else you would like to say about . . . ?
- Can you give me an example of that?

Then you can involve the rest of the group by asking:

- How do the rest of you feel/what do the rest of you think about that?
- How does what she said compare with your experience?

Remember, as leader you are setting an example of open, caring communication. In a conflict setting where divergent opinions are being expressed, your job is not to fix the problem, defend the Church, explain what should have happened, or instruct the person in how she should have felt. Your job is to listen and understand and help the speaker *feel* understood. If you try to short-circuit the process, the person will not feel understood and it will simply add to her pain. Also remember that there are other group members present who may add their resources in helping the situation.

But what about the third situation when the speaker seems motivated by malice, is taking critical pot-shots, or seems to be causing trouble for the sheer sake of causing trouble? This is a situation that calls for your leadership, not only because such tactics prevent people from dealing with the task but also because it will damage the relationships of those in the room. Such situations do not happen often in the Church; but if they do, the leader can say something like, "I can understand you have a problem with [describe the problem] that is very important to you. Dealing with this problem is not the purpose of the meeting, but I will be glad to meet with you privately when we have an uninterrupted stretch of time so I can really listen. For now, we must move ahead with the work of the group."

In our scene from Plainville Second Ward, the elders quorum presidency is faced with the problem of building the quorum into a real team. They know that some members of the quorum carry out assignments, while others don't. There is less than full participation, with all of the dynamics of resistance, resentment, guilt, and passivity that go along with such a situation. Certain activities—such as home teaching—just don't get done. The presidency then carries out a plan to get all of the quorum members fully committed to working together as a functioning team.

Plainville Second Ward:
The Elders Quorum

At the weekly meeting of the elders quorum presidency, the four men were deep in discussion. The president, Dean Suzuki, was making a point. "I feel good about the action we've taken as a quorum since Bishop Pratt gave us the Zion challenge," he said earnestly. "We've each written out what our stewardships entail, and we've set some goals as a quorum. Lars, would you go over those with us?"

The second counselor, Lars Whitehead, a heavy-set man in his late thirties who managed school-bus maintenance for the district, cleared his throat and read: "Number one, to make sure that every quorum member feels connected to the quorum; number two, to help each member and his family grow and develop spiritually; number three, to faithfully carry out all assignments; and number four, to help quorum members implement the three-part mission of the Church: to perfect the Saints, proclaim the gospel, and redeem the dead." Lars pulled off his glasses and frowned. "And your question, Dean, is how do you think we've been doing?"

The first counselor, Terry Harvey, the science teacher and football/basketball coach at the junior high, responded: "Well, since the bishop outlined what he wanted in terms of home teaching, I think everyone is doing a better job there, and families are just living better. I know mine is. But I'm not sure that we're carrying out our assignments any better. We are still following the same assignment procedure I've seen since I was old enough to be in a priesthood quorum. Somebody stands up and says, 'We need ten men out on the welfare farm this Saturday (or to clean up the chapel grounds, or whatever). How many feel they can go?' A few faithful raise their hands and the presiding person says, 'Well, we sure need you brethren. I'll pass around a sheet, and if you can go sign your name, or check with your wife and give me a call.' The sheet goes around, nobody else signs it and no one calls, and then we have to scramble around Friday night dredging up people to go at the last minute. The stake's mad, the members who didn't want to go are mad, and the leaders are frustrated. There's just got to be a better way."

Dean drummed his fingers on his clipboard. "Why don't people volunteer for quorum assignments?"

Darrel Hodges, the secretary, slapped his hand emphatically on the table. "Well, speaking for myself, if you really want to know the truth, it's because I'm fed up. I know that I spent two Saturdays last month pruning apple trees in the rain, and then on Sunday I'd look around the quorum and see everybody who had their feet up watching the football game. I said to myself, Why should I volunteer again when these others haven't done their part?" He paused, a little surprised at his own temerity. Dean nodded, listening intently. Darrel wrapped up: "We just don't show any commitment to each other. There's no common bond of brotherhood and teamwork. I know I'm making a judgment, but that's really how I feel."

Terry was nodding, too. "I know I've felt like Darrel lots of times. But there's another problem too. I'm one of those who's heard the phone ring Friday night and somebody wants me to do something the next morning when Marsha and I have been planning to visit her folks or take the kids to Portland for the day or when we have company coming. Frankly, I haven't appreciated the feeling that I'm supposed to drop everything. Even when they've announced it in church the previous Sunday, if I've got something already planned for the weekend, I'll sometimes try to

juggle things so I can do the assignment too; but if I can't, I figure that my family takes precedence."

Dean glanced at the other faces. They looked a little sheepish
yet defiant. He grinned quickly. "I think we're getting at some
reasons other quorum members would probably subscribe to as
well. It's an issue of fairness, isn't it?"

"Darn tootin'," muttered Darrel.

Dean continued. "If we were to summarize, then, there are
two major obstacles to getting volunteers for assignments. Because we wait for volunteers, the most willing people get worked
to death. They feel it's not fair. Also, because of how the assignments are allocated, people don't know when an assignment's
coming so they feel plans already in place take precedence. I think
these are legitimate reasons. The Church shouldn't ride rough-
shod over family schedules, and people shouldn't be unfairly bur-
dened by assignments. But there should be a way to accomplish
both family and quorum goals."

"Right," interjected Lars. "And without making quorum officers the bad guys."

"In fact," added Terry, "we're just talking about avoiding the
negatives. We don't just want people not to be mad at us. That
should be the minimum. I think the maximum should be that the
men feel they can be good at both things—their families (or, Darrel, their vast and extensive social lives) *and* their quorum responsibilities."

Dean grinned as the twenty-six-year-old secretary grumped:
"Oh yeah? Have you ever tried to find a date in Plainville? Talk
about frantic Friday telephone calls!"

"I don't know," Dean began mildly, "but when I was praying
about the feeling in the quorum, I didn't put my finger on these
problems. I live in Utah, you know," he pulled a pious face,
"where elders quorums complain to the bishop if they aren't allowed to work on the welfare farm every other Saturday." As the
others chuckled, he continued: "But I was looking in the scriptures for ideas about how quorums should work together, and I
found a few scriptures. Let's read them together and see if they
give us some ideas:

"Wherefore, now let every man learn his duty, and to act in
the office in which he is appointed, in all diligence.

"He that is slothful shall not be counted worthy to stand, and
he that learns not his duty and shows himself not approved shall

not be counted worthy to stand. Even so. Amen. (D&C 107: 99–100.)

"Again, the duty of the president over the office of elders is to preside over ninety-six elders, and to sit in council with them, and to teach them according to the covenants (D&C 107:89).

"I say unto you be one; and if ye be not one ye are not mine (D&C 38:27).

"And every decision made by . . . these quorums must be by the unanimous voice of the same; that is, every member . . . must be agreed to its decisions (D&C 107:27).

"For it is required of the Lord, at the hand of every steward, to render an account of his stewardship both in time and in eternity (D&C 72:3)."

"Okay," growled Lars. "So it's not all peaches and ice cream. There are duties. They have to be done, and done diligently. We're responsible for helping the men learn their duties."

"That much would be like the army," interposed Terry, "except that we're supposed to be united in spirit and heart. Not 'one' the way an army is, but 'one' spiritually. We need to sit in council together. We need to see how the Lord feels about our stewardships and what he wants us to do about them."

"That's the way I feel, too," said Dean. "Everybody's got personal duties. Family duties. Darrel, you may not be married, but I know you spend a lot of time with your mother and your sister's kids in Red Gap. We're all sons and brothers and neighbors. Most of us are husbands and fathers. These are important duties. In fact, they probably should come before quorum duties."

"But the problem with quorum duties," interrupted Terry excitedly, "is that the *system* is wrong. When we just ask for volunteers, there's no feeling that we've made decisions about quorum assignments together. Only the people who feel that the job is really part of their stewardship volunteer, and that's too haphazard."

Dean nodded. "You're on to something, Terry. How can we get the men to feel committed to each other and be responsible for all that must be done? We need to sit down with each brother and get his commitment to accept welfare duties as part of his responsibility to the quorum."

"And in a way that's fair to everybody," Darrel interposed.

Lars had been writing a list on his yellow notepad as fast as he could drive the pencil. Now he flipped the pad around and showed it to them. "Look. We know that we can pretty well count on these assignments." He read off the list of seasonal work in the orchard, cleaning up the stake property, providing chaperonage at girls camp, Boy Scout fundraising, service projects for the needy throughout the year and especially at holidays, helping move-ins and move-outs, and doing set-up and clean-up at the ward parties. "What have I left off?" Lars queried. "Let's figure out how many men it usually takes for each job, factor in a few extras for emergencies, and divide by the active men in the quorum."

Darrel whipped out his calculator, exclaiming, "And we can keep a kind of floating cushion because some people will move in or out. Or get activated. . . ."

Within a few minutes, they had determined that if each quorum member would accept four assignments a year, they would easily meet all of their responsibilities. Dean suggested: "Let's split up into two teams and divide the quorum between us. Let's visit each man, explain the duties of the quorum, and ask if each man would be willing to accept four assignments a year. We'll ask about schedules—you know, vacations, family reunions, weddings, National Guard, shift work, and so forth. People probably won't know for a whole year, but we'll ask them to let Darrel know as soon as they have a good idea of their schedules."

Lars chimed in happily: "Then, when an assignment comes up, we call the guy and tell him this is one of his four assignments. If he can't go, he's responsible for trading with someone or getting a person to take his place and letting us know."

"Sounds good!" Terry exclaimed. "We never ask for volunteers, everybody gets an equal number of jobs, and the assignments aren't favors to us or pay-offs for a guilty conscience, but just part of a man's quorum duties. And we can check on how he feels about the system and about the individual job in the quarterly priesthood interview."

"Well, hey," said Dean. "What have we got to lose but our frustrations? We can't just lay this on 'em, though. Remember Doctrine and Covenants 107:27?"

The next Sunday, Dean presented the plan at priesthood meeting. He wanted the quorum to consider its own group effectiveness, and he wanted every man to think how the plan would affect him personally. He read Doctrine and Covenants 107:27 to them about quorum decisions "by the unanimous voice." "That means," he explained, "if this plan really isn't going to work for even one of you people, then we need to figure out how to change it so that it will. Let's talk about it. We're here to listen. If we're going to be of one mind and be truly united as a team of brothers in the gospel, we need to learn to make decisions together that we all agree on."

Quorum members mulled the idea around slowly. Doug Pixton, one of the few who always volunteered, commented: "I sure don't mind the fact that there would be a way to spread it around. Nosirree. I'm in favor of this."

Paul Sorenson raised his hand. "Is there some way to maybe let it be known that you're more available for some kinds of assignments than others? I'm pretty sure I could get Tom Reynolds to help someone move in, but I think he'd run a mile in the opposite direction if I suggested that we go provide priesthood presence at the girls camp. And I think he'd do something with me where he probably would just say no if you called him up out of the blue."

"Great idea," said Dean. "Darrel can keep a 'Notes' section of special requests or team members. And probably—" he grinned at Warren Gardner who had his arm in a cast from a disastrous water-skiing expedition with the priests quorum the previous weekend— "we wouldn't want to ask Warren to climb a ladder just yet."

David Chun queried, "What do you do if there are work assignments and some members have honest conflicts?"

Dean hesitated. "We would ask each person to see if he could rearrange his schedule, or if he could swap with somebody. Would that be okay?"

Burt Snow said dubiously, "I dunno. What if an emergency comes up and nobody has time to make plans?"

"In that case," said Dean, "we'll just have to admit that it's an emergency and ask for volunteers. And we know that it'll happen at least a couple of times. It's inevitable."

"Hey, I've got an idea," suggested Lars. "If it's pretty inconvenient and takes quite a lot of time, why don't we say that you can get credit for two assignments?"

Burt Snow brightened considerably. After considerable discussion and some modifications, the quorum members present voted to adopt the new procedure unanimously. For the next couple of weeks, Dean and Darrel as one team and Lars and Terry as the other visited every elder. Most of the men in the meeting were actually enthusiastic, agreed to try out the new system, and reported their schedules as far as they knew. There was less enthusiasm among the inactive members; but even so, the quorum presidency was pleasantly surprised by how often a man conceded that he "wouldn't mind giving you a hand every now and then." Darrell fussed around with various kinds of charts and finally implored some help in organizing jobs, capabilities, schedules, and preferences from the indefatigable Jeff Burns, who calmly suggested giving each member a page in a notebook with a "No Job" column for the few assignments a member couldn't take, rather than sixteen columns for what he could do. In addition there would be a column for schedule notes and another column for contents.

"You'll need a one-sheet chronological log of incoming jobs and who has taken assignments as the first sheet in the book," he pointed out. "And why don't you organize the sheets by members' first names? That way a paper-clip will tell you where to start phoning on the next job but it won't be as mechanical and predictable as organizing it by surnames."

Then the presidency waited nervously. The first assignment was a request from the stake activities people for five men to work on repairs and clean-up in the stake girls camp area. "I'll try it first," said Dean. He picked up the phone, turned to the first sheet, and called Art Bateman. "Here's your first assignment, Art," he said cheerfully. He filled him in on the details.

"Okay, sure," said Art.

Dean continued down the list: Brad Wilson, Chet Shumway, David Chun. Doug Pixton was out of town—they were attending Evelyn's sister's wedding in Seattle. David had a convention on fire-prevention methods to conduct for the county. "I'll get somebody, Dean, and tell you who it is," he promised. Fred Palmer was the last.

"Would you drive and pick up the rest?" Dean added. "Here are the names of three of the other four, and David Chun will be calling me about the fourth one. I'll call him and have him tell his man to give you a call about the ride."

He hung up the phone with an unreal sense that it had all been too easy. But to Dean's surprise, relief, and delight, the whole activity went off without a hitch. From then on, no more assignments were made in quorum meetings. Everyone felt better about people having equal assignments and then being held accountable for their own stewardships. Naturally there were hitches and difficulties from time to time; but in almost every case the problems were worked out, and in general things went well.

With home teaching picking up momentum through the system of quarterly stewardship interviews, and the problem of assignments solved, the presidency next turned to Sunday meetings as a way to work on their first and second goals: making sure that every quorum member felt connected and wanted and helping each elder grow spiritually. They wanted to have every Sunday meeting of the quorum be a meaningful experience, so they decided to try to reach the goal of connection by finding ways of letting members share significant spiritual experiences. Out of their brainstorming emerged a variety of ideas.

For instance, instead of having lessons on the fifth Sundays, they asked three or four men to come prepared to share a ten-minute sketch of their lives that included a significant spiritual experience. Not too many men kept journals, but the presidency asked selected men to go back to their missionary journals or letters to find an experience, to write a letter to a member of their family about a significant experience that they could share in a larger group, or to write a letter to a son or daughter to be opened on that child's twenty-first birthday as a way of identifying important values to that man. They were not surprised when journal-keeping acquired new importance to many of the men.

The presidency also asked quorum members to write down a problem, issue, or concern they had; every couple of months, the presidency would arrange time during the quorum meeting for the person best able to deal with the matter to talk. Sometimes the topic was dealt with briefly if it was a procedural matter, but sometimes a whole lesson was taught on the topic.

One of the most rewarding innovations the presidency initiated was the Appreciation Session, a five- or ten-minute session at the end of class every few weeks. During this portion of a meeting, the presidency would give the name of a quorum member and anyone who wanted to could tell what he appreciated about that man. It was a little embarrassing to the man being featured, but although their ears turned red sometimes, they felt their hearts warm. These direct expressions of affection and respect had a dramatic effect on men's self-esteem and feelings of connection to the quorum.

With the heightened feelings of trust and respect in the quorum, it was almost inevitable that the lessons got better. Peter

Quinn, the teacher, had always presented interesting and stimulating lectures, but now he found himself asking more questions. The quorum members, in turn, were much more willing to respond, to volunteer information, to ask each other questions, or to observe, "Well, I think So-and-So probably has something to say on that topic."

While this quorum feeling of brotherhood was building on the basis of the stronger Sunday meetings, Dean, Lars, Terry, and Darrel also moved on some organizational issues, restructuring the quorum around some standing committees. Temporal and Spiritual Welfare Committee had several subgroups. The social subgroup planned and made assignments for firesides and quorum socials. The assistance subgroup helped the ward employment specialist to look after the employment needs or welfare needs. The sports and physical fitness subgroup planned for team or other sporting activities. When Peter, the dispatcher in the county sheriff's office, complained that he needed a fitness program that matched his chained-to-the-desk lifestyle, other quorum members also liked the suggestions that the subgroup found for Peter. The Family Histoy and Temple Committee focused on temple activities, family history research, and preparing quorum members and families to go to the temple. There was also the Missionary Committee, which developed a plan to fellowship new members and part-member families; assisted in community projects, which were plentiful in Plainville; and helped the full-time missionaries when they were needed. One guideline given by the presidency was that activities must meet the needs of members, and there should be no activities that the quorum members were supposed to support just for the sake of supporting. As a result, both activity and enthusiasm went up.

Members who had been on the periphery of activity for a long time found themselves drawn irresistibly toward the brotherhood, affirmation, and spiritual growth they could feel happening in the quorum. During one fifth-Sunday session, Dean Suzuki found himself swallowing hard as Jerry Mason, one of these reactivated elders, explained haltingly:

"I didn't have too much to do with the quorum for about ten years after I started working at the sugar beet factory. It only runs in the fall and winter; but after I missed my meetings nearly every week for three months, I wasn't any too anxious to start coming back. But I guess I was curious this spring. When Chet and Larry brought by the bishop's message about the ward, I guess I came back because I was curious to see what it would be like. I wasn't more than half-prepared to give it a fair chance, I admit it. And"—he faced Dean squarely—"I wasn't sure about having you for the president, Dean. My brother was killed on Okinawa during World War II, you know, and I've never had much use for Japanese people. But there was something here that just made me want to be here.

"Chet really put me on the spot when he started talking about family prayer. I'd never done it before and I felt awkward. It used to be that Bonnie would nag me by saying something like 'Aren't we ever going to have family prayer?' and I'd get irritated and say, 'If you want it, why don't you get something going?' It wasn't a very good environment for spiritual things. But that's changed. My Howard and Russell were scrapping all the time. They've really softened toward each other. And Kaye used to smart off to me and Bonnie all the time. I don't know—there's just a new feeling of respect. I'm willing to listen to them. They're willing to listen to me. And when I come here, I feel better. I feel the way I want to be all the time, even when I'm out on the tractor."

Discussion

This experience may sound idealistic, even romantic. Certainly it passes silently over the many hours of conferring, collecting information, discussing, negotiating, evaluating, and readjusting that have to occur in a group of real human beings. But the process itself is emotionally satisfying, because it communicates respect and caring. It lets quorum leaders and members nurture and minister to each other.

The presidency of Plainville Second Ward elders quorum recognized that the quorum was a long way from functioning as a united body of priesthood brothers. They analyzed the situation and made serious plans to build the quorum into a spiritual team.

1. The presidency had earlier developed a set of goals for the quorum which the quorum had accepted. However, there was a conspicuous gap between accepting the goals and actually getting to an action list. Although they felt good

about home teaching, which had received the first emphasis, they could tell that Sunday lessons were not powerfully
effective in meeting the goals and that the periodic service
assignments were actually detrimental.

2. The presidency had developed a good team spirit. They
    discussed the problems openly and personally, were not
    defensive about past practices, and used the scriptures not
    as a handbook but to set the spirit which any new solution
    must match.

3. A plan that stressed fairness and acknowledged personal
    differences was the key to solving the assignments prob-
    lem. The president set the criteria of open discussion, hon-
    est sharing, and a commitment to stick with the process
    until everyone could feel good about the results.

4. Deliberately strengthening the Sunday activities had three
    purposes: it let the quorum members learn about each
    other and express appreciation to each other, it helped
    them cope with their problems, and it improved the
    lessons by increasing the amount of personal interaction.

5. The committee structure let people associate on the basis
    of their interests, involved more people in leadership activ-
    ities, and involved the members in planning and carrying
    out important functions. These functions were need-
    based, eliminating activities that the members did not
    want or enjoy and thereby reducing the guilt they felt for
    not wanting to support an activity they perceived as pe-
    ripheral.

6. In such an atmosphere of increased trust and respect,
    members felt free to share with the others their experi-
    ences of change, learning, and growth. Not only did they
    become examplars of change but also such expressions of
    trust actually worked to increase trust.

As this case study shows, leaders in a Church group can begin
to assess the team's strengths and weaknesses, can plan for
changes with the total team membership, and can improve and
grow together. I have spent years of my professional life helping
business staffs and work units in organizations develop teams. It is
hard to overestimate both the importance of effective teams and
also the difficulty of team-building.

It would be great if all Church units learned to build a unified team with the example set by stake presidencies and bishops. The process for building teams would flow down through the stake as each officer taught the people with whom he or she worked. But team building can also flow from the ground up. If a family learns how to become a close, spiritual unit, then they can teach by example and, when there are appropriate occasions or invitations, more explicitly.

Even in situations where the formal leadership is lacking in vision, informal leadership can often point a better way. The Young Women's presidency in Plainville Second, for instance, was slow to catch the vision. Nola Gardner, the president, hadn't come to the first executive meeting; but Marjean Suzuki, a counselor and Laurel teacher, could see what her husband was achieving with the elders quorum. She called Nola after a few weeks and said, "I've really been impressed with the changes the elders quorum has made, and I know how happy Dean is with how things are going. Would it be useful to have their presidency come and talk with our presidency to see if they're doing anything we could learn from? Or if you think the tasks of the two organizations are too different, I could talk to Dean and bring back some ideas that you might consider. I'm not trying to do your job; but if the presidencies met together, we might learn from them and they might learn from us."

Nola didn't quite see how the new assignment rotation applied to Young Women but invited Marjean to discuss at the next presidency meeting some principles she thought relevant. For Marjean, the most important transfer was the possibility of finding a new way to consult with the teachers and set up a rotating calendar of planning activities, many of which had been somewhat haphazard and dull from being put together at the last minute by an overworked group. It was the beginning of better consultation and more effective team-building for the Young Women.

6

Teaching

And thou shalt teach them ordinances and laws, and shalt shew them the way wherein they must walk, and the work that they must do (Exodus 18:20).

Appoint among yourselves a teacher, and let not all be spokesmen at once; but let one speak at a time and let all listen unto his sayings, that when all have spoken that all may be edified of all, and that every man may have an equal privilege (D&C 88:122).

And the Spirit shall be given unto you by the prayer of faith; and if ye receive not the Spirit ye shall not teach (D&C 42:14).

The Principle

Should teaching appear on the list of leadership responsibility? Actually, yes. If we examine the functions of leaders in any organization, we see that all of them must, as a built-in part of their position, spend some time teaching others. Leaders are teachers. This process has various names—training, coaching, counseling, performance review, orienting, or sharing—but it all adds up to one thing: the leader tries to help others gain increased understanding, insight, and effectiveness in important areas of their responsibilities.

LDS leaders have an additional responsibility. Each executive has the duty to see that the teaching in his or her organization is effective. Bishops are thus indirectly responsible for the teaching in the entire ward. Think of the amount of teaching that goes on every Sunday! Sunday School, priesthood quorums, Relief Society, Primary, Young Women, and sacrament meeting.

The most effective way for leaders to help teachers be effective is (1) to hold regular stewardship reviews, (2) to maintain an ongoing program of visits and evaluation, and (3) to support teachers with a specific and helpful quarterly teacher-training meeting for all teachers that is organized and conducted by the ward teacher development coordinator.

The scriptures give relatively little instruction about *how* we should teach. In the Doctrine and Covenants the Lord states, "The elders, priests, and teachers of this church shall teach the principles of my gospel, which are in the Bible and the Book of Mormon, in the which is the fulness of the gospel." Thus, this scripture identifies the primary teaching texts. Two verses later, the Lord also states, "And the Spirit shall be given unto you by the prayer of faith; and if ye receive not the Spirit ye shall not teach" (D&C 42:12, 14). Quite apart from the usual interpretation of this statement that one should not teach if he does not have the Spirit, this can be taken as a pointed warning: we will not *teach* unless we have the Spirit of the Lord; that is, without the Spirit what occurs will not be teaching as the Lord means the term.

Looking to the forthcoming temple and its learning environment, the Lord set a teaching pattern appropriate to all Church classes: that there should be one teacher, that all should listen as he or she speaks, and that the teacher then should allow every other person the opportunity to speak so that all may be edified (D&C 88:122). I think this also means that class members who are expressing their faith, their testimonies, and their understanding of gospel principles strengthen themselves through the exercise of struggling to express powerful but often inexpressible feelings and concepts.

The Lord tells priesthood leaders that it is part of their calling to teach those under their leadership what their duties are (see D&C 107:85–89) and presumably this applies to other leaders too; and parents, who unquestionably are the leaders in the home, are directly commanded to teach their children very specific things: repentance, faith in Christ, baptism, and the laying on of hands for the gift of the Holy Ghost (see D&C 68:25). If parents have neglected these teachings as part of the child's preparation for baptism, their negligence is called a "sin." The same section also counsels parents to teach their children to pray, to observe the Sabbath day, and to labor at their assigned duties. Parents must teach their children, by both precept and example, to be neither idle nor greedy, but rather to seek for the riches of eternity (D&C 68:26–31).

In this chapter's scene from Plainville, a discouraged Sunday School teacher is about to abandon his class of unruly teenagers. The teacher's file leader, a counselor in the Sunday School presidency, is an effective leader in supporting the teacher emotionally and helping him acquire the skills to deal with this situation.

Plainville Second Ward:
The Sunday School Teacher

Class 13 was behaving about as usual this hot July Sunday morning, and Ron Hardy was ready to drop the manual and walk out. Even as he tried to explain the five R's of repentance, he saw Judy and Amy with their heads together, stifling hysterical giggles about something, Troy was dozing, Allen and Hal were examining a pocketknife, and Yvette, Audra, Ken, and Brett were flirting elaborately, not even bothering to keep their voices down. The class was utterly chaotic. Ken and Brett had even turned their chairs around, to pen Yvette and Audra into a back corner.

Ron drew a deep breath and kept determinedly talking; but his frustration, irritation at their rudeness, and despair at knowing what he could do overwhelmed him. He'd taught other classes before, but his oldest child, Sandra, was only ten and he couldn't possibly imagine her acting like this. "I just don't understand teenagers," he thought dismally.

He'd been the teacher since February, and he'd never once taught a lesson he felt good about. Sunday was the worst day of the week. He dreaded seeing the weekend approach. "I'm like Daniel going into the lion's den," he'd told Pamela just that morning, "but the lions are winning." He'd tried everything. He had yelled, praised, brought treats, brought in the Sunday School president, called some parents—but nothing had made a difference for longer than a week or two.

When the closing bell rang, he breathed a great sigh of relief, called on Audra to give the closing prayer, and dejectedly left the classroom. That afternoon, listlessly making a place on his mashed potatoes for the gravy, he announced to Pamela: "Well, today was my last day. I just can't go through this every Sunday. I am going to tell the Sunday School presidency they have to release me. I'm not doing the kids any good, and it's threatening my sanity."

Pamela smiled sympathetically and handed him the peas. "I have really mixed feelings about this whole situation," she said. "I know how hard you've tried and how frustrated you've been. You've given it your best shot, and it just hasn't worked. I hate to see you frustrated and upset like this. Maybe someone else *would* handle the class better, but I don't know anyone who could have tried harder."

"Well, thanks, honey," said Ron, spooning some peas on four-year-old Lisa's plate. "I hate to give up. I hate to think of myself as a failure in anything, but they've just got me licked."

That evening Ron drove over to the home of Gene Thompson, the first counselor in the Sunday School presidency, who was responsible for the thirteen-year-old class. Gene welcomed him warmly and took him out on the deck with a glass of lemonade. Ron nervously gulped a swallow of the lemonade, choked, coughed, and banged the glass down. "Gene, I'll get straight to the point," he blurted out. "You'll just have to get a new teacher for that class of mine. The kids aren't learning anything, and it's getting so frustrating for me I've just got to give it up."

Gene ran his hand through his thinning hair and then quickly patted Ron's knee. "I'm kicking myself, brother," he said. "I know you've really tried, and I also know thirteen-year-olds are a tough group to handle. But I hadn't realized things had reached such a stalemate with the class. I feel as though I should have been in better touch. Crummy job I'm doing."

"No, it's not that—," began Ron uncomfortably.

"But admit it," pressed Gene. "You basically just got dumped into a pool of piranha, didn't you?"

Ron laughed. "I guess that's a good way of putting it."

"Well, listen," said Gene. "I won't try and talk you into it; but before you leave this assignment, I wonder if you'd try an experiment with me?"

"Is this to make *you* feel better?" Ron growled.

Gene glanced at him guiltily, and they both laughed when Ron flashed him a big grin. "So tell me. What do you have in mind?" Ron asked.

"Ever since the bishop has asked us to try and live as close to a celestial law as we can, I've been trying to identify what the Lord has said about teaching. What I'd like to do is go over these scriptures on teaching, see what they might mean for you, and ask you to try to follow these directions in this class. If they won't work, then I'll treat you to a steak dinner in lieu of combat pay and we'll buy monogrammed straitjackets and gags for the entire class and bring my old top sergeant out of retirement to teach it."

"Actually," Ron responded wryly, "I'm kind of interested in the straitjackets. But let's go over the scriptures and see if there's anything there I haven't already tried."

Gene walked in the bedroom and came back with two sets of scriptures and a yellow notepad. The top page was filled with neatly printed references, followed by a phrase or two of summary. "Here," he said, handing Ron a set. "You can use Meredith's. I was pretty impressed with how many times teaching comes up in the scriptures," he said, half-apologetically, "but don't let me get obnoxious about it. Let's just go through the three or four with stars by them and then see what the applications would be like in your class."

The two of them began reading, taking turns reference by reference:

"And again, the elders, priests and teachers of this Church shall teach the principles of my gospel which are in the Bible and the Book of Mormon, in the which is the fulness of the gospel. And they shall observe the covenants and church articles to do them and these shall be their teachings, as they shall be directed by the Spirit. And the Spirit shall be given unto you by the prayer of faith; and if ye receive not the Spirit ye shall not teach. (D&C 42:12–14.)"

"Appoint among yourselves a teacher, and let not all be spokesmen at once; but let one speak at a time and let all listen unto his sayings, that when all have spoken that all may be edified of all, and that every man may have an equal privilege (D&C 88:122)."

"And let them journey . . . preaching the word by the way, saying none other things than that which the prophets and apostles have written and that which is taught them by the Comforter through the prayer of faith (D&C 52:9)."

"[But the priests] were to receive the grace of God, that they might wax strong in the Spirit, having the knowledge of God, that they might teach with power and authority from God (Mosiah 18:26)."

"Okay," Ron summarized, after they had finished. "It's pretty clear that a major theme is having the Spirit. Second, we should teach from the scriptures and what the prophets have written. I guess we should also teach with power and authority."

"I'm with you so far," said Gene. "But what about Doctrine and Covenants 88?"

Ron hesitated. "That one threw me. I mean, I understand about the one teacher, but it was the 'equal privilege' part I didn't get. Now that I think about it, I guess it means that everybody should have a chance to speak and everybody should listen. Taking turns, kinda?"

Gene nodded his head, "You see exactly the same four things I do. Now, if you look at your teaching in light of these principles. . . ."

"Well, I know I haven't had a good spirit in that class for a long time," Ron said unhesitatingly. "To be honest, I've had a reluctant, even a resentful spirit when I have gone to teach. It sure hasn't been the Spirit of Christ. Sometimes I've really dreaded facing the class one more time."

Gene nodded. "Pretty depressing. Another scripture says, 'If ye are prepared ye shall not fear' (D&C 38:30), and my guess is that it would be impossible to dread the class if you felt the Spirit."

"That's what I *want*!" Ron exclaimed. "But how do you get that fear out of your heart and feel the Spirit?"

"Well," Gene hesitated. "I'm not really sure, but the scripture that just popped into my mind was from Paul's letter to Timothy: 'For God hath not given us the spirit of fear; but of power, and of love, and of a sound mind' (2 Timothy 1:7). Is there any help there, or is it too general?"

Ron blinked. "I'd have to say that a lot of it is really relevant," he answered slowly. "When I've prepared the lesson, I've just tried to get a logical sequence in mind. I haven't thought about an approach powerful enough to hit those kids where they live. I sure haven't spent any time thinking about loving them. And having a 'sound mind' seems like it's telling me to really use basic common sense. I haven't even thought about what would interest teenagers as teenagers. And—well, Gene, Paul says these are things God gives us, and I don't think I've even prayed specifically about any of them."

"Well, that's quite a payoff from just one scripture about having the Spirit," said Gene mildly. "Any observations about the other points?"

"Well, we read the scriptures in our family, but I don't think I've tried to prepare each lesson with the scriptures in mind."

Gene nodded. "What about involving the kids in the lessons?"

"I've actually tried *not* to," Ron admitted. "I've tried to have enough material that I can have something to say all the time. I get nervous even thinking about giving those kids an opening—not that they listen to what I have to say anyway."

"Okay, then," said Gene. "Now, let's plan an attack." Together, the two men agreed on a procedure that they felt would incorporate the points identified by the scriptures:

1. Ron would first read over the lesson and pray for the Spirit to help him approach the main idea with power, love, and clear understanding.
2. When he had a clear focus for the lesson he would write it down and build his lesson around it.
3. He would think of a situation that everyone in the class could understand and ask each one of them to respond to it. In some cases, he might ask a class member or two to come prepared to respond to the central theme of the lesson.
4. Ron would ask class members to bring their scriptures to class every Sunday, and in class they would look up the references that related to the lesson.
5. To speak with power and authority, Ron would relate a personal experience that was important to him. After all, as Gene pointed out, "you're the world's expert on your own experiences."

As they said good-bye, Gene said, "I'm really anxious to know how this is going to turn out."

Ron was grinning. "I'm actually anxious to try it—but keep that straitjacket catalogue handy."

The next lesson was on baptism, and Ron put his new process to the test. As he prayed and thought about the lesson and the class, he felt impressed to focus on one idea: how baptism applied to these thirteen-year-olds. He asked himself what he knew about them. Amy, the second oldest of Mariah Dalton's five children.

The divorce had come when she was eight. Audra Wilson, one of the brightest girls in her class but very chatty, just like her mother, Barbara. Hal Gardner, who had a reputation for being a little reckless. He'd been driving the boat when his dad, Warren, broke his arm on that water-skiing party. Ron realized humbly that, even after several months, he knew surprisingly little about them as individuals. And what kind of commitment could he expect them to have about the class?

Then he had an insight that made him pick up the phone and call Gene. Gene listened and said, "Absolutely. I'll clear it with Kent and we'll stand by." Pamela was praying silently as they drove to church the next Sunday, but Ron was actually whistling cheerfully.

When the members of Class 13 slowly gathered in the classroom, Ron was waiting for them, conspicuously pleasant in contrast to the tense and sour face they were used to. He greeted them by name and, with a firm hand on Ken's shoulder, steered him to a seat between Judy and Amy and planted Allen and Hal on opposite sides of the room. Then he walked briskly to the front of the room and announced: "Class, I'm giving you a choice of three options, and you won't get into trouble no matter what you choose. First, you can stay here in the class and participate in the lesson. That means you answer questions, read scriptures, listen when someone else is talking, and think about the ideas. Second, if you want to visit with each other, you can go in Room 14 and a member of the Sunday School presidency will check in on you from time to time. If you want to read a magazine or a book from the meetinghouse library, you can go out in the hall. You can't leave the meetinghouse. What'll it be? I want an honest answer from each one of you."

The class members, stunned, were speechless, glancing at each other nervously. Ron continued: "I've cleared all three options with the Sunday School presidency. You really can choose. I know I haven't been the greatest teacher, but I'm determined to give you lessons that are really worth your while from now on, starting today. But you're free to choose."

"Wow, that's great!" giggled Amy Dalton. "Let's go talk, Judy!"

Judy glared. "Are you crazy? My mom would have a fit. And so would yours."

"No," Ron interrupted. "I'll talk to your parents and explain that these are real options for you. Do you want to try it?"

"Not me," Judy said firmly. "My mom is always talking about how I'm supposed to be here to learn the gospel."

"How have you done so far?" inquired Ron.

She blushed, then laughed when she saw he was grinning at her. "Well, I guess it's never too late," she conceded cheerfully. "I'll stay."

"Amy? If you stay, you have to participate in the lesson. It's not a place to visit."

"I guess I'll stay," she mumbled.

Hal, grinning broadly, got up. "I'm outta here. Coming, Allen?"

"Well," Allen said cagily, "if I don't like the lesson, Brother Hardy, can I shift to one of the other options?"

"You can shift next week," said Ron firmly, "but you have to choose at the beginning what you'll do that week. You can decide something different every single week if you want to."

"I've decided," announced Hal, walking to the door. Allen got up indecisively and trailed along.

"Fine," said Ron. "See you later."

Defiantly Hal opened the door. Gene Thompson, who had been lounging against the wall straightened up.

"Hal and Allen want to go to Room 14," said Ron.

"Okay," said Gene agreeably. "Anybody else?"

"Well," said Audra, "nothing against you, Brother Hardy, but the lessons are really boring. I'd rather read the *New Era*."

"Fine," said Gene. "Why don't you go down to the library and get an issue. Then pick a chair in the foyer. I'll check with you later. Is that all?"

Ron swept the class again. "Choose out loud, not by default," he insisted. "Troy?"

"I'll stay."

"Yvette?"

"I guess I'll stay."

"Ken?" Audra cast Ken a commanding look. "Reading means silent reading in the foyer. Visiting in Room 14 only," Ron reminded. Ken subsided. "Okay," he mumbled. Brett nodded in answer to Ron's questioning look.

Gene gave him a wink and closed the door.

"Okay," Ron began. "We're talking about baptism. I was baptized at age eight. Were all of you?" The students nodded, except for Ken Harvey, who had waited until he was nine so that his grandfather, who was on a mission, could baptize him. "Well, when I was fifteen," Ron continued, "I knew my ordination as a priest was coming up, but I'd been messing around quite a bit that year. At school, I was hanging out with two or three kids who weren't religious in any sense of the word. I'd tell my parents I was going to the library and then meet them in the park. Johnny Stark was already sixteen and had a car, so we'd all pile into it and go riding. He nearly always had some beer. I didn't like the taste, particularly, but I didn't say no when the bottle got to the back seat. Another time, Carmody came up with a fifth of whiskey. Dolan used to shoplift *Playboy* from the 7-11 and it went around the back seat too. I always said no to cigarettes and wouldn't stay in the car if they smoked, because my parents would jump on me if they smelled it, but that was about the only thing I said no to."

Amy Dalton was staring wide-eyed at him, her mouth gaping slightly. Troy and Brett had exchanged a quick glance during the part about the beer and then stared studiously at the blackboard, their faces carefully neutral.

Ron continued: "So there I was. I didn't like what was happening. I knew I wasn't worthy to become a priest. I needed to repent, but I wasn't sure how. I spent a lot of time thinking about these questions." He swung around and jotted down on the chalkboard:

- If I could be baptized again, it would wash away my sins, but how can I be forgiven when I can't be baptized again?
- How could I repent?
- Did God hold me more accountable than Johnny and Splits, since I was a Mormon and had the priesthood?
- How did the Atonement apply?

"So what do you think?" he asked mildly and waited. No one spoke. The silence made Ron nervous but he forced himself to keep on waiting.

Finally Brett raised his hand and spoke slowly. "I'm not sure about some of those questions, but I know that you've got to stop doing what's wrong if you're serious about repenting."

"I think God *does* hold you more accountable," Amy interjected suddenly, "because you *know* what you're doing is wrong."

"The sacrament has something to do with it," Troy began uncertainly, and Judy interrupted, "Yeah, but if you take the sacrament when you know you're doing something wrong, that just makes it worse."

Suddenly, hands were flying up all over the room and the air was full of questions and comments. Ron steered the discussion, reminding them to take turns talking, asking another question if a particular approach seemed to stall, and interjecting his own comments. When the bell rang, Troy groaned with dismay. Surprised, Ron glanced at his watch. They hadn't even got to Alma the Younger, so he assigned all of the students to read that account, called on Ken for the closing prayer, and ushered them out.

As they spilled into the hall, still talking, Hal and Allen came swaggering defiantly out of Room 14. "Boy, did you geeks miss a great lesson," Yvette informed them scornfully.

Ron bowed his head, his heart swelling with thankfulness. When he looked up, Gene was standing in the doorway, one eyebrow raised. Ron smiled. "Forget the straitjackets."

The next week when Ron gave the class members their choice, nobody moved. Gene, who was waiting in the doorway, winked as Ron said, "I guess we don't need you today."

Discussion

The stereotype of the unruly teenage class is not entirely without foundation. Young teenagers are simultaneously dealing with their own raging hormones, experimenting with the balance of autonomy and authority, and engaging in complex social experiments with the opposite sex. Add the expectation of education to this mixture, and it may seem like too much.

Ron Hardy, the hapless teacher, has what can be considered a typical experience. He wants to be successful and works hard, but he doesn't understand teenagers, is baffled by their rudeness, and finds himself dreading the assignment. His initial strategy is to concentrate on the lesson material. He reasons that if he has a lot of material to cover, he can stay in control. In contrast, the Lord's instructions are to concentrate on first obtaining the Spirit as a prerequisite for teaching principles derived from the scriptures. The instruction to "observe the covenant and church articles to do them" clearly means that the teacher must be living worthy of the Spirit or, in more modern parlance, should "walk his talk," then pray earnestly for the Spirit.

The Sunday School counselor provides effective leadership. He accepts responsibility for his part in this unpleasant situation that has developed, does not criticize or blame Ron but listens to him, shares his own feelings, searches the scriptures with him, and acts as a resource as Ron formulates a plan for teaching.

Ron's preparation is focused on a clearly relevant idea: how does a baptism at age eight apply to thirteen-year-olds? To solve the discipline problem, Ron uses a very effective judo device: he sidesteps it by giving the students other options. His admission that he has not been very effective but now feels better prepared is one teens seldom hear, so it intrigues them. When he follows through on the options and lets students leave the class—also extremely unusual in a Church setting—he communicates respect for both those who leave and those who stay. His four discussion questions are carefully framed on a thirteen-year-old level, and the fact that he uses himself for an example—especially a negative example—is an almost certain attention-getter. Not only do the students experience the intellectual stimulation of engaging directly with the topic but also they solve the discipline problem by informing the absentee students about what they're missing.

The scene ends with Ron experiencing real success—for the first time. It is not likely that he will use the same format for each lesson. As he studies the lesson and prays for spiritual guidance, studying things out in his own mind about teaching methods, he will almost certainly be impressed to try new and different ways of involving the class. As the students experience the power of the gospel principles coupled with the "sound mind" of true relevance taught by a teacher who has prayed and has prepared with love, it will be hard for them to stay away.

Teaching is a crucial Church role. It covers much more than an hour's instruction on Sunday morning. All parents and grandparents are teachers in their families. Parents preparing a family home evening lesson are under the same general instruction to seek the Spirit, teach basic principles of the gospel from the scriptures, live the principles they teach, and teach their children as individuals. There should be an opportunity for all family members to participate so they can edify each other. Parents should speak with the authority of personal testimony and personal experience.

This pattern of teaching is also relevant to home teachers and visiting teachers. They should read the lesson suggested in the *Ensign*, pray for the Spirit to let them know the emphasis they should give for each of their families, plan the lesson with variations that accommodate the diversity of the families or sisters they visit, and build into it opportunities for all to participate and share their ideas and feelings.

The Lord's church is a teaching church. One of the main goals emphasized for the whole Church in our day is to instruct and edify the members of the Church in the principles of the gospel. This is done in the home, during visits to the home, and in all Church meetings. Good teaching is an essential part of the millennial path, and leaders have the responsibility to be effective teachers themselves and to help teachers under their stewardship become more effective.

During my Church service, I have been a bishop, a stake president, a high councilor, and a member of the Sunday School General Board. During that time, I have noticed that some people have a gift for teaching while others struggle with teaching assignments. Can every person become an outstanding teacher? I suspect that some will always be better teachers than others, but I strongly believe that a teacher who truly wants to be more effective can measurably improve by following the principles outlined in the scriptures.

I am also aware that some who have been called to a teaching position have never seen a really good teacher in action. In such a case, I would suggest that the newly called teacher find out who has a reputation for being really effective with the age group the new teacher has been called to serve, then go and observe that teacher. It's all right to do this in another ward or branch.

It can also be helpful if this new teacher's leader is helpful and nonthreatening and, with the new teacher's permission, can observe the class and interview class members. On the basis of what he or she learns, the leader is then in a position to make specific, constructive suggestions that will accomplish two purposes: first, communicate unmistakably to the teacher that the leader also has a stake in his or her success, and second, help the teacher experience that warm thrill of success that makes classroom teaching one of the most satisfying assignments in the Church.

7

Helping

Let us therefore come boldly unto the throne of grace, that we may obtain mercy, and find grace to help in time of need (Hebrews 4:16).

But whoso hath this world's good, and seeth his brother have need, and shutteth up his bowels of compassion from him, how dwelleth the love of God in him? (1 John 3:17.)

The Principle

Every leader can expect to face two kinds of helping situations. First, she sees someone who appears to need help of some kind. She must evaluate how to check out that perception with the person, evaluate the kind of help that seems beneficial, and decide how to offer help in a way that the other person can accept. Second, a person seeks out the leader and tells him directly: "I need your help."

There is a common dilemma in the first situation. Even people who desperately need assistance—direct physical labor, a helping hand, counsel, or support—may feel ashamed or embarrassed to ask for help, refuse it if it is offered, consider a question about their situation an invasion of their privacy or an attack on their self-image, or feel demeaned if their perception is that they have become a "service project." Part of this reaction is a phenomenon of American culture, and hence we may need to consider a variety of approaches in offering help: (1) "You know the blessing of helping others. Please don't deny others the blessing of helping you." (2) "We all have seasons of giving and seasons of receiving.

This is your season to receive." (3) If the service is an obvious one (such as shoveling snow from a walk), an older person who would proudly refuse an offer of assistance will be grateful to find the walk shoveled, with or without permission.

Different approaches are effective with different people, and this requires true sensitivity on the part of a leader. Almost totally ineffective is the meaningless invitation, "Please call me if there's anything I can do." The person will almost certainly never call. Psychologically, the offerer can feel satisfied with making the offer but no service needs to be expended. Another "kill-service" question is, "What can I do to help?" It almost invites an answer of, "Nothing, thanks. I can manage by myself." A more effective question is, "What are the problems or concerns that seem most pressing right now?" This invites the person to simply describe his or her situation, and the service that the individual may actually consider most valuable may not be obvious at all.

A dilemma in the second situation is that a few people have learned to depend on others rather than looking first to their own resources. They are more skillful in looking for ways others can give them assistance than in helping themselves, and often consider the Church an "entitlement" program upon which they can draw for welfare, money, free child care, and endless emotional support. Again, the leader must be sensitive, encouraging more self-sufficiency in a supportive way.

The situations in a ward that become opportunities for service are endless: helping a person move; caring for the sick, the aged, and the infirm; giving support in times of grief or tragedy; putting in a lawn; repairing a car; taking someone to the store; baby-sitting; helping with a wedding reception, ward banquet, or house cleaning. One of the most sensitive areas of offering help is in the area of financial assistance, where someone may need real help to find a job so he or she can support a family.

The gospel that Christ taught has always emphasized that we should all be our brother's keeper, should love our neighbors as ourselves. This includes being concerned about our neighbors in an economic sense as well. The New Testament Saints, following the ascension of the Savior, lived briefly with all worldly goods in common. Joseph Smith, inspired by not only this story but by the newly revealed information about the City of Enoch in the Pearl of Great Price and by revelations on the subject, instituted the

United Order. However, neither the Saints in former days nor the Saints in latter days have been prepared to live this economic order permanently.

Almost certainly the millennial life will deal more successfully with the shattering problems of poverty and economic inequity that currently burden our society. In the millennial world, no one will be content unless all others are as materially well off as he or she is. People will want to see that others are helped in a material sense. Therefore, we may appropriately ask what attitudes and action are important to observe. Clearly, we are to pay an honest tithe and a generous fast offering. We are also encouraged to support missionary work and to share our surplus informally, without being commanded, as we encounter those who are less fortunate. Furthermore, every priesthood quorum, acting as a brotherhood and following the counsel given by priesthood leaders, is expected to know the economic condition of each quorum member and actively help those in need. This includes the widows of quorum members. The Relief Society bears the primary responsibility for being aware of the needs of single women and women married to nonmembers. In practice, however, the Relief Society is usually more aware of the needs of families headed by an inactive priesthood holder than the priesthood quorums are.

It has been the standard of the Church from the beginning to help all people to help themselves—to become self-supporting. Almost every bishop and branch president also gives direct welfare, but this aid is always thought of as a temporary measure, a situation in which the Church member quickly regains financial self-sufficiency. The order of the Church is self-sufficiency within a network of support and resources: first, one's own; next, the resources of the extended family; and finally, the resources of the Church.

The Plainville scene for this chapter shows how a quorum leader with the right perspective moved effectively to help a member who was in real economic difficulty. In the area of economic or occupational help, the leader will first try to understand the other person's need. With that understanding, the leader will give help that allows the other person to retain his personal sense of dignity and self-worth. Help is not "helpful" if the assistance given leads the other person to either become dependent on the help or to become so defensive and angry that he rejects any form of help.

Plainville Second Ward:
Chris Scott, Unemployed

The Scott household was in an uproar. Chris was yelling in rage at the four children: "I'm sick and tired of you kids goofing off and not helping. You think just because I'm not working that I should do all the work around here!" He glared at his wife: "And that goes for you too, Carol. Just because you're working as a checker at the grocery store doesn't mean that you can't help a little more, too!" With that verbal blast he grabbed his hat, slammed out the front door, and roared away in the pickup, tires squealing.

Carol, lips trembling, put her arms around ten-year-old Tammy, who was sobbing brokenheartedly. Fourteen-year-old Toni looked both defiant and near tears. Twelve-year-old Don stalked off to his room, but not before six-year-old Cal, wide-eyed and apprehensive, asked, "Why is Dad so mad?"

Carol said more calmly than she felt: "It's hard on your dad to be out of work. You know he never yelled like this when he was working. He'll be all right when he is able to get another job."

Chris had worked for Pacific Plywood for fourteen years; but ten months ago, in September, the company had cut back to a skeleton crew because of problems in the lumber industry. While Chris was sick at heart, since he liked his work and the company, he at first felt optimistic that something would come up soon and that unemployment compensation would cover the family needs. But as he made the rounds, his optimism sagged. His only skill was making plywood, and jobs were nonexistent in that area. He found nothing in construction or working with heavy machinery. Aside from a short seasonal job driving truck for the potato harvest, he had had no work all fall. Winter was worse. Now a corrosive spring had come and gone. Immersed in his own difficulties, Chris had barely noticed the change in the ward bishopric in May. Now it was July. He had spent the hot Sunday afternoon looking at the want ads from a neighbor's borrowed newspaper and feeling black despair. As usual, there were only a few jobs available at fast food places, but Chris's pride shrank from waiting on his neighbors and being the new employee next to more skilled high school students. He was thirty-seven years old. He was still young, able-bodied, smart. There had to be something!

Carol, dark circles under her eyes, set up the Clue board, popped some corn, and coaxed Don out to join the other children, chattering cheerfully. After Thanksgiving, she'd resolutely gone to their neighborhood store and interviewed for a job as a checker. She didn't tell Chris until after she'd actually gotten the job. He had been angry, but she, thinking of his own uncertain future, had calmly insisted, "It's only until you find something, honey."

"I suspect that Mrs. White perpetrated the vile deed with the candlestick in the lounge," she announced, moving the candlestick from the study. "Don, do you have any evidence?"

"I have some evidence," Don intoned in sepulchral tones and gave her a furtive peek at his card. Carol, who was playing partners with Cal, whispered, "Mark off Mrs. White." As Don rolled the dice, Carol thought drearily, "Those stories in the *Ensign* always talk about how adversity creates greater closeness in the family and greater reliance on each other. And somebody walking into the kitchen now would think we looked like a family off the cover of the family home evening manual. Except that there's one person missing."

Her job was within walking distance of the house. The children were good about taking care of themselves and each other when she had to work afternoons and evenings. Thank heaven the store was closed on Sunday. She dreaded Saturdays when all the children were home. She never knew what she would find when she got off work at 6:00 P.M. Sometimes it was a shining house, a hot supper on the table, and the children finishing up their homework. Sometimes nothing. Yesterday, Chris had been home, but he was slumped in one of his terrifying spells of immobility in front of the television, ignoring them. Toni had whispered that she'd made scrambled eggs and toast for everyone for lunch. The week before, Chris had been gone all day and ten-year-old Tammy had cut her finger opening a can of soup for lunch. Carol's job provided enough income to barely meet regular expenses. The car was old, but Chris had been able to keep it running. The pickup was newer, but the insurance was higher on it, too. They'd bought school clothes before Chris got laid off, but these wouldn't last forever. Even a birthday present required painful scrimping. Nobody had been to the dentist all year. The dishwasher had gone out in January—it was fortunate it wasn't the washing machine. Their savings had barely lasted through Christmas.

They had talked the whole situation over quite sensibly at family home evening in October, and the kids had all said they would help. Toni had tried out for the junior high drill team and been accepted; but the uniform cost almost two hundred dollars. She told her friends she was too busy and told the advisor that she couldn't participate anymore. She and Don both got paper routes and delivered papers every day after school. Carol was immensely grateful for that. There seemed to be an endless number of demands for school fees and projects. On their own, the two oldest quietly handed her ten dollars a week "to help out with the groceries."

Toni was clowning with a fake British accent for Tammy: "I say, what, what? I suspect that it was Colonel Mustard with the pipe wrench—nahsty things, pipe wrenches—in the dining room, don'tcha kneow."

"They are really good kids," Carol thought, tears unexpectedly pricking her eyelids. "But they *are* just kids, and kids don't always do their chores on time and they don't see what needs to be done and do it without being told. This is the second fit Chris has thrown this week. The kids have been avoiding him for a long time. And I'm so tired . . ." She fought back the thought. She had to keep going. She had to.

Carol knew the family was in jeopardy. If Chris didn't get work and he continued to be irritable and punishing to everyone, she knew something would have to give. Toni had already yelled back at him when he had snarled at Cal about something, and Chris had hit her. He'd apologized later, but it had made Carol realize how much Chris's sunny temperament had deteriorated. What would happen if it weren't for the Church? What if Chris's commitment to their temple marriage and Church standards didn't stand between him and drinking or another woman? She was afraid that Chris might walk away from the family out of guilt, or their own relationship would disintegrate so far that it might not recover, even if he found work, or the children would develop a lasting bitterness toward Chris. And what if he *didn't* find work? It was looking less likely every day. Carol knew Chris's immense pride in being self-reliant, so she tried to walk the fine line between being available and supportive and not giving advice. Had it been a mistake to let Chris try to manage things himself?

As it gradually became clear that Miss Scarlet had assassinated Mr. Boddy in the library with the rope, her resolution also clari-

fied. Since spring—really since George Pratt had become bishop—
Carol had been turning over an idea for a plan to help Chris.
Their home teacher, Terry Harvey, was also first counselor in the
elders quorum presidency. Terry knew about the job situation and
had asked Chris several times if there was anything he or the
Church could do. Chris had always thanked Terry warmly but refused and said he could handle things on his own. Carol knew
Terry was both tactful and sensitive. Since Christmas he hadn't
asked how the job search was going, but he didn't miss much.
He'd sent thirteen-year-old Ken over several times to help Don
with his newspaper route when storms had lashed the little town
in February and March and had seen to it that Chris got hired on
when the junior high laid new sod on the football field in April.

Carol's intense prayers had led her in the direction of feeling
that Chris needed a plan that made sense and would give him the
feeling he was moving ahead and not just drifting. She prayed
again before she went to bed, then lay turning the details over in
her mind. It was after midnight when Chris came home to the
darkened house.

From work the next day she called Terry, who was spending
his summer vacation from junior high putting in a new patio.
"Could you meet me during my lunch break?" she asked. "I need
to talk to you."

"Sure," said Terry. "I'm going to bring you over here. Marsha
is trying a new German potato salad recipe. Then I'll run you
back to work."

She was grateful for his and Marsha's tact in organizing the
children into a picnic in a tent in the backyard so she and Terry
could talk quietly. On the brief drive, she had told Terry succinctly
about conditions in the family. Now she said: "Terry, I know the
Church has a program for helping people with problems like ours.
We need help, but I don't think Chris will ask for it. We don't
have any family to speak of. My parents are both dead, and my
two brothers are in Arizona trying to keep the hardware store
going. Chris's sister is taking care of his mother in Minnesota. I'm
about at the end of my rope. Is there any way you could come up
with a plan for Chris that he would feel good about and accept? If
it means relocating so he can get a job in another part of the
country, we'll do that. But Chris has looked for work everywhere
around here and just can't find anything."

Terry poured more water in her glass. "Carol, I'm so glad

you've asked me. I've been really concerned about both of you. Let me talk with the elders quorum presidency and see what we can work out. We'll come up with some ideas and check with you before we talk with Chris. But you don't have to carry this alone."

As he dropped her off and went by the lumberyard to pick up more redwood planks, Terry began to wonder exactly what the quorum could do. He knew the job market was tight. Chris was neither stupid, undereducated, nor lazy. He knew how hard he'd looked for a job. At the house, he set fifteen-year-old Todd and Ken to unloading the truck while he went in the house and phoned Dean Suzuki at the Sears warehouse where he was in charge of inventory control. He filled him in on the problem, then asked, "Could we talk about this at our presidency meeting Wednesday night?"

"The sooner the better, Terry," replied Dean. "I'm really glad Carol talked to you. Must mean you're being the right kind of home teacher. I've been wondering if Chris isn't sliding into a depression. Plan to take the whole meeting if you need it."

At the meeting two days later, Terry reviewed the Scott situation to put Lars and Darrel into the picture. Then he added: "I've looked at the welfare manual and the bishop's handbook and the scriptures. Just being sure that the family doesn't suffer material want is easy. But they don't really need that, and Chris definitely doesn't want welfare. There's another need here, and everything I see indicates that we have a clear responsibility to help Chris solve his employment problem, if at all possible."

He continued: "Let me just read a few verses from the Doctrine and Covenants that have impressed me, particularly in light of the goal we accepted to try and become a true community of Saints:

'Nevertheless, in your temporal things ye shall be equal, and this not grudgingly, otherwise the abundance of the manifestations of the Spirit shall be withheld (D&C 70:14).

'But it is not given that one man should possess that which is above another, wherefore the world lieth in sin (D&C 49:20).

'For if ye are not equal in earthly things, ye cannot be equal in obtaining heavenly things (D&C 78:6).'

"That's pretty straight doctrine," Terry continued. "I don't know if we're ready to have everyone equal in temporal things, but Chris Scott certainly is below anyone else in our quorum right now, and I think we need to get him the help he needs. I called the stake employment director, and he gave me his current job listings, but my guess is that Chris has already checked these out."

Dean said respectfully: "Terry, I'm impressed with how much you've done in just two days. You're setting an example for all of us—both as a home teacher and as a member of the presidency. And I think we all agree with you that we need to help Chris." He glanced at Lars and Darrel, who nodded. "Where would you like us to begin?"

Terry did not hesitate. "Let's begin by brainstorming all the things we can think of that would help Chris. Let's be as creative in our thinking as possible. No matter how wild an idea seems, spit it out. Don't evaluate anyone's suggestion, not even your own. Just get as many ideas out on the table as possible. Then we'll see which ideas are workable."

In less than ten minutes, the four men had come up with a sizeable list of ideas:

— Get a list of jobs in the lumber industry from other states.
— Hire him as the church custodian.
— Get him a loan to go back to school.
— Help him put an ad in the newspaper.
— Get him a spot on a TV program.
— Get a newspaper reporter to interview him as an example of the problem of the unemployed.
— Get him Church welfare assistance.
— Find a person who will teach him a new skill or trade.
— Get him enrolled in a trade school or the community college.
— Get him a franchise so he could go into business.
— Help him start a new business of some kind.
— If he doesn't know how to interview for a job, help him learn to interview.
— Help him prepare a good resumé.
— Help him write a good letter of application.
— Have the members of the quorum chip in money.
— Help him get a loan to go into business.

"Okay," said Terry when the flow of ideas slowed. "Let's go over these." A few ideas were clearly not feasible. The Church custodial system didn't allow much local flexibility. Chris's personality would not let him accept Church welfare assistance or a gift from the quorum members. But all of the rest seemed to have at least some merit.

Dean summarized: "It seems to me the ideas can be grouped into four areas: (1) Help Chris find a job like his old job, here or somewhere else. (2) Help Chris develop better job-search skills: resumés, letters of application, interviewing techniques, and so on. (3) Help Chris develop an entirely new skill. (4) Help Chris set up his own business. Is that how you see it, Terry?"

Terry nodded. "What do we do with this list now?"

Lars spoke up. "Why don't we do some homework? If we came up with some concrete recommendations in each area, we could sit down with Chris and have something specific to suggest. You probably know more about libraries than I do, Terry. Could you go to the library and get copies of the help-wanted sections from some of the big metropolitan dailies, like Portland and Pendleton and maybe even into California? I know the state employment office has the addresses and phone numbers of the same office for all the states in the region. I could pick that up."

Quickly Dean volunteered to find out about franchises and see what kinds of loans might be available through the bank. Darrel volunteered to talk to Les Curtis, the stake employment specialist, and find out who was an expert in interviewing, resumés, and applications. "I'll drop in at the community college in Roseville, too, and see what kind of vocational and trade programs they've got. They might know about government aid, too." They agreed to meet in a week, pool their information, and see if they were ready to make a concrete proposal to Chris.

The next Wednesday they had a solid list of interesting resources. They had a list of job search firms from a number of areas with addresses and phone numbers of people to contact. A business communications instructor at the Roseville Community College offered to help Chris with his resumé, letter of application, and interviewing skills. So did Les Curtis. He also loaned them three Church-produced video tapes about job search skills that Chris could view at home. The state Chamber of Commerce had a list of firms and organizations who handled franchises, including the typical cost of setting up a business. Lars, who knew nearly everybody in city government, had prowled the offices, asking if they had any suggestions of new jobs that Plainville needed. "Look at this!" he flourished his list. "They say traffic is bad enough downtown that a parking terrace would be a good idea.

There's only one dry cleaning service, no appliance repair service. There's a janitorial service for businesses, but no housecleaning service. No business that specializes just in carpet and drape cleaning."

Darrel had a list of direct-vocational programs offered at Roseville Community College, how long each took, and how much they'd cost. Just in the course of asking around, the presidency had found three men who would be willing to take Chris on as an apprentice—in furniture sales, water systems repair, and auto mechanics.

"And now," said Dean, "we need to figure out how to present these options to Chris."

"I told Carol we'd check back with her before we talked to Chris," Terry reminded him. "Why don't I do that and get back in touch with you?"

"Okay," agreed Dean. "And if it's okay with Carol, why don't we move on it as fast as we can? I'm free tomorrow night. Is anybody else tied up?"

"If we could meet with Chris early," Darrel nodded, "that would be fine. I've got a date with the secretary at the registration office of the community college for the 8:30 movie."

"Us married folks," rumbled Lars cheerfully, "keep regular hours. Anytime is fine with me."

On Thursday, Terry left a message at Sunrise Market for Carol to call him. When her break came, she quickly keyed his number. As he described what they had done, she sagged against the wall in the employees' room, overcome with relief and gratitude. "I can't tell you—" her voice wavered—"how I feel about this."

"Well, we've still got the biggest hurdle to go," Terry reminded her. "Your husband's well-developed male ego. How do you think we should approach him?"

She laughed. "Maybe we can work on the ego after he doesn't need it quite so much. I think if you invited him to visit with you at the meetinghouse, it would be better than coming to the house. It would look more official, and it would take him out of the house where he might think he has to put on an act for me and the kids."

"Consider it done!" Terry said cheerfully. He called Dean back and relayed the suggestion. "Okay, brother," Dean said. "Will you call the others and tell 'em 7:00 P.M.? I'll phone Chris." Chris sounded listless when he picked up the phone. Dean was brisk and businesslike. "Could you meet with the quorum presidency at the chapel at 7:00 P.M. tonight?" he invited. "We have some job information we thought you might find helpful."

Caught off guard, Chris mumbled, "Well, sure, I guess."

"Okay, see you then. Good-bye."

That night Chris was on time but looked a little apprehensive as they sat down together in the Scout room around the table. Terry offered the opening prayer, then Dean explained: "Chris, as a quorum presidency we feel that we have a responsibility to help you look for employment. Terry, as your home teacher, has really taken the lead in this effort. He knows how hard you've looked and how difficult it is to keep on looking when things are as discouraging as they are now. He's involved us as a presidency. We've worked and prayed and have come up with some information we think you'll find interesting. Can we show you what we've found?"

Chris nodded, somewhat grudgingly, but listened attentively as Terry showed him the four areas they had explored. Each presidency member described the data he had collected. Chris looked stunned as they laid out the lists of firms, officers, courses, and possibilities. When everything had been reviewed, Chris cleared his throat and said: "Brethren, I'm overwhelmed. I can't tell you how much I appreciate your concern and what you've produced. You have more ideas here than I've been able to come up with by myself in ten months."

Dean grinned warmly. "Let's hope some of them pan out, then. Why don't you look at all the possibilities and see what your first choice would be and how to explore that, the second choice, and so on, until we've a complete plan of action that makes sense to you."

Chris heaved a huge sigh. "Well, my first choice has always been to stay in Plainville and work in lumber. But I can't live forever on the hope that things are going to change at the mill. So let's start looking at the other options."

"Do you want to see if you can find a job in the lumber business somewhere else?" asked Terry. "Or stay in Plainville and learn a new trade?"

"Everything I hear from the guys at the plant says that lumber is depressed all over," responded Chris. "It might make more sense to stay in Plainville and move into a whole new line of work. Let's look at that list again."

The five of them huddled over the list, discussing each possibility in depth and suggesting some spin-offs. Going into any business would require capital, and Chris was reluctant to go into debt. He also admitted: "I'm really not sure I want to go back to school and compete with younger people. I went to college a year before my mission; but when I got back, I found a summer job in the mill, Carol and I were going together by fall, and, well, I just didn't have any burning desire to go back. Besides that, even in a vocational course, I'd feel sort of like I was marking time. You don't know how bad I want to *work*!" He glared fiercely at the table.

"Well, then," suggested Darrel cheerfully, "how about one of those apprenticeship possibilities?"

"I've always done most of the work on my own car," admitted Chris. "If I could learn auto mechanics and make a little while I learned, I think that would be best for me."

Terry grinned. "Well, let's try 'er out. It's Clive Wilson at Wilson Wheels. Do you know him?"

Chris shook his head. "Just to say hello to is all."

"He's Brad Wilson's older brother," Terry continued. "You know Brad from the elders quorum?" Chris nodded. "Hasn't set foot in the church for years, but he's really a nice guy. I think you'd enjoy working with him. His boy Casey has been on my basketball team all three years. A great kid. I'll check with him and see what time he'd like to see us tomorrow morning."

"Well, if *that's* settled," said Darrel, "Jennifer's waiting."

Chris said nothing to Carol that night about the meeting. When Terry called a half-hour later with the appointment, he merely acknowledged it briefly, unconsciously releasing a deep sigh of tension as he hung up the phone. Knowing where he had been and guessing what the phone call meant, Carol realized with another pang how sternly he was keeping his hopes in check and what a heavy toll the last ten months had taken. She realized, too, that he wasn't telling her anything until he knew whether the job appointment was going to work out. Our marriage has turned into a relationship where we keep things from each other, she thought. Me from him, and now him from me. It's got to change. She went off to Sunshine Market the next morning with a prayer in her heart.

At 10:30 A.M., Terry and Chris parked their cars almost simultaneously in the side lot next to the Wilson Wheels service station.

Clive came to the door to meet them, sizing up Chris quickly with a twinkle in his eye. As Terry listened, the two men came to a quick agreement: "Mac Hawkins has been a mechanic since horsepower meant hooves," Clive said, "but he's starting to slow down. He and I will teach you everything we know and involve you in working on as many different makes and models as we can, nine hours a day, six days a week, minimum wage for three months, as long as you're working hard, showing progress, and not scarin' off the customers. At the end of three months, it should be clear whether staying on here seems like a good idea from our perspective. If it is and you agree, you've got a job at fifteen dollars an hour and benefits."

"And if I want to apply somewhere else?"

"Your choice, and I'll write you a letter of recommendation," Clive assured him. "Can you start Monday?"

The two men shook hands on the deal. In the parking lot, Chris shook hands with Terry. "I feel like the whole world has been lifted off my shoulders. For the first time in months, I feel alive and full of hope. I'll never be able to repay you for what you and the others have done. All I can do is to try and do something for someone else."

Terry smiled. "Paid in full, brother," he said. "Now I'll bet you've got somebody you'd like to share the good news with."

Carol ripped off the cash register receipt and handed it to Lori Reynolds with a smile. "Have a nice day," she said, and turned to greet the next customer. It was Chris, holding a pink rose from the bush by the sandbox. "Hi, lady," he said. "Take you to lunch?"

Discussion

Financial problems present a challenge to sensitive leadership. Church members have always been willing to respond to those who are sick, have had an accident, or are experiencing grief at a loss. Food and emotional support are quickly offered. But what do you do in the case of a Chris Scott who, though hardworking and intelligent, is demoralized by long unemployment and protects himself through a prickly pride? Church welfare, even if he would accept it, is not an answer to an able-bodied man of thirty-seven with four children.

Helping the one in need means first getting accurate information about that person's needs. In the current Church system, it is the work of the home teachers and visiting teachers to assess the needs in the family. However, Chris was reticent to talk about his situation and refused direct offers of aid. Part of the problem was denial, but it was obviously affecting his marriage as well. It took courage for Carol to go to Terry and ask for help.

The presidency meeting demonstrates a general process of helping one in need. Based on Carol's information, they discussed the situation privately and in depth, identified options, spent their own time doing research, and went the second mile by making contacts. They wanted to provide help that Chris would want to accept in a way that would leave his dignity intact. Their efforts paid off. The way they organized the information clarified Chris's situation to himself, provided him with useful options, and moved him from emotional depression and financial despair to hope and optimism.

It is not exactly clear what the economic conditions will be during the Millennium. Will people have the same kinds of jobs they have now? Will there be any unemployment? Will people still have economic needs to which others should be responsive? The agriculturally based models of the United Order of Joseph Smith and Brigham Young may not be the best basis for predicting the millennial economy. However, even though we do not know the answers to these questions, surely people worthy to live in that thousand years with Christ will want to share all they have with others. Meeting the needs of someone who is less fortunate than themselves will be a matter of highest priority both individually and collectively.

While Chris Scott's problem is economic, there are many other forms of help ward members need. My family and I have received help from many people through the years, but one incident always stands out. Bonnie was hospitalized for three weeks with a spinal fusion and, naturally, needed several months to regain full functioning. I was a busy faculty member. We had four children under the age of ten. Even though they were in school or tended during the day, the evenings and weekends simply overwhelmed me: trying to visit Bonnie, feed the children, do the dishes—the list was endless. I was done in by laundry, flattened by vacuuming, drowned by bath-time.

But I felt I owed it to my own image of a competent person, I suppose, to put on a positive face. We received many sincere offers of help, but I always announced, "This is a wonderful opportunity for us as a family to learn to pull together," even while I noticed that all of the plants in the living room were shriveled from lack of water and that somebody had plastered his pizza on the wall above the couch.

But one marvelous woman didn't ask. Somehow, when I was at work the second week, she got in the house, stripped the beds and collected all of the laundry. When I got home at night, the beds were freshly remade, the boys' bureaus were full of clean socks and underwear, and crisply ironed shirts were hanging in the closet. I was filled with gratitude for this woman who had given help I desperately needed but couldn't ask for.

The parable of the Good Samaritan says, "But a certain Samaritan . . . *saw* him [the wounded Jew], [and] he had *compassion* on him. And *went* to him and bound up his wounds, pouring in oil and wine, and set him on his own beast, and brought him to an inn, and took care of him" (Luke 10:33–34).

How different the whole parable would have sounded if the scripture read, "And the Samaritan, when he saw him, had compassion on him, and went to him and asked, "Please call if there's anything I can do to help."

The Lord's way of helping is for us to have clear-seeing eyes and sensitive hearts to gather information about the needs of those around us. Then out of our compassion, we should act to do something that is helpful. Any person at any age can be a leader in providing help according to this definition. No title or authority is necessary—just eyes that see, a compassionate heart, and willing hands.

8

Counseling

> The teacher's [leader's] duty is to watch over the
> church always and be with and strengthen them;
> And see that there is no iniquity in the church,
> neither hardness with each other (D&C 20:53–54).

The Principle

A sensitive part of the leader's role is to counsel those who
have personal problems they feel they cannot solve alone. Stake
presidents, bishops, and branch presidents are especially expected
to assume the counseling role to help members deal with their individual burdens. But to a certain degree, home teachers, visiting
teachers, and quorum/auxiliary leaders may also be seen as
sources of personal counseling for individuals who trust them and
rely on their inspiration and good judgment.

In the Church, the instructions about who should deal with
certain problems areas is clear. If the matter involves a serious violation that could jeopardize one's membership (fornication, adul-
tery, drug use, child abuse, crime, etc.), the bishop or stake president is the person with the authority to represent the Church.
However, individuals struggling with marital problems, difficulties
with children, family or neighborhood conflicts, loneliness, depression, anxieties and fears, rebellion, hostility, and despair may
go to the person in the Church they know best—and that may or
may not be the bishop.

In these cases, what should such leaders do? The scriptures indicate that, when people are afflicted with physical and/or emotional distress, we should help them bear their infirmities, not to

condemn them or avoid them. (See D&C 42:52.) The Lord has also indicated that those in responsible positions should be with and strengthen Church members, particularly when they feel weak and inadequate (D&C 20:53–54).

Very few Church leaders have been trained as professional counselors. How does an untrained leader deal with what may be difficult personal matters? While some cases may genuinely need referral to trained counselors and psychotherapists, usually available through LDS Social Services, in a great many cases a caring nonprofessional can follow a few simple steps and be effective and compassionate simultaneously.

First, the leader should listen to the person with the problem. It is crucial for the leader to understand before he or she can help. Suppose a person asks you, "Could I talk with you? I have a problem I've got to ask somebody about." An appropriate response— one that establishes a welcoming atmosphere and some ground rules simultaneously—may be: "I'll be happy to talk with you. I'll try to understand the nature of the problem. If I'm not the right person to help, I'll help you find someone who can." Thus, our "contract" with the person who comes for aid is to listen and understand, determine in consultation with the individual what kind of help is appropriate, and (if necessary) get that person linked up with a resource that would be truly useful.

This means that the leader needs to know his or her own resources and capabilities. Can he or she give the desired assistance directly or does the person need to connect with a more effective resource person? It is critical that, in this process, the leader be guided by the Spirit of the Lord so that decisions can be made consistent with the will of the Lord. If a person has problems that are clearly beyond the experience of the leader (deep emotional disturbances, severe marital problems, sexual difficulties, etc.), the leader must indicate that he or she does not have the resources to deal with these problems effectively and should arrange for more professional help, which probably means going through the bishop.

However, if the leader feels prompted to give counsel, certain guidelines are helpful. The role of the leader as counselor is to help the other person deal with his or her problem—not to take it over and make the other person dependent on the leader. Thus, a good approach in most cases is a problem-solving approach—supporting the person while he or she solves the problem. Counseling is different from advice-giving. Advice-giving is usually phrased, "If I were you, I would do such-and-such." You are not the other person. What might be both simple and logical to you may be utterly impossible for the other.

In a problem-solving counseling session, the leader/counselor first helps the counselee to define the problem clearly. Often the counselee's first description of the problem may not be the real problem. Frequently, someone who is used to getting advice from family or friends may define himself or herself as the problem and need some help disentangling the two. It is classic, for instance, for battered women to accept the view that "if I were a better wife, he wouldn't do this." Take time to listen carefully. Here are some basic questions to keep in mind that may help you be sure you're getting the whole story:

- Who are the people in the situation?
- How is the counselee involved?
- What has the counselee done up to this point?
- What does the counselee see as the immediate future if the situation continues? the long-range future?
- What options seem to be available?

With this background, the leader then helps the counselee to look at all of the alternatives that seem to be available. For example, a young woman may come to a leader with a courtship decision: "I have been going with this fellow for two years. He wants to get married, but I'm not sure he's the right person for me. But he's active in the Church and seems to be a good person. If I say no, I may never find anyone as good. What should I do?"

The counselor may need to ask some clarifying questions about the young man's behavior, his future, how their families feel about the relationship, what kind of relationships this young woman has experienced in the past, how she sees her own future, and so forth. But a crucial question is: "What do you see as your alternatives?" The young woman says, "Either get married or break up." The counselor can help her broaden this range significantly, including getting some premarital counseling and testing to see how compatible they really are; agreeing to a short separation to test their feelings; using an engagement period as a test of the relationship rather than as time to prepare for the wedding; talking candidly with their parents, if this hasn't been done; going away to school or work; and serving a mission. Then the counselee, faced with a broader range of options, can test her own feelings against a variety of background settings and work with the counselor in setting up a plan to solve her own problem.

Bishops and stake presidents are not the only people who find themselves giving counsel to others. An important aspect of parenting involves counseling with children. Both in and outside of the Church, many American parents today must bear the burden of giving counsel as a single parent.

Anyone who has a real friend has often been in the situation of "just talking things over" and feeling the burden lift as a result of thinking out loud in a friendly presence. Few of us are trained in counseling, but all of us who try to help each other can keep the same ground rules in mind: Listen. Try to understand. Don't give advice. Help the other person see a different range of options. You do not have to "fix" the problem for the person. You do not have to be responsible for the outcome.

Sometimes a person does not want counseling, only catharsis. In that case, your role is simply to listen. In another case, people do not want counsel but direction. I have often had a desperate person say, "Just tell me what to do and I'll do it." Although their sincerity is commendable, the attitude is not. From the time of our premortal existence, people have wanted someone to tell them what to do so they would not have to take responsibility for the consequences of their own actions. Counseling is a process of helping the counselee sort through his or her own feelings, needs, and wants so that he or she can begin to make better choices for himself or herself.

And counseling is not therapy. Therapy is a long-term process of healing from emotional or mental distress. It requires special commitments and special skills. Sometimes, in the case of deep-seated emotional problems, the act of a true friend is to see that the troubled individual gets professional help.

In the Plainville scene, a husband and wife who are having some marital problems ask Bishop Pratt for help. They are constantly quarreling, seem to have different goals, and feel very dissatisfied with their marriage. George Pratt uses this problem-solving approach to help Norm and Helen Berry deal with their difficulty constructively.

Plainville Second Ward:
The Berrys, Heading for Divorce

Norm and Helen Berry were ready to call it quits. It was a bitterly depressing thought to both of them. They had both grown up in Plainville and attended high school, where they started dating when Norm was a senior on the track team and Helen was a junior, pretty, popular, and intelligent. Their relationship became more serious when Norm graduated and began working in the men's department of Plainville's Sears store. Both were members of the Church, but the activity pattern of the two families was very different.

Helen's parents, Hy and Alice McDougall, were very active. Family prayer, scripture reading, and a blessing on the food were daily occurrences. Hy took the spiritual lead in the home, ensuring that Helen and her two older brothers received blessings in time of need, taking the family to Church every Sunday, and presiding over a weekly family home evening.

Norm's background was quite different. His father was an inactive adult Aaronic Priesthood holder who was a good provider, a kind father, and a companionable husband. Norm's mother made sure that the children were baptized and sent them to church but often did not go herself if Darwin wanted her to do something with him on Sunday.

Both sets of parents had approved of the relationship when Helen and Norm began dating, glad that their son or daughter was dating a Church member. Helen's parents wanted her to graduate from college and marry a returned missionary. Nobody in Norm's family had gone to college or on a mission, so his parents were pleased when he graduated and got a good white-collar job with a promising future. When the question of a mission came up, Norm's boss told him that if he were away for two years there would be no promise of a job when he returned. Norm's father encouraged him to stay with his job, and his mother said he could go on a mission later. Besides, there was Helen. It didn't seem very likely that she'd still be around when he got back.

Helen and Norm had been dating for more than a year when she graduated from high school. With some misgivings, she went to Brigham Young University for a year, then got a job as a bank teller for the summer. She and Norm began dating very seriously.

Norm had now been working for two years and saving his money. He'd already been promoted to assistant manager in the sporting goods section, and his boss told him that he was the kind of young man who had a future with the company. He asked Helen to marry him. The McDougalls did not disapprove of Norm, but they had other goals for Helen. Helen was torn between wanting to fulfill her parents' dream, as her two brothers had, and the sweetness of her feelings for Norm. Hy and Alice were supportive as she tried to decide what she really wanted; and when the end of the summer approached, she felt that she simply couldn't leave Norm. Finally she told her parents that what she really wanted to do was marry Norm, and they gave their approval, rather than create more conflict.

Helen and Norm were married in the Seattle Temple and settled down in a nice apartment. With two incomes, they managed quite well financially and were able to save significantly toward a home. Just before their first child was born (named Lucy after Norm's mother), they moved into their own home. Helen left her employment; and two years later, Eddie was born.

Helen had her hands full with the house and babies. Norm's schedule was a rotating one at the store, sometimes keeping him there when the store was open in the evenings and sometimes keeping him away on weekends. When Helen was called to play the piano in Primary, Norm gallantly took over the children. Lucy was old enough to go to the nursery, but Eddie was a handful. After a few weeks of walking the halls, Norm found it easier to stay home with the children, bringing them to sacrament meeting during the last hour of the meeting block. But the pattern gradually developed of missing this meeting, too. "They were too fussy, honey," he would explain to Helen. Or, "Eddie had just fallen asleep and I didn't have the heart to wake him up." Alice McDougall noticed, too; and although she was careful not to interfere in Helen's marriage, she knew Helen was unhappy about the situation.

Helen knew there was nothing magic about serving a mission, but she wondered if this was the reason Norm seemed to take religious responsibilities so casually. She had assumed Norm would be like her father, routinely initiating family prayer and scripture reading, presiding at weekly family home evenings, and scheduling regular trips to the temple or at least going on the stake's quarterly excursions. But Norm had not experienced any of these activities in his own home, and he was somewhat irritated that Helen kept pushing him about religious matters.

"Aren't we going to have family home evening this week?" "Who should say the blessing on the food?" "Are you going to say the family prayer or should I?" "When are we going to go to the temple?"

Norm felt that Helen was always on him with one or another of these questions every day. His stock answer became, "Why don't you do it?"

Helen could tell that Norm felt nagged, so she asked less and less frequently, hoping that he would be more active if he felt less pushed. But the upshot was that they had family prayer, home evening, and scripture reading less often. She wanted to talk to her parents but felt that it would be a criticism of Norm if she did. Besides, what could they do? Periodically, her resolve to be the loving and supportive wife the Relief Society lessons seemed to mandate would slip and she would comment acidly: "I don't see why you can't find time to go to the temple. You can find time to play basketball with your friends"; or "Just once I'd like to see you get us all together for family prayer. Why do I have to suggest it all the time?" Norm, stung by such criticisms, would say nothing but would become sullen and resentful.

As soon as Eddie was eighteen months old and could go in the nursery, Helen resolutely brought both children to church every Sunday. Lucy, at three and a half, could usually manage sacrament meeting fairly well, especially in the lap of her doting Grandpa McDougall, but Eddie was nearly always frantic by that stage. Grimly, Helen doled out the Cheerios and Alice outdid herself with quiet books, both of them ignoring Norm's whispered: "Honey, he's climbing the walls. Let me take him into the lobby." Helen felt she was doing what a righteous woman should do and had her mother's wholehearted support.

But the latest incident had made Helen question whether they had any kind of marriage left. The regular stake temple excursion was the third Saturday in May, and Helen had cajoled Norm into going. He agreed; however, the night before they were to leave, he called from work and said: "I can't go, honey. Glade's sick and I've got to cover his shift." Disappointed, Helen canceled the baby-sitter. But when she was pushing Eddie on the swing at the park, she heard a familiar voice coming from the basketball court and, incredulous and enraged, saw Norm racing downcourt.

Deliberately she put Eddie in the stroller and, taking Lucy by the hand, walked slowly past the basketball court on the way home, making sure Norm saw her. When he came home for lunch, he was apprehensive and defiant.

"Okay, okay," he began, "you don't have to say it. I made up that part about Glade being sick because I wanted to play in the game."

"So you lied to me," Helen said flatly.

"Yes, I lied!" Norm exclaimed belligerently. "I knew if I told you the truth you'd nag me for days. This basketball team is important to me, but all you want to do is Church work. I get so sick and tired of you pushing Church activities at me all the time that I feel like quitting the whole thing."

Helen felt so chilled that her lips moved stiffly as she said: "Norm, if you ever leave the Church, that will be the end of our marriage. I simply will not raise my children in a split-family home."

Norm flared: "They're my children, too, just in case you've forgotten. And also, just in case you've forgotten, *I* was raised in a split-family home, and I turned out all right—at least you thought so when we got married."

Tears came to Helen's eyes. "Norm, I still think you're all right, but I want something more in our family. I just don't see the kind of strength and unity I want in a family coming from the way things are working now."

Norm shrugged, stomped into the family room, turned on the TV, and pretended to watch a program. Neither spoke much to the other for the rest of the day. That night, each stayed strictly on opposite sides of the queen-size bed. The next morning, they silently got ready to go to church, each dressing one of the children. Helen was relieved that Norm apparently planned on going, but she felt trapped in the situation. How could she say that what Norm had done was all right?

This sacrament meeting was the day Bishop Pratt presented to the ward his vision of extraordinary goals, trying to be of one heart, completely supporting each other, and living as they would be expected to live in the Millennium.

Both Helen and Norm were deeply moved by the bishop's talk and the testimonies that followed. The outpouring of the Spirit made both of them feel that they had to do something about the impasse and ugly feelings that lay between them.

When the meeting was over, Helen whispered anxiously: "Norm, I feel we ought to talk with the bishop and see if he can help us deal with these barriers between us. What do you think?" She waited nervously while Norm hesitated for an instant, then agreed. They waited patiently as dozens of ward members shook hands with George, expressing their appreciation for the meeting and the goals he had articulated. The couple made an appointment to visit with him that evening.

Sunday afternoon was still uncomfortable, especially after Eddie fell asleep. Norm took Lucy for a walk. When he came back, he asked Helen, "What do you think we ought to tell the bishop?"

Helen was careful in her response: "Norm, I think we've got to be completely honest and tell him exactly how things are. If he doesn't see the real picture, how can he give us any help?" Norm nodded in agreement. Alice McDougall arrived early to take care of the children, being brisk and matter-of-fact, giving Norm no chance to shoot an accusing "You've-been-talking-behind-my-back" glance at Helen.

At the bishop's office they took their seats, carefully not looking at each other. George welcomed them warmly and offered them an opening. "Lots of people had things to say after the meeting, but I got the impression that you wanted to talk about something different. Am I right?"

Norm nodded and blurted out, "It's about us."

Helen continued: "Bishop, we're both miserable. We just seem to have so many problems between us that we don't know what to do."

George said: "Well, I've been a bishop almost exactly six weeks and I'm not quite sure how this is done, but let me suggest something. Helen, first you explain the situation as you see it and tell me your concerns about it. Norm, you and I will just listen or ask a question if there's something we don't understand. After she's finished, then you can describe the situation as you see it. We'll decide whether I, as your bishop, can help you or whether we need to find a professional marriage counselor. Is that all right?"

Helen had been afraid she would sound bitter and carping—and also that Norm would just clam up and be sullen. Norm was afraid of being unjustly blamed but also felt honestly indignant about what he felt were excessive demands. But what George heard were two people, bewildered and grief-stricken over the impasse in which they found themselves, frightened that they wouldn't be able to get out. As they poured out their fears, anxieties, hopes, and despairs, George felt impressed that he could help.

When they had finished, he asked: "Well, what are your options at this point? Do you see any action you can take to deal with these problems?"

Norm said, low-voiced: "We're at the point where we feel that we aren't resolving anything. We don't know what to do. Helen even said something about a separation."

The bishop asked, "Is that what you want?"

Both shook their heads. "But we can't go on this way," said Helen.

"Well, then," said George, "you have some work to do. Let me sum up the impressions I have. Tell me if it seems fair. It sounds as if Helen wants a certain kind of husband—something like her father, and Norm gets quite defensive about that." Helen nodded. "Norm feels committed to the marriage, but he doesn't see why all these religious practices have to be observed so strictly. In fact, he feels so outraged at the pressure that he feels justified in lying."

Norm gulped. "That's about the size of it."

"I don't want to minimize those differences. They're quite different orientations. And I want you to know that I don't think one of you is more righteous than the other. I think you have different scripts for acting out your religious feelings, and those scripts don't match. But here's a place to start. Will you go home and make a list of the things you appreciate about each other? It can be a short list or a long list. Then write down one or two things—no more—that you feel are the most important things the other person needs to do to get the marriage back on an even keel. Then list a minimum of two things *you* can change to make things better between you. Don't show each other your lists. But I'd like to meet with you again—Wednesday night, if you can make it—review your lists, and see if we can make a plan based on those feelings. Are you willing to do this?"

They both agreed and got up to leave. George noticed with satisfaction that Helen reached out and took Norm's hand as they walked out.

They arrived home, took over bedtime chores from Alice, and tucked Lucy and Eddie into bed. Then Norm took a deep breath, put his hands on Helen's shoulders, looked at her squarely and said: "Helen, I'm deeply sorry for what I have done. I never should have lied to you. I really felt the Spirit at the meeting this morning. I felt the bishop was inspired then and in our session with him tonight. Inside me was a terrible feeling. I knew that you and I have not been of one heart, and I have this feeling of distance between us. I know that this has been mostly my fault, and I'll do anything to make things better."

Tears flowed down Helen's cheeks, and she buried her face in Norm's chest. Through her tears, she said: "My dear, I'm as much or more at fault than you. I've thought a lot about us, and I see what the bishop pointed out—that I've wanted you to be like my father and for us to have a family like my parents had. How could I have been so stupid? You are you, and our family is ours. I forgive you with all my heart, if you will forgive me."

He stroked her hair wordlessly, the look on his face communicating his whole heart. "Norm," said Helen, "let's decide the kind of family *we* really want. It's all right if there are some areas where we don't agree. I think we can work things out so that we can accommodate those differences. If we love each other and work at it and keep close to the Lord, I know it will be right for us."

They sat together holding hands and talked deeply and truthfully about what they wanted to accomplish together. There were so many things they wanted to say that words poured out between them. They both wanted to have spirituality in their home, but Norm had always felt Helen was more religious then he. He had simultaneously let her lead out and resented her doing so. Helen volunteered to reduce her expectations, but Norm pointed out, "We're not going to build prayer as a habit if we don't both pray." They agreed on a kneeling family prayer at breakfast and supper. Family home evening would be either Sunday or Monday, depending on Norm's work schedule, at 6:30 P.M., and they would find ways to make it meaningful for themselves as well as Lucy and Eddie.

Norm admitted that scripture reading was hard for him and that going to the temple was more of a duty than a pleasure, but he was willing to work at both. They decided to follow President Benson's counsel to read the Book of Mormon. "I can handle a chapter a night," Norm laughed.

"Becky Sorenson told me she likes to listen to the scriptures on tape," suggested Helen. "Why don't I borrow one and see if that makes it any easier?" They decided to go to the temple at every quarterly excursion; if Norm's work interfered, they'd arrange to drive up separately on his day off when Alice could take care of the children, or on Saturday if they could find someone to go with them.

Helen felt radiant with hope. And when Norm said, "I think we owe the Lord a prayer of thanksgiving right now," her heart melted. She was wise enough to know that neither she nor Norm was perfect and that they not only faced their considerable differences but also the hard work of implementing their plan. But she felt they were working on it together, instead of at cross purposes. She sensed a new depth to their unity. With the Lord's help, they were walking on the millennial path together.

The next day, Norm called George at work. "Uh, Bishop," he began, "we didn't actually make those lists we said we were going to."

George tensed. What had gone wrong? "How come?"

Then Norm was laughing. "We were too busy solving the problem!" As he described what had happened, George let out his breath in a long sigh. "Bless you both." He hung up the receiver feeling thankful—and also thinking realistically, "Would that it could always be this easy!"

Discussion

Experienced bishops know that many marital relationships are deeply conflicted and that a little good advice and an encouraging pat on the back are inadequate to solve them. Yet the case of Norm and Helen Berry is not completely unrealistic. At least one study shows that most LDS women want their husbands to be the spiritual leaders in the home, the one who initiates family home evening, prayer, fasting, and visits to the temple.[1] Nor is the source of this expectation hard to find. Church lessons, talks, and manuals stress the husband's responsibility of spiritual leadership; it is unfortunate that they often do so at the expense of describing the spiritual partnership that seems to characterize most of the healthy marriages we observe. As a result, the wife is often con-

---

1. William G. Dyer and Phillip H. Kunz, "Problems Facing LDS Families," unpublished research, 1982.

signed to a "supportive" role that leaves her confused and often feeling guiltily responsible for her husband's behavior. This is an unfair triple-bind for a woman. If she makes sure that the family has prayer, she is "usurping" her husband's responsibility. If she doesn't, she is "neglecting" her family's spiritual welfare; and if she tries to get her husband to do it, she is "nagging."

Interestingly enough, another recent research finding is that "the best single-item predictor of long-term marital success among the couples they studied was, 'Husband voluntarily participates in the housework.'" Carlfred Broderick, a former stake president, father of eight, and director of the Marriage and Family Therapy Training program at the University of Southern California, suggests that the reason this item is such a powerful predictor is what it shows about "attitudes. The husband who pitches in to do his share without having to be cajoled is clearly a team player. His enemy is not his wife; she is his invaluable ally in the unceasing battle against the common enemy—those famous and all-too-familiar 'slings and arrows of outrageous fortune.'"[2] In my opinion, what's true of physical housekeeping goes for spiritual homemaking as well. Partnership is simply better than specialization and rigid role definitions, because it lets both partners concentrate on what they want to achieve, not on how well they're performing.

A healthier response—and it is certainly no quick fix—is to avoid the power struggle of "rigid spiritual roles" and embark instead on the long and difficult process of negotiating expectations, needs, and wants. The important thing is that husband and wife communicate openly. In my opinion, it is better for the children and for the couple for the wife to matter-of-factly hear the children's bedtime prayers, call on someone to give the blessing, and take the children to church alone and pleasantly than to have constant tensions, nagging, resistance, and quarrels about religious behavior. In other cases, the mother assumes the spiritual direction of the family and the husband "goes along." There is no tension, but the children never see their father as a spiritual role model either. Only through discussion can they find areas of spiritual leadership that even a reluctant husband may be willing to assume.

As another example, the form of family home evening is important, but far more important is the content and the feeling that

---

2. Carlfred B. Broderick, "Marital Danger Zone," *This People,* Summer 1992, p. 19.

family members are left with about each other. A little creativity and good will can go far toward finding a solution to many of the "form" problems, leaving the whole family free to experience the religious "content." One family I know with five children assigns one person to be voice for all of the family prayers on that day of the week; they report a real sense of contributing to the family spiritually on their "prayer day." In another family, Dad calls on someone for family prayer at supper, while Mother calls on someone for the breakfast family prayer. In all these examples, they agreed that family prayer was important and found a way to sidestep the disagreements that seemed to center on "who's in charge of making it happen."

In the case of Helen and Norm, getting an outside view proved very useful. George wasn't a trained counselor, but he knew how to listen and ask clarifying questions. Because neither one of them really wanted a divorce, he suspected that finding a different pattern for them to talk about their problems besides mutual recrimination and resistance would in itself be helpful. The "appreciation list" that he suggested was something he remembered from a family home evening lesson and he wasn't at all sure it would work, but he thought it probably wouldn't hurt. And besides, it would help them think about each other in a different context than the problem offered.

As it turned out, he was right. After he had commented about Helen's desire for a husband like her father, Helen suddenly realized how much of her marriage was controlled by that unarticulated expectation. And Norm, who was basically decent, could see how childish he had become—lying, sulking, and shouting because he felt so pressured.

With the foundation of the bishop's observation, Norm and Helen could carry the dialogue a step further, clarifying their own expectations and reactions. Quickly they acknowledged how they had each contributed to the problem; and since both of them genuinely wanted a spiritual home and a good marriage, the resistance to asking for forgiveness and working mutually on the problem disappeared. Naturally, these patterns of living had become ingrained in the six years of their marriage, and it would be optimistic to assume that there would be no more disagreements, no more mismatched expectations, and no more strains; but at least Norm and Helen would meet these tensions with a stronger sense and history of mutual commitment.

9

Assisting the Less Fortunate

Pure religion and undefiled before God and the Father is this, To visit the fatherless and widows in their affliction, and to keep himself unspotted from the world (James 1:27).

Thus speaketh the Lord of hosts, saying, Execute true judgment, and shew mercy and compassions every man to his brother:
And oppress not the widow, nor the fatherless, the stranger, nor the poor; and let none of you imagine evil against his brother in your heart (Zechariah 7:9–10).

The Principle

Throughout all the scriptures runs the admonition to care for those who are less powerful. The widows and the fatherless receive special mention, no doubt because the scriptures were written in a time when muscle power—human and animal—supplied the main sources of energy for food production. Consequently, the absence of a man's physical strength from the household usually meant penury and want for a woman and her dependent children. Reflecting this context, the scriptures most often mandate protection and material assistance; however, in our day when easily available energy makes muscle power a less significant economic issue, we can more easily see that many women who are widows, divorced, or single parents need not only material help but also friendship and social support. Men have equally powerful needs for social and emotional support.
The scene that follows from the Plainville Second Ward shows

how one neighbor, Ann Simonson, reaches out to a widow who has some unlovable characteristics but who still needs those who will "visit the . . . widows in their afflictions."

Leadership is a process, exercised either formally or informally, of exerting influence on others so their behavior is altered. Ann Simonson is an informal leader, acting not by assignment or request but because she sees a need and feels the strength within herself as a Christian to respond. She has caught the bishop's vision of a millennial goal and willingly extends herself in love to reduce the pain in another's life.

Plainville Second Ward: Jane Campbell, a Widow

Ann Simonson lived only a few blocks from the chapel. When she and her husband, Kent, had moved in six years earlier, the neighborhood had just gone through a kind of crisis. Some neighbors had reacted strongly when the chapel was started eight years earlier. One rumor was that the Mormons were building a temple, and "everyone knew" that Mormons brought dead people to the temple to be baptized. Wisely, the stake president asked the members in the area to visit their neighbors, tell them exactly what a chapel would be used for, and invite them to attend LDS meetings so they could understand the Mormons.

The chapel had been completed just a few months before Ann and Kent had come to Plainville, and a number of Mormon families had moved into the area. Consequently, it was becoming a heavily Mormon neighborhood. Ann and Kent had chosen their home carefully, and the proximity of the chapel had been an important element in their selection. Their children were within walking distance of both church and school. Kent was president of the Sunday School, and Ann loved his steadiness and devotion to their children and the Church.

The week after Bishop Pratt's announcement to the ward, Ann saw a moving van stop at a two-story Tudor-style house three doors from her modest brick home. On her way to her part-time job at the city recorder's office, Ann wondered who could be moving in and she made a mental note to greet the family with a loaf of homemade bread.

When Ann returned from work shortly after noon, the movers were still busily hauling furniture, appliances, and boxes into the house. Ann made a batch of bread, and as soon as she had whisked it out of the oven she wrapped a loaf in a pretty tea towel and walked down to the larger home, wondering who the family was and whether the children were the same ages as her own children. The door popped open almost as soon as she took her finger off the bell, and a tall, sword-straight, gray-haired woman appraised Ann unsmilingly for a moment while Ann's cheerful smile faltered on her lips.

"I saw you coming," said the woman abruptly. "I'm Jane Campbell. I'm a widow. My children are all married and gone, and I hope this is a quiet neighborhood."

She looked so stern and formidable that Ann gulped and struggled to recollect her welcoming speech. "I know you're busy moving in, but I want to welcome you to our neighborhood. I'm Ann Simonson. Kent and I live in that brick bungalow three doors down." She smiled, her warmth returning, and held out the bread. "We have four children and they're pretty lively, but I think this is a fairly normal neighborhood. I hope you can use this?"

Jane unthawed slightly. "Come in, come in. Let me find a clean place to put this bread and I'll give you back your towel. But I'm afraid there isn't even a place to sit down yet. We used to bring bread to new neighbors where I grew up in Idaho, but I haven't seen this done in years."

Ann followed her into the cluttered kitchen, where Jane had obviously been scrubbing cupboards. "By the way," Jane added, "do you know where the Mormon chapel is? The realtor said there was a chapel of my church in the area."

Ann gasped in delight. "What a coincidence! I'm a member of the Church, too. My husband is president of the Sunday School. How nice to have another member in our neighborhood. I'll show you where the chapel is; and if you like, I'll take you to church on Sunday and introduce you, especially to the other neighbors who are Mormons."

For the first time, Jane really smiled. "What a relief to know that there are some LDS people around. I was afraid I would be all alone without any neighbors who would take an interest in an old woman."

The two women smiled at each other, and both felt a bond of sisterhood, although twenty-five years separated them in age.

"Sister Campbell—," Ann began.

"Please call me Jane," the older woman interrupted. "I hope we can be on a first-name basis."

"I hope so, too, Jane," Ann replied. "Now, I'll finish scrubbing these lower cupboards while you unpack your dishes. Let's see how much we can get done before my children come along from school about three-thirty. They're so excited that there's just another week before summer vacation."

"I remember how my three were during the last week of school," Jane reminisced, and the two women settled comfortably into their work. Jane was a "talker" and willingly filled Ann in on her background. She had been reared in Idaho and had met and married a fellow from Oregon when both were students at Ricks College. In Portland they had reared their two sons and daughter. Now one son was in Connecticut working for a computer firm, another was a career officer in the Air Force on assignment in Europe, and her daughter, a financial officer with a bank specializing in Latin American contacts, was living in Dallas.

When Jane's husband had died three years ago, Jane had felt disoriented in the big, older home where they had spent a quarter century. Worse, the neighborhood was in transition. Boarding-houses and small businesses sprang up around her home, and Jane didn't feel comfortable walking around the area. Ralph and Darlene, her son and daughter-in-law in Connecticut, invited her to come and live with them, but Jane liked her independence and preferred Oregon's climate. She decided to move to a quieter community. Plainville was close enough to Portland that Jane could drive back to visit friends or have them come and see her. She was also fairly close to the Portland airport. Surely the children could fly in regularly for visits.

When Ann could see her children coming down the sidewalk, she intercepted them, introduced them to Jane, and then left for the afternoon, feeling quite pleased. On Sunday, the family stopped by for Jane. Ann introduced her to the sisters in Relief Society. She also made a point of mentioning Jane to the other LDS women in the neighborhood and commented on how much Jane enjoyed visits. Ann took Jane to work with her a couple of times. Jane explored the library where Becky Sorenson worked and the downtown area, then the three women sometimes met for lunch.

It was not a perfect relationship. Ann quickly learned that Jane's appealing independence and candor had a down side. Jane liked to make decisions, not only for her own life but for others; and Ann became adept at turning aside volumes of advice on how to arrange her house, raise her children, and develop political opinions. Ann dropped by Jane's house for a few minutes nearly every day so she could leave when she needed to, rather than inviting Jane over where Jane dominated the conversation, criticized the children, and stayed for hours.

Nearly everyone in the ward was friendly, but most of the women kept their distance. Not only did Jane dominate most conversations, but she also complained. She complained about how noisy the ward was, that the visiting teachers didn't come on the same day of the week every month, that the bishopric was too young, that the garbage collection was haphazard, and that dogs ran loose across her lawn. After listening to this stream of complaints, few women in the ward visited Jane, and many avoided her, even at church.

Even Kent shook his head after one evening when they had had Jane to supper and to family home evening. It had ended pleasantly only because Kent had jettisoned the lesson and seized the first opportunity to break into Jane's monologue about irresponsible teenagers to suggest they have refreshments and play croquet on the lawn. To Ann he murmured: "How do you put up with the constant complaining? Why do you keep visiting her?" When Ann laughed and shrugged, he persisted, "Surely there are others who are more rewarding to be with."

Ann responded thoughtfully: "I agree it's not always fun, and I don't like having to screen the children from her the way I do. But—well, Bishop Pratt asked us to try and live as a ward would in the Millennium. I just don't think a Zion people would reject or avoid anyone. Yes, Jane's a real pill in a lot of ways, but I've spent enough time with her to see past that. If we only spent time with friends we personally enjoyed, we'd leave out a lot of people who need friendship, warmth, and inclusion. I know I don't have to do it, and I'm not doing it out of obligation. She doesn't really like to drive to Portland, and not many of her old friends come to see her. Her children do phone regularly, and she appreciates that, even though she usually carps about how infrequent it is. And besides that, it's really not all uphill. She has a great sense of humor, really knows how to tell a story well, and is a very loyal friend. She honestly tries to do things for others. I really like her in a funny sort of way."

But even Ann's commitment was put to the test with Jane. One drizzly afternoon in early September when Jane came down with a cold, Ann took her a plate of cookies. Jane answered the door in her bathrobe, looked at the gift, and said shortly: "I don't like chocolate chip cookies. You should give them to somebody else."

Speechless, Ann turned away and walked home, the unwanted cookies in her hands, rain beading on the surface of the plastic wrap. She was shocked by Jane's rudeness and struggled to master her own feelings of resentment. She clearly identified her own first impulse—to give not only the cookies but also her time and her attention to someone more appreciative. Ann faced these feelings clearly. Deliberately, she began to give herself another message: I know Jane truly likes me. I also know she would not consciously try to hurt my feelings. So the rudeness must be Jane's unfortunate way of expressing herself. I really want to love my neighbor as myself and to love Jane as the Savior loves me. I know the Savior would want me to forgive Jane. So I need to put this incident behind me and go on being a friend to Jane.

She walked up her front steps. "But how?" she asked through gritted teeth.

"Oh, boy," shouted seven-year-old Ian as she came in. "Great! She didn't want 'em. More for us!" He seized the plate. Ann grinned in spite of herself, even as she automatically ruffled his bright red hair and said, "Only three, then no more till supper."

She took off her raincoat and, as she hung it in the closet, breathed a silent prayer asking Heavenly Father to eliminate her hard feelings for Jane. She felt a quiet sense of well-being and happiness steal over her. Amazed but completely at peace, she went briskly into the family room to ask eleven-year-old Betsy about her homework. A couple of hours later when she was stirring gravy, she made a brief phone call to Jane, asked about the cold with her usual concern, and listened to a complaint about the commercial on TV before laughing and saying: "Well, I've got to feed this bunch. Talk to you soon."

When she told Kent about the latest development, he scowled in mock indignation. "And what did Ian do with all those cookies? Is that why we only had two apiece for dessert?" Then he looked at Ann thoughtfully. He knew Ann was both motivated and rewarded by a true sense of charity, or the pure love of Christ, for another human being whose unfortunate personality made it difficult to attract friends. He felt a little guilty because he had thought often—and suggested more than once—that Ann make it easier on herself by detaching herself from Jane.

But he had noticed some interesting changes in both Ann and Jane. Ann had never associated with older people before. Her close contact with Jane had helped her understand and appreciate the trials of the widowed person twenty-five years older. Kent could see that Ann had expanded her circle of love and could more easily include people with whom she had formerly felt no common ground. And Kent admitted that Ann had helped him grow in the same area.

Kent had also noticed some changes in Jane. At first she took from Ann and others—their friendship and acts of kindness—without giving much in return. But then he heard her invite Ann and some other women to lunch because it was "my turn." She had become less critical. Occasionally she would praise the young people in the ward and grudgingly admit that the bishopric was remarkably wise and caring for men so young. Kent could clearly see what would have happened to Jane Campbell if his wife or someone like her had not gone the extra mile. Jane could have become a lonely, bitter woman—disliking the ward and the members.

"What are you looking at me for?" Ann inquired, wrinkling her nose at him.

"You're a blessing, my dear," he said tenderly. "And not even in disguise."

Discussion

Ann Simonson is an informal leader and a second-miler—one who goes beyond what most would be willing to extend. She reaches out to Jane Campbell, at first out of Christian compassion and her own general good nature, but also because she soon discovers likable traits in the older woman. Jane needs friends but has forgotten how to be a friend or how to make new friends in a circle of people who are not habituated to her personal idiosyncrasies.

Ann's thoughtfulness and her commitment as a disciple of Christ represent not only how we should reach out to the lonely in our current situations but also our responsibility to turn the other cheek and go the extra mile. Our life in the community, our interactions with each other, and our relationships as brothers and sisters in the gospel can be rich and rewarding; but they can also be very challenging, frustrating, painful, and disheartening. Sweet sentiments will not be enough to keep us committed during the rocky passages when our contact with ward members injures us, whether the wound is intentional or accidental. The scriptures are a soberingly realistic handbook of principles for interpersonal in-teractions, and the instructions on forgiveness are both powerful and specific:

> I, the Lord, will forgive whom I will forgive, but of you it is required to forgive all [people] (D&C 64:10).
> Verily, verily, I say unto you, my servants, that inasmuch as you have forgiven one another your trespasses, even so I, the Lord, forgive you (D&C 82:1).
> But I say unto you, Love your enemies, bless them that curse you, do good to them that hate you, and pray for them which despitefully use you, and persecute you (Matthew 5:44).
> For if ye forgive [others] their trespasses, your heavenly Father will also forgive you:
> But if ye forgive not [others] their trespasses, neither will your Father forgive your trespasses (Matthew 6:14–15).

The Savior knew that it would never be easy to love those who commit an act of enmity toward us, or who despitefully use us—even unintentionally. It is easy to love our friends, or those who always do nice things for us. The test of a millennial person is a willingness to stay in relationships, to return kindness for unkind-ness, and to pray for those who may seem to treat us despitefully.

Many people who have difficult personal circumstances, un-fortunate family situations, handicaps, or even mental or physical illness, sometimes try to protect themselves with an outward shell or set of defenses. Being a real neighbor means "abiding" with these people, getting behind their defenses with gentleness and sympathy, and developing the pure love of Christ so that we may see in other children of our Heavenly Father the eternal worth that he sees in them.

Ann's reaction when Jane rebuffs her gift—and, by extension, her concern and her friendship—focuses on one of the dilemmas of service. Can there be such a thing as truly "unselfish" service? Some would argue that everyone who does something for another has selfish motives—if only the desire to feel good about himself or herself. True selflessness is a fiction, they argue; it will never be achieved, now or in the Millennium.

According to those who hold this view, Ann is unconsciously motivated by a desire to store up "treasures in heaven" because of her good works. Even the scriptures talk about the rewards that await the righteous. For example, 1 Corinthians 2:9 promises: "Eye hath not seen, nor ear heard, neither have entered into the [human] heart . . . , the things which God hath prepared for them that love him." We are also told that if we cast our bread (our service) on the waters, it shall be returned to us after many days (see Ecclesiastes 11:1). From this cynical perspective, all service is selfish; and if the millennial world is made of people of one heart and one mind, then they have all colluded to help each other gain the rewards each wants.

I could not disagree more strongly. It is true that people sometimes engage in acts of service out of mixed motives. A great deal of visiting teaching and home teaching is done out of a feeling of duty or obligation or self-righteousness, not out of love for one's neighbor. I have seen missionaries go to the field for the wrong reasons and couples marry in the temple as a result of family and social pressure.

But as a Church leader, I also have observed the value of being patient with people as they work through mixed motives. A teenager who signs up grudgingly for a service project and shows up reluctantly may have exactly the kind of experience he deserves with that attitude, in addition to poisoning the project for others. But it is also possible that the quiet, irresistible miracle of love may work for him, too; and he may feel the disciple's reward of experiencing the pure love of Christ—for himself and for the person he is serving. At least he is in the right place at the right time for the miracle to happen. A woman who complacently checks off visiting teaching for six months in a row as "done," may, in the seventh, feel real compassion spring up in her heart for the women she visits.

Our motives and attitudes must be refined as we work to build Zion and prepare for the coming of the Savior. That means we need to be prepared for a certain amount of "dross" in our own motives and in those of people around us. If we are making progress and helping others to progress, I believe that the Lord's patience with us will be eternal and his mercy infinite.

Furthermore, my own experience tells me that unselfish service is not only a reality but a *common* reality. Ask the father of a seriously ill child whether his sleepless nights and minute-by-minute nursing are motivated by the thought of a personal reward. Ask the parents of a missionary what motivates their prayers for her safety, spirituality, and service.

My wife, Bonnie, has always been a compassionate, sensitive person, even as a young woman; but in the forty years we have been married, she has astounded and humbled me at her ever-deepening compassion for the widows, the ill, the depressed, and the sorrowful in our neighborhood. I live with someone for whom selfless service is a way of life. Selfless service is not only a possibility but already, for many informal leaders, a millennial reality.

10

Managing Diversity

And he denieth none that come unto him, black
and white, bond and free, male and female; and he
remembereth the heathen; and all are alike unto God,
both Jew and Gentile (2 Nephi 26:33).

[God] hath made of one blood all nations . . .
for to dwell on all the face of the earth, and hath
determined the times before appointed, and the
bounds of their habitation (Acts 17:26).

The Principle

All Church leaders know that the people they are expected to
lead are very different in many ways. They differ in age, personality, sex, experience, health, spiritual maturity, emotional maturity,
interests, intelligence, length of time in the Church, marital status,
family configuration, needs, motivation, strength, physical appear-
ance, personal goals, prejudices, and a wide range of other factors.

While leaders are aware of this fact, sometimes they ignore it
and assume that only resemblances are important. It is true that
resemblances *are* important and that a minimum community of
interests is necessary for people even to be associated voluntarily
with each other, but it is a mistake to think of individuals as inter-
changeable in staffing a ward or as being so similar that everyone
will be interested in the same activities and programs. Usually, if
such an assumption prevails, the leaders do not consult or survey
the membership before making decisions. Instead, the leaders simply assume that they already know the group's interests, understand the group's needs and how best to meet them, and believe

that the group shares the leaders' personal interests. Even more frequently, consultation and information gathering are restricted to the leader's counselors or to another small group of personal associates. When leaders add to this decision-making style the claim that their decisions are always "inspired," then full participation and integration can become very difficult for members who do not fit that model.

When leaders do not recognize, acknowledge, accommodate, and even celebrate diversity, they repress and can even oppress members. Those with different interests or circumstances often feel frustrated and disappointed when what they would like to do is not taken into account. Not all boys like to play basketball. Not all girls are fascinated by fashion and discussions of marriage preparation. Not all members are in traditional family situations, and not all family situations are ideal.

How do leaders inform themselves about the diversity of those whom they lead so that these differences can be considered? Here are some suggestions:

1. Surveys and questionnaires. Remember that the information is only as good as, first, the questions, and, second, the interpretation.
2. Interest inventories. Remember that such inventories are necessarily shallow and may not explain motives.
3. Intensive and systematic discussions with third parties such as leaders of quorums and auxiliaries, visiting teaching and home teaching supervisors, class teachers, and so forth. In such cases, remember that the information is still indirect and is being filtered through the consciousness of a third party.
4. Focus groups. These are one-time discussion groups, lasting an hour or two, comprised of eight to ten people who share the characteristic, situation, or problem that the leader wishes to learn more about. Examples are divorced men, converts of less than a year, and so forth. The focus group provides open-ended and personal responses that are as specific as possible about the situation under study, how it makes them feel, and what they would like to see happen.
5. Personal interviews. As a practical matter, the first three methods must be used as surrogates and shortcuts simply because of the press of time. But the most accurate way of

collecting information about diversity is for the leader to talk personally, confidentially, and candidly to individuals. If time were unrestricted (which, of course, it is not), this would be the ideal way to collect information in every single organization or group.

Here are some sample questions a leader might ask to encourage responses:

- What are your goals?
- What do you like to do?
- What would you prefer not to do?
- What is rewarding for you about your interactions at church?
- What types of things make Church activity or service hard for you?
- What changes would you like to see occur that would make things here better for you?
- What can *I* do to make things work better for you?

Our broader American society has evolved certain culturally defined—but unfair—ways of dealing with some differences. If we use the example of race, for instance, we all know that members of racial minority groups have been stigmatized, marginalized, and stereotyped. The ways in which they can contribute are limited by custom to a shorter list than the ways majority members can contribute, and those contributions are usually seen as less valuable than the contributions made by majority members. Such individuals, regardless of their spiritual maturity and their ability to forgive, bear deep wounds that have been unjustly inflicted upon them. It is sad but true that some of these social customs persist in the Church, just because we are limited human beings. It is also true that a few members of the Church are not just insensitive but bigoted; part of their own self-image is wrapped up in being able to scorn other groups. Worse, they wrest some teachings or historical practices of the Church to make it appear that their actions and attitudes have a theological basis.

I simply reject such claims out of hand. The Church is now truly international in scope, with members from every race, nationality, and ethnic background. The voice of the scriptures is clear: "Black and white, bond and free, male and female . . . all are alike unto God, both Jew and Gentile" (2 Nephi 26:33).

It is my firm belief that most members of the Church will behave better as soon as they know better. When they become aware that some of their behaviors or attitudes are less than fully Christian and are a source of pain to their brothers and sisters, they will repent. Some examples of offensive behavior which members will, I believe, discontinue as soon as they understand more completely the profound inclusiveness of the gospel are pejorative nicknames for certain racial and ethnic groups, automatic assumptions about people's interests or capabilities, and jokes that use ethnic, racial, or gender stereotypes.

Gender stereotyping and injustice are particularly important in the Church because the fact that only men are called to hold the priesthood is, I believe, improperly used by some men to justify, in the treatment of women, all kinds of differences that have nothing to do with priesthood. Women have been working hard in recent years to get society to accord them equal regard. No member of the Church should need to be reminded to treat women with respect as the equal partners of men in family life and as equal colleagues in building the kingdom. I regret that women are still sometimes referred to by Church members by such stereotypes as "the weaker sex," or that they have stereotypes attributed to them such as gossiping more than men or being more emotional (and hence less rational) than men. It is unfortunate that women still tend to be assigned gender-stereotyped tasks as "women's work"—for example, taking minutes, doing kitchen work, providing child care, and cleaning up. Women's voices are also an underutilized resource in planning, decision-making, and evaluation in many Church units.

Leadership that provides spiritual direction to prepare a people for the Millennium must include a sensitive appreciation of and attention to the diversity of Church members and an honoring of the diverse gifts of all members of the Church.

As LDS congregations become more diverse, the challenge for those desiring the millennial path is to overcome past socialization and learned prejudices and instead to reach out and fully accept all members—with their differences—as brothers and sisters.

Plainville Second Ward is not completely free from prejudice, but the bishop's enunciation of higher principles had already made a difference in the anti-Japanese feelings Jerry Mason had about Dean Suzuki. The Chun and Martinez families sense no racial discrimination; however, the first black family ever baptized in Plainville is about to meet the missionaries. Many ward members react very positively, but others discover that they unconsciously harbor the vestiges of prejudices whose origins they can barely identify. Leaders in all of the ward organizations, whether they have conscious feelings about blacks or not, must appraise how they will respond.

Plainville Second Ward: The Bowens

Elder John Donaldson and his junior companion, Elder Mike Archuleta, were absolutely ecstatic. They had finally found a "golden" family. The two elders had been laboring in Plainville for two months and had received a few invitations to discuss the gospel with people who were interested in finding out more about the Church, but this family they had met just two weeks before Thanksgiving was so incredibly right that they could hardly believe it.

It had started out as just a routine tracting day. They had gone to an area of town where some new homes were being built, knocking systematically on all the doors in the subdivision. At one door, a pretty little black girl had answered. They asked to talk with her mother. Patricia Bowen greeted them graciously and listened with interest while Elder Donaldson explained that they were Latter-day Saint missionaries with an important religious message they would like to present to the family. He elaborated: "We have a message about new revelations given to humankind about the mission of Jesus Christ. It is our testimony that this message will bring great joy to those who will receive it. All we ask is for an opportunity to share this message with you. You can then decide if what we say is as important as I have indicated."

Mrs. Bowen liked the conviction and sincerity of the clean-cut young men who were almost too soberly dressed in suits, white shirts, and ties. Smiling, she said: "We're interested in religion, even though we have our own church. If you'd like to come back after supper, we'll listen to your message. How long will it take?"

Elder Donaldson had an impression that this would be an important contact and told her they would appreciate an hour. They made an appointment for seven-thirty that evening.

As they walked toward the next house, Elder Donaldson asked his companion, "What do you think?"

Elder Archuleta was all but bouncing along the sidewalk. "In five months, that's the most positive first contact I've ever seen. That lady had such a good spirit about her you could just tell that she's the kind of person who's waiting for the gospel." He hesitated, then asked, "Have you ever taught a black family before?"

"No," answered Elder Donaldson, "but I've always wanted to. There aren't many blacks here in Oregon. I wonder if it will be any different? I wonder what they know about the priesthood ban before 1978." He took a deep breath. "Well, we'll find out tonight."

Promptly at seven-thirty, the two elders rang the Bowens' doorbell. Steve Bowen answered the door and said: "Hello there. You must be the Mormon missionaries. Come right in. We're anxious to talk to you."

The next hour was like a dream for the two elders. They could not remember anyone who had been so receptive. The Bowens freely filled them in on their background. They were both originally from Atlanta. Steve Bowen had been an outstanding athlete in high school but had damaged his knee sliding into second base while playing baseball. This cost him a chance at a college scholarship, so he went to work for a national chain of stores selling tires and automobile parts. Patricia was also on the sales force, and their friendly rivalry developed into a warm friendship, then rapidly into love. They now had three children, ten-year-old Max, seven-year-old Melissa, and four-year-old Roger. Four years earlier, Steve had been promoted to assistant manager of a store in Ventura, California, and was now manager of a store in Plainville that had been open for only two years. They had moved in just three months earlier and were still adjusting to the climate, the distance from their families, and the new city.

They had been active Baptists in both Atlanta and Ventura; but although the Baptist Church was desegregated, their own congregations had been composed almost entirely of black members. They had never really been a part of a predominantly white congregation, like their present local congregation. The racial composition, however, was not as much of a problem as the distance. They had to drive almost fifteen miles to the chapel and were still nervous about driving on Oregon's famous black ice. Between the move and the October storms, they had been back only twice after their initial visit. Still, they felt a need for more spirituality in their family and had been talking about finding a closer church when the two elders called. Neither had heard much about the Mormons except for the Tabernacle Choir, which they both enjoyed; polygamy, which they considered somewhat fantastic; and the historical fact that at one point blacks couldn't be ordained to Mormon priesthood. Patricia asked about that item with characteristic candor.

Elder Donaldson clarified that in 1978 a revelation, given to the prophet and canonized by the Church membership, offered the priesthood to all worthy men regardless of racial background.

"Revelation?" queried Steve. "Prophet?"

Elder Donaldson could not have asked for a better transition. Even the children settled down and listened intently as he explained first how the Savior had established his Church with Apostles and had presented the first principles of the gospel to the people. The Church continued for a time after the Crucifixion, but the priesthood and authority were lost and the true principles corrupted. He then told about Joseph Smith's first vision, the visitation of Moroni, the coming forth of the Book of Mormon, the restoration of the priesthood, and the eventual establishing of the Church. He bore his testimony that he knew by the power of the Holy Ghost that the true church had indeed been established in these last days, and invited them to investigate the Church. He asked if he and Elder Archuleta could return and present their full message.

Steve and Patricia glanced at each other as they thought about what he had said. Then Patricia said quietly, patting Roger who was getting fussy: "I've felt the Holy Spirit with us as you talked. I think you're telling us the truth, and I want to know more."

Steve nodded. "I don't know what it was," he said, "but something about your message really felt good to me. I think we ought to hear all that you have to say."

Elder Archuleta's hands were shaking as he wrote the appointment down for four days later, and they left feeling dazed with excitement, gratitude, and humility. The next few weeks were deeply satisfying to the two elders. They lived for their twice-weekly appointments with the Bowens. In turn, the Bowen family became more and more attached to them, as well as connected with the message of the Restoration. Patricia invited them to Thanksgiving dinner; and the elders, without any regrets, passed up a district get-together to come.

The two elders were pleased and excited when they told John

Emmett, Plainville Second Ward's mission leader, the good news about their new investigators. And Brother Emmett was nearly as excited as the full-time missionaries. The ward had never had a black investigator or member before, and he wanted to be sure that the integration of the Bowen family into the ward was done right. He arranged with the elders to have some of the stake missionaries from Plainville Second meet the Bowens, one by one attend some of the discussions, and start initiating a regular contact with the family. Then when they started to attend church the family would be familiar to several ward members. Brother Emmett would be the first stake missionary to attend a discussion and meet the Bowens.

After a slight hesitation, the Bowens agreed to having John Emmett come to their home for the next discussion. He soon became a familiar face to the Bowen family, and he was present when the missionaries challenged them during the second discussion to begin reading the Book of Mormon. Steve and Patricia agreed promptly and began reading it aloud as a family the first night. After a few days, they asked for another copy, because Steve was taking the family copy to work to read on his lunch hours. When Elders Donaldson and Archuleta asked them to come to church, they quickly agreed; but Steve had to go to a managers' district meeting the first weekend; Melissa and Roger had flu the second weekend; and after nursing the children, Patricia was sick the third weekend. As a consequence, they still had not attended church by the first week in December.

In the second discussion with the Bowens, Elder Donaldson had talked about being "born again"—that is, being born of the water (baptism) and also of the Spirit (the Holy Ghost). He had suggested that the Bowens consider accepting the gospel fully and being baptized into the Church. Steve and Patricia had both replied that they felt it was too soon to consider such a step, that they needed to know more about the gospel. However, at this present point, a few weeks later, the two elders had fasted and prayed, and they felt it was time to seriously challenge the Bowens—Steve, Patricia, and Max—to be baptized. This they did.

Choosing the words of his response carefully, Steve said: "Elders, Patricia and I knew that you would ask us about baptism. We truly believe that Joseph Smith had a visitation of the Father and the Son and that he restored the Church. That is not our concern. We're worried about going to church. Will you Mormons include a black family? Will our children be discriminated against? I know nobody's perfect, but I'm not going to take my kids into a situation where people aren't going to want them."

"You see," Patricia added gently, "we have testimonies of the Church, but what if people in the true church of Christ don't act like Christians?"

The two elders looked at each other and then back at the Bowens. Here it was. "Look," said Elder Archuleta earnestly, "we're not going to pretend that people in the Church are perfect, so we're glad that you don't expect them to be. And to be honest, I think there's more of a chance of racial prejudice against blacks than almost any other group, just because they pick it up from the larger society." He was sweating a little. "I've heard my own granddad call blacks . . . well, call them names; but that's American prejudice, not Mormon. You ought to have heard what he called my parents when my family joined the Church! We've been Catholics for hundreds of years, and he thought we were betraying the family. But the priesthood revelation was almost fifteen years ago—almost my whole life—and I promise you that I've never heard anybody in the Church call blacks names, even though I've heard people say things like 'They must be lazy or they could get out of the slums.'" He drew a deep breath and looked at them anxiously. "I'm being just as honest as I can. You deserve it."

Elder Donaldson added: "I've heard one of my uncles question whether President Kimball's revelation was really inspired. It embarrasses me to think about it. But I think you know that Elder Archuleta and I have a pure love for all of you, and I think that most of the Church members will be like us."

"I understand that there might be prejudice in your family, Elders," said Patricia, "and we're certainly not holding you responsible for your relatives. But can you tell us what the local ward is like?"

At this point John Emmett spoke up. "Let me speak to that point. I have been a member of this ward for years and I think it truly is unusual. Right after the early discussions, I told the bishopric, the elders quorum president, and the Relief Society president that the elders were teaching you and they all said, 'Great! We are anxious to meet them.' Just last week the Relief Society president asked me how you were doing and wanted to know if you needed any help when she heard that Sister Bowen was sick."

Patricia raised her eyebrows in astonishment. Brother Emmett continued: "Bishop Pratt challenged the ward members last spring to try and build a Christlike community, and I think the people are honestly trying. There are no other black families in the ward that I know about, but the elders quorum president is Japanese, there's a Chinese-American family in the ward, and a couple of Hispanic families, too. I don't know if any of them are converts, but there's a good spirit there. It just doesn't feel like the kind of place where people get looked down on."

"We're willing to give it our best shot," said Steve. "But I think we have to know that we'll be accepted—really accepted, no discrimination and also no phony sweetness and light—before we can talk about the baptism question."

"And since everybody's had the flu already," smiled Patricia, "I don't see any reason why we can't come on Sunday. What are the meetings like?"

Relieved, the beaming elders explained the three meetings in Plainville Second Ward's block schedule, which met from one to four in the afternoon.

Max gasped, "That's the whole afternoon! And the Cowboys are playing the Raiders on Sunday."

Melissa had an equally strong opinion: "I don't want to go in a class without Mommy!"

Patricia was also dubious: "Three hours of church for a four-year-old? Or even a seven-year-old? I don't know." Her voice trailed off. She glanced at Steve.

Steve added: "I'm not crazy about the idea of splitting up, either. We want to be with our kids."

"Hey, let's just play it by ear," suggested Elder Archuleta. "We'll all be together in sacrament meeting. If you want to, you can come to opening exercises in Primary with the kids or even to classes with them. Nobody's going to squawk. If it gets too much for the first day, you can leave. We don't take away your car keys at the door."

Elder Donaldson grinned. "And to break up the three hours, bring a snack for the little kids. Everybody used to feed their kids Cheerios during sacrament meeting when it was the last meeting of the three instead of the first. I don't think the three hours will seem too long. And during Primary, they get to move around and sing songs and do activities in their classes."

The elders' cheerful flexibility relaxed the Bowens, but Steve said firmly, "Only sacrament meeting this first week."

The elders didn't push, but made an appointment for twelve-thirty, so that they could accompany the Bowens to the meeting. When they left the Bowens, they drove straight to Bishop Pratt's and summarized the discussion. "They were really straight with us about the possibility of discrimination," Elder Donaldson told him. "I can't tell you what a neat family this is, and I just feel sick at the possibility that somebody could say something or do something inadvertently. They're not going to be looking for offense, but they're really going to be checking us out."

Elder Archuleta chimed in worriedly, "Bishop, do you think anything should be done to prepare the ward members and tell them to be on their best behavior?"

George looked at their concerned faces and remembered his own missionary days with a pang of nostalgia. He considered Elder Archuleta's request thoughtfully for a moment and then shook his head. "I don't think so," he replied. "This is a test of our members. If I tell them to watch their behavior, how will we ever know how they really feel and act? But I'll be praying, and I'll bet you will be, too."

He was right. In fact, the elders began fasting Saturday afternoon and prayed long and fervently before they left for the Bowens'. The answers to the elders' prayers began immediately. Patricia and Steve radiated only anticipation, no wariness, and the children were obviously in a good mood, even Max, who was missing his football game. When they reached the meetinghouse, they had barely entered the foyer before Bishop Pratt came out of his office. "Hello, Elders," he said. "These must be the Bowens!"

Elder Donaldson performed the introductions, and George shook hands all around, beaming. He said, warmly and sincerely: "The elders have told me what a wonderful family you are. Welcome to the ward. I hope you'll feel at home with us."

He shook hands with the children, and they smiled with pleasure when he already knew their names. "Mommy, there's a Christmas tree," pointed out Roger in a stage whisper. Melissa was pleased to recognize the Christmas carols that Katherine Whitehead was playing as a prelude. Before the meeting began, Jocelyn Smith stepped across the aisle and shook hands warmly with Patricia, introducing herself and asking if any of the flu symptoms had lingered. "Will you be staying for Relief Society?" she asked.

"Not today," replied Patricia, smiling.

"Maybe another time," said Jocelyn.

George was conducting and introduced the Bowens to the congregation as an investigator family originally from Georgia. The whole congregation, including the Bowens, appreciatively laughed as he made a time-honored Oregonian joke about "webbed feet." Steve and Patricia sang "O Little Town of Bethlehem" with familiarity, blending their voices in the harmony. The children also followed along in the hymnals with ease. But Steve and Patricia had noticed some of the children whispering and pointing during George's introduction, and it was obvious that they were the only black family in the chapel.

It was a good, if not exceptional, meeting. Well-briefed, the Bowens passed the sacrament trays on to the missionaries without taking bread or water, then settled down to observe. Fourteen-year-old Ted Hainesworth gave a short talk about the importance of sharing with others at Christmas, reading a poem from the *New Era*, and finishing with obvious relief. Tina Quinn, age seventeen, followed with a polished short talk on prayer, drawing on an example of how her father, as the police dispatcher, communicated with the patrol cars. Linda Potter sang "What Child Is This?" in her clear soprano.

Then the Rovetti family, who had recently moved into the ward, took the balance of the time. First, four-year-old Kevin climbed up on the footstool George positioned for him and, obviously enjoying the attention, seized the microphone in both hands, and bore a loud testimony that he loved his family, knew the gospel was true, and recited a verse from "Away in a Manger."

Max stared at Kevin in amazement and leaned over to whisper to Roger: "He's just as old as you are. Think you could do that?"

"Sure," hissed Roger back at him stoutly.

Kay Rovetti, about seven months pregnant, continued with the theme of prayer. She told of times when their prayers had been answered—of finding someone who could fix their old Pontiac when it broke down on their last vacation, of the whole family fasting and praying when Kevin was born with acute jaundice, of their prayers for the health of the baby who was coming, and of the many prayers Mary must have offered during the months of her pregnancy with the Savior.

Then Anthony Rovetti spoke on how to pray. He quoted the Savior's instructions to his disciples not to pray simply to impress others and not to give long, repetitious prayers. Prayers, he said, should be given from the heart, be specific, and be honest. He gave the example of the one-sentence prayer of the publican in the New Testament, "O God, be merciful unto me a sinner," and also gave Joseph Smith's prayer in Liberty Jail, "O God, where art thou?" as an example of a sincere longer prayer.

The elders could tell that the Bowens enjoyed the service, and they were silently grateful that their own prayers—that the speakers would not be boring, long-winded, or "weird"—had been answered.

When the meeting was over, a number of people came up and introduced themselves, making progress out of the chapel slow. Elaine Chun singled out Melissa. "The missionaries tell me that you're seven, Melissa," she greeted her. "Is that right?"

"Yes," nodded Melissa.

"I teach the seven-year-old children in my class," said Elaine, smiling. "I hope you'll come visit the class and see if you like it."

"Sure!" said Melissa excitedly.

"We're not staying for Primary today," said Steve, interrupting his own conversation with Dean Suzuki, "but perhaps another time."

Max had dropped behind to discuss the Raiders' chances with Tim Reynolds, who was in his fourth-grade class. The whole family reached the sidewalk feeling quite comfortable about their welcome.

As they drove home, Elder Archuleta asked, "Well, what did you think?"

Patricia promptly said: "I really felt a good spirit there. I liked what the family said about prayer, and nobody was rude or pushy."

"Your bishop certainly seems like a fine man," added Steve. "I felt he meant it when he welcomed us there."

"Yeah, well they only hold Ku Klux Klan meetings on alternate Tuesdays," laughed Elder Donaldson. "How do you feel about going to the meetings regularly?"

Steve glanced at Patricia. She nodded slightly. He said: "I think we have to at least try it seriously before we can talk about baptism. But it sure helped to have you elders along, too. Can you keep coming with us for a while?"

"Sure!" Elder Archuleta all but yelled. "Brother Emmett will stay with you, and I'll go to Primary with you, Roger. I'll bet you and Kevin Rovetti will turn out to be great friends."

"I just wonder," Patricia said softly, grinning, "what they're saying about *us*."

The experience of having a black family at sacrament meeting came up at a lot of dinner tables that Sunday. Comments varied widely:

"To have a black family in the ward would be a great experience for us all. I hope they'll join the Church."

"My dad would turn over in his grave if he saw a black family in a Church meeting. I'm sure he never thought they would really be given the priesthood."

"Did you see how attentive those children were? I'm sure they'd enjoy Primary."

"We've got a ten-year-old daughter. How would you feel in six years if she wanted to date that oldest boy?"

All during December, the Bowens were regular attenders at Church meetings. Phyllis Pratt and Jocelyn Smith between them made sure Patricia Bowen had a friend beside her in Relief Society. Elder Donaldson went with Steve Bowen to priesthood meeting, and Elder Archuleta attended Primary opening exercises with the children, then took them to their classes. Roger still wanted to be with his parents for a couple of weeks but couldn't resist the status of having Elder Archuleta sit with him in his Star-A class until he suddenly decided he was old enough to go on his own.

On the surface, everything seemed to go smoothly. The Bowens attended the ward Christmas party, and Steve brought his specialty, Chinese coleslaw, for the salad bar. Everyone was cordial and courteous. The teachers made a point of asking the Bowens for their opinions. In fact, Steve and Patricia conceded, everyone was so nice that they felt uneasy, as though they were outsiders being treated with kid gloves rather than as brothers and sisters. "Is it because we're not baptized yet?" they wondered, "or because we're black? Are we just being supersensitive? And how can we tell?"

The Bowen children had no such qualms. They said the other kids were really nice to them. The only event that came even close to being potentially negative occurred when the irrepressible Ian Simonson asked Melissa why her skin was dark. Melissa responded promptly, "I got it from my parents and grandparents just like you got your red hair and freckles." All the kids laughed and went on to talk about something else.

When Tim Reynolds asked Max if he wanted to join the Cub Scout troop, Max eagerly accepted. The Reynolds and Bowen families matched exactly in ages. Patricia and Lori soon discovered that Carrie Reynolds and Roger Bowen enjoyed playing pirates and building Lego constructions as much as the two seven-year-olds, Brittany and Melissa, loved snow forts and jigsaw puzzles. Soon Patricia and Lori were amiably swapping child care after school at each other's houses, a real boon with Christmas shopping to do. Lori, afire with new happiness at her family's reactivation, couldn't say enough good about their home teachers and the bishopric. Patricia absorbed it all.

At Brittany Reynolds's birthday party and sleep-over two days after Christmas, Melissa was an excited guest but came home with business in her eye. "Brittany's eight now," she announced firmly to Steve. "And her daddy's going to baptize her next Saturday. I'm going to be eight in March and I want you to baptize me."

Steve swept her up in his arms. "Do you want to go to Brittany's baptism?" he asked, adroitly changing the subject.

The distraction worked, but he and Patricia had another long, thoughtful conversation that evening when the children were in bed.

On New Year's Day the elders had dinner with the Bowens, bearing their testimonies anew about the great gift of the gospel and hopefully asking them again about baptism. The Bowens insisted that they needed more time. That evening, Paul and Becky Sorenson hosted a singalong and board-game marathon for the Bowens and the Reynoldses. In the kitchen, as Patricia helped Becky and Lori stir up the punch, she casually said, "The missionaries asked us again about being baptized."

"What did you *say*!" squealed Lori excitedly, clutching the can opener.

"I said we're still thinking about it," said Patricia.

Becky laughed. "If you'd said yes, Lori would be rocketing through the ceiling now." Her quick quip made it easy for all three women to laugh. Becky put her hand on Patricia's arm and said sincerely: "Patricia, you and Steve have to make the decision that you think is right for you and your family, but"—she was astonished to hear her voice break and feel tears rise in her eyes—"but if you decide that you don't need us or that we don't need you, it will break my heart. Is there anything we can do to help make that decision?" She put her arms around Patricia and hugged her fiercely.

Patricia, returning the embrace, said, shaken, "I think you have," then reached out to encircle Lori, too.

That night, Patricia told Steve what had happened in the kitchen and added: "Steve, I think we have to be true to our own feelings about the gospel. If the Church is true, it's true, and we should go ahead and be baptized. If this turns out to be some kind of cover-up and people can't really accept us, then that's their problem. But I can't believe Becky and Lori didn't mean it."

Steve smiled. "You're right. I was thinking tonight in that group that it would be hard to think of anyplace I wanted to be more right then. I love the gospel, I like the people, and that's got to be enough to help me stop being so suspicious."

The next day, they talked to the children and explained their decision. "Can you be baptized on Saturday at the same time as Brittany?" shrieked Melissa.

"I don't know how long it takes," returned Steve, "but if we can, we will be."

"What about you, Max?" Patricia asked gently. "You're old enough to be baptized with us, but it has to be your own decision."

"Just try and stop me," grinned Max.

Laughing, Steve phoned the elders and told them their decision. Breathless with joy, the missionaries assured them that they could be included in the Saturday services, explained the interviews that they would need, and found out which evenings they'd be free to meet with the zone leader. Then Steve and Patricia called their families in Atlanta, braced for negative reactions from both but were pleasantly pleased to hear Patricia's mother say, "I can tell that you feel closer to Jesus and that's the only thing I've ever wanted for my children."

Next they called Tom and Lori. Then they phoned the bishop, then Paul and Becky. Lori had already called them. The phone rang the instant they set it down from this last call. It was Sister Emmett, John's wife, calling with congratulations and checking on the size of baptismal clothes they would need. And that was just the beginning. When they were chatting with the bishop after their interviews with the zone leader, they commented on how dazed they were by the outpouring of rejoicing. George Pratt chuckled. "We've been holding off so long, not wanting to seem pushy, that you have no idea how much steam has built up!"

When the baptismal service began at ten o'clock on Saturday morning, it seemed as if the whole ward was in attendance. The Reynolds and Bowen families clung together, Melissa basking in Brittany's reflected glory. John Emmett, who was conducting the service, quickly sized up the situation and announced that opening exercises would be held in the chapel. It was standing room only in the font area. Tom baptized Brittany, Elder Archuleta baptized Max and Patricia, and then Elder Donaldson baptized Steve. As Steve came up out of the water, his face split in a grin of irrepressible joy, and the congregation burst into spontaneous applause, laughter mingling with their tears.

Rather than receiving the confirmations immediately after the baptism, the Bowens chose to be confirmed Sunday morning in testimony meeting. Blaine Hainesworth, who was conducting, bore his testimony of the great spirit that people had felt at the baptisms the day before. Looking directly at the Bowens, he said, "I feel a great love for you and hope you will be of one heart with all of us." At his invitation, Max, Brittany, Patricia, and Steve each bore testimony about the truthfulness of the gospel: their love for their families, the missionaries, and the other members of the ward; and their desire to be fully involved members. Lori Reynolds, aglow with happiness, bore a thrilling testimony about the transforming power of the gospel, her joy at seeing her husband baptize their daughter, and her equal joy at seeing her cherished friends join the circle of brotherhood and sisterhood within the Church.

The family was deluged with well-wishers afterward, some of whom had tears in their eyes as they shook hands with the Bowens. Quietly, John Mueller pulled Steve a little aside and said: "My dad was always very prejudiced against blacks. I never particularly thought I was, but I don't think I was particularly accepting either. I just want you to know that in the weeks you've been coming to church, I've grown less and less comfortable with those old feelings. I've prayed and asked the Lord to lift those feelings from me. I feel that he has. I'm telling you now that I feel like a brother—a real brother—toward you." Speechless, Steve gripped John's hand, reading the older man's sincerity in his eyes.

Elder Donaldson was transferred almost immediately after the baptism, but as Elder Archuleta and his new companion watched proudly, Steve was ordained a priest, and he and Patricia promptly received callings as home and visiting teachers. Steve was recruited for the elders quorum basketball team, and both of them began singing in the ward choir.

One evening in March, Steve and Patricia attended a study group of eight or ten other adults in the ward, hosted by Ron and Pam Hardy. The discussion focused on diversity, and Steve felt compelled to ask: "What made the difference in your feelings toward us when we were baptized? Before then people were just as polite and as nice as they could be, but somehow we never felt really included."

Ron responded grinning: "Oh, so you noticed? Seriously, I think it mostly takes time to develop friendship and trust, to learn what it really means to love our neighbors. I don't know about the others, but when you and Patricia first started to come to the ward, I wondered how *you* felt about *us*. I could tell that you were looking us over, and I really felt on exhibit."

Nola Gardner added: "When you were baptized, I knew that you were fully committed to the Church, and I felt that also meant you had decided to commit yourself to us, the members. In return, I felt a total sense of acceptance for all of you. If I could do it again—and I hope we have another chance with another family—I'd try to show you my full acceptance from the very beginning."

The fact that ward members felt free to respond candidly to Steve's question was deeply confirming to him; but a full feeling of acceptance came a few weeks later in an elders quorum meeting. A discussion developed around what was meant by the "church of the devil" or the "whore of the earth," as described in the Book of Mormon. Steve said he thought this must mean the Catholic Church. Immediately Anthony Rovetti said: "Steve, I disagree with you. I know that some people feel the same way, but I've seen too much good among the Catholics in my own family and the Catholics among whom I grew up to believe in this kind of blanket condemnation."

"Yeah," chimed in Elder Archuleta. "If the Catholic Church was as bad as all that, my family wouldn't have had enough desire for truth to join the LDS church."

"Wait a minute," objected Hy McDougall. "I'm not casting aspersions on anybody's religion, but if you know a little history, the way Nephi describes this church really does fit the history of the Catholic Church at some periods."

The discussion was a lively one with no holds barred, and Steve participated fully. Afterwards, he could not remember the summary and conclusion Peter Quinn pulled together. Instead, he remembered that he was treated as an equal among others. He had spoken his mind freely, and others agreed or disagreed on the merits of his ideas and evidence, not taking special pains to accommodate his opinions. For the first time, Steve truly felt at home in Zion.

Discussion

Race is certainly an aspect of diversity about which many people have very strong emotional responses. Although racial and ethnic diversity is proliferating in all wards and branches, Plainville Second Ward is probably not unlike many units in the United States and Canada even today. While members know that the blessings of the gospel are available to all persons regardless of race, many of them have never known representatives of some ethnic or racial groups personally. Feelings of prejudice that may have been implanted early can lie dormant for years, surprising individuals with unexpected reactions when they need to deal face to face with members of these groups.

The missionaries respond to the Bowen family with the pure love of Christ, but they are aware of racial tensions in their own backgrounds and are concerned about how the Bowens will be accepted by the ward. When they express these concerns to the bishop, he wisely decides not to make any special preparations for the Bowens but instead waits to see how the members will honestly respond.

The Bowens almost instantly sense the polite cheerfulness and careful courtesy with which they are accepted, not realizing until after baptism that they are responding to the ward in the same way. The ward's children accept the three Bowen children with a minimum of curiosity. Patricia feels quickly at home, perhaps because of her rapidly developing friendship with Lori Reynolds. Steve Bowen crosses an internal threshold within himself only when he feels himself accepted without distinction in a vigorous exchange of opinions. Obviously, personal definitions of "acceptance" are at play here as well as the natural process of developing trust, which can occur only over time.

Although we do not follow George Pratt's reactions to the situation, he knows that there has never been a black family in the ward before and that some members harbor prejudices or, at least, reservations. What should he do? He feels that if the members have a vision of the totally Christlike community, they will wrestle with their own feelings and respond appropriately. By the same token, he cannot help them grow spiritually if he uses subtle, coercive pressure on them to "be nice" while the black family is with them. His patience in letting the situation develop over a matter of weeks and in letting each class teacher, the Relief Society, the elders quorum, and personal relationships take their normal course is important. It means that the Bowens retain the initiative in their responses.

Leaders in the Church have a most delicate balance to achieve. Although each person is different, it is not possible to design a special program for everyone. There has to be a common ground and commonly shared values, but programs must be flexible enough to take into account "the one" who is different—not only as a matter of administrative wisdom but because in no other way can the one be ministered to. Leaders must be clear role models of Christlike behavior. Their actions must communicate both an acceptance of those who are different and a willingness to admit and then abandon any language or actions that in any way discriminate against anyone who is outside the common mold.

Some may feel that the problems of Plainville Second Ward are not really problems at all. The ward is relatively homogeneous in education, socioeconomic class, racial composition, and American culture. The differences are minor: some women are employed while others are not; some people have more education than others; some adults are single or single parents; some couples are childless; some are more active than others.

But what about wards in urban ghettos where black, Hispanic, Asian, and European ethnic groups mingle, some of whom have been Americans for up to five generations and some of whom are so newly arrived that they do not yet speak English? Predictions of more Spanish-speaking than English-speaking Church members in the near future bring the issue closer to home. Other challenges would be posed by a ward that had sharp economic divergences, one where several families were struggling with drug and/or alcohol addiction, or where some members were involved in crime. Since the 1850s, the Church in Utah and surrounding states has developed a strong cultural homogeneity into which members have been integrated as they have accepted the gospel; but since the explosion in Church membership outside the United States beginning in the 1960s, the Church can no longer be viewed realistically as a cultural monolith.

One inactive Aaronic Priesthood holder with whom I once worked said, "I don't really feel comfortable calling people 'brother' and 'sister.' I don't *feel* like a member of the same family. I really feel more like a third cousin." I had to laugh, but he had a point. Is there room in the Church for a third cousin?

The issue of diversity will increase in intensity in the future. It will adversely affect our ability to relate to each other in a Christ-like way unless we find ways of hearing, encouraging, and celebrating the voices of diversity.

One of the great challenges in preparing for the Millennium is this: can we be of one heart and one mind with many kinds of people, finding bridges in the gospel to connect us in spite of the differences that divide us? The Savior's message is clear: We must.

11

Dealing with Repentance, Change, and Forgiveness

Come now, and let us reason together, saith the
Lord: though your sins be as scarlet, they shall be as
white as snow; though they be red like crimson, they
shall be as wool (Isaiah 1:18).

I, the Lord, will forgive whom I will forgive, but
of you it is required to forgive all men (D&C 64:10).

The Principle

One of the most important functions of a leader, particularly
for those who have chosen a millennial path, is to help in the repentance process of those they lead. Repentance is a term almost
synonymous with change. If one becomes aware that he or she is
behaving in inappropriate ways (bad temper, gossiping, failing to
carry through on promises, and so forth), then the appropriate action is to repent—or change—by replacing the old behavior with
new, more effective or more righteous actions.

In the sense that repentance means changing behaviors, all
leaders have the responsibility to help others improve. When the
behavior of another is morally wrong and could affect his standing
in the Church, then the person who is designated as the one to
help in this process of repentance is the bishop or the stake president.

The processes of repentance and change are very similar:

1. One must begin by recognizing that one has either sinned
   or has behaviors that need changing.
2. Recognition is not enough. One must then have a desire

or motivation to want to do things differently. This has been referred to as "a godly sorrow" (in the case of repentance) or having a "felt need" strong enough to expend the time and energy to change.

3. After recognizing the desire to change or repent, one must involve someone else in an appropriate way, perhaps by confessing the sin to the wronged person or to the bishop or by finding another person to provide support during the change.

4. If one's transgression has harmed another, then some restitution is required. If one stole property, then one must return or replace it. If one offended or personally hurt another, then one must apologize and ask for forgiveness, and any misunderstandings in the minds of third parties must also be corrected. If one has sullied another's reputation, then one must go back and make amends.

5. With the goal of eradicating the sin, or making the change, one now engages in new behaviors and/or abandons the old, sinful ways.

6. One feels a sense of freedom from guilt or sin, or a feeling of growth and accomplishment.

These six steps are the actions to be taken by the person who is repenting or changing. But what about people who have been hurt, distressed, or outraged by the behavior of the sinner? On this point, the teachings of the Savior are very clear. No matter what the other person may have done to us, it is required of us to forgive all who may have trespassed against us. (See D&C 64: 8–10.)

I do not want to oversimplify or cheapen this process. It has become apparent in recent years that survivors of incest, for instance, carry deep and complex wounds that require a long time and often professional help to heal. Although similar cases lie outside the scope of this chapter, I hope that individuals struggling with such processes will receive the kind of support they need to come to the point where they can forgive and, hence, move forward with their lives. Such situations are frequently complicated by the perpetrator's refusal or inability to repent and change; in other situations, such as assault, murder, rape, and fraud, the physical damage may be irreparable. Even so, refusing to progress toward forgiveness or waiting for the perpetrator to "repent" before setting the forgiveness process in motion will seriously impede our own spiritual progress.

This chapter deals with a more ordinary situation: someone has broken one of the laws of the Church. Perhaps no commandment is more important in a millennial society than for us to acquire the emotional and spiritual maturity to truly forgive each other as an offender recognizes and repents of his or her sins. The scriptures tell us that during the Millennium Satan will be bound for a thousand years. "And because of the righteousness of [the Lord's] people, Satan has no power; wherefore, he cannot be loosed for the space of many years; for he hath no power over the hearts of the people, for they dwell in righteousness, and the Holy One of Israel reigneth" (1 Nephi 22:26).

One of the acid tests of whether the Saints are ready for the Savior, the Holy One of Israel, to reign on earth is whether they will repent of all their sins and will forgive each other their sins.

The members of the Plainville Second Ward, in the scene that follows, are faced with a trying situation in which a teenage couple commit a sexual sin, the young woman becomes pregnant, and the young man is reluctant to assume full responsibility for his share of the situation. It is unfortunate but true that our society has always weighted the penalty for sexual activity more heavily for women than for men; that also is one of the realities that the young woman and the ward members must struggle with.

Plainville Second Ward: Colleen Dalton

Early one frosty January morning before the bishop went to work, the phone rang at the Pratt home. Phyllis, who was helping Susan pack a sack lunch for a field trip, picked up the receiver. George heard her say, "Sure, Colleen. I'll call him."

Colleen Dalton. The oldest of Mariah's five children. A senior in high school and working long hours at the Frostee-Creme to save money for college. Very pretty and very nice. She had been Mariah's right hand during the divorce five years earlier, a gentle and reliable second mother to the four younger children when Mariah had started working full-time.

The voice on the other end sounded very young. "Bishop, this is Colleen Dalton. I need to talk to you as soon as possible. Is there some time we could get together?"

She was in some kind of trouble. His heart smote him even as he replied cheerfully, "How about this evening at seven at the bishop's office? Or if that's not soon enough, let's arrange a time during the day."

"Oh, it's not an emergency," she said, with a small, mirthless laugh. "I'll see you this evening. Thanks."

George was there early, but Colleen was early, too. It was not quite seven o'clock when her heels clicked down the hall. He rose to greet her, shook hands, and fussed a bit getting her settled in the chair, but she was pale-faced and tight-lipped. It was obvious that small talk was not going to relax her. As soon as he pulled his chair near her and leaned forward attentively, she announced flatly, almost defiantly, "Bishop, I'm pregnant."

George gasped, but he realized he wasn't really surprised. Somehow he'd been dreading this identical announcement. Still he *was* shocked. He heard himself asking weakly: "Colleen, how did it happen? Are you sure? Does your mother know?" *Get a grip on yourself, George,* he rebuked himself. *How do you **think** it happened?*

Colleen answered the second question. "I'm over a month late with my period. I bought one of the self-testing kits at the drugstore, and it shows that I'm pregnant. And no, I haven't told my mother anything yet."

George had by now regained his composure. "Colleen, thank you for confiding in me. You know I love you, and I'll be with you all the way. Now, tell me how this happened."

Colleen poured out her story. She had been going with Alex Eastman, a boy she'd dated since her junior year. He had graduated last spring, was attending Oregon State, and was working at the lumber mill on weekends and holidays. He was nineteen, a good boy. George relaxed a little. He knew Alfred and Dorothy Eastman, not members of the Church but a good solid family. At least Colleen hadn't been taken in by some sleaze artist.

Colleen spoke steadily, courageously. "We've been going steady since the summer. We love each other. We're planning to get married sometime. Alex wants to finish college and that's what I want, too, for me and for him." She took a deep breath and looked down. "It was Thanksgiving weekend." She raised her head and he saw the terrible torment in her eyes.

"Bishop, we only did it once, and we both felt terrible after-wards. We never thought that I could get pregnant; but after I missed my period, we really got worried, and now the test has confirmed our worst fears. What are we going to do?"

George had been thinking while she talked. Now he said care-fully: "Colleen, the first thing we need to do is to confirm the pregnancy. The kits are pretty good, but they're not always accu-rate. I'll arrange an appointment for you at Dr. Eccles's clinic to-morrow afternoon. Don't worry. I'll talk with him and there won't be any embarrassing questions. Then we'll be sure. But, as-suming that you're pregnant, are you prepared to get married?"

Colleen glared at him and gave an angry, half-hysterical sob. "Prepared? Of course we're not prepared. We're not *prepared* for anything. But if you mean whether we *would* get married . . . I just don't know." She slumped suddenly and spoke dully, looking at her hands. "Alex and I talked about that. I feel that we're both responsible and that the right thing is to get married and have the baby. Alex doesn't feel that way. He's sorry it happened and he wants to help me, but he wants to finish school. I know that mar-riage just isn't what he wants right now." She raised her head sud-denly and looked defiantly at George. "He's not just trying to run out on me. It's not that way at all."

George could hear how many times she'd told herself the same thing and asked gently, "Colleen, I assume that Alex hasn't talked to his parents either."

Colleen nodded.

"Well, let's just take things one step at a time. First, let's get the exam and the test. Then we'll get together and see what's to be done next. I know you're terribly worried, and I know you feel heartsick, both for the transgression and the possibility of a baby. But it's not the end of the world. I know that this is mostly a mis-take and too much trust in your own willpower, that committing this sin was not what you really wanted. We can pull the pieces back together so that you'll be able to get on with your life. Ex-cept for murder and for the sin against the Holy Ghost, we can re-pent of anything if we want to. Would you like me to give you a priesthood blessing? It would be a comfort to you right now."

For the first time, tears came to Colleen's eyes. "Would you, Bishop? I would like that so much. I didn't think I was worthy of a blessing. And my dad. . . ."

George was glad she had said yes. He wanted to bless this frightened young woman who was so bravely determined to handle the situation. He stood behind her chair, placed his hands gently on her head, and poured out his soul to the Lord—Colleen's basic goodness, her need at this time, and her desire to put her life in order. By the power of his priesthood, he promised that she would have a sense of comfort in taking these first steps toward repentance, and pledged his own help during the days that lay ahead. "The Spirit of Lord will strengthen you and lead you, step by step, in the decisions that lie ahead," he promised.

Relieved and subdued, Colleen left the office. George Pratt knelt in prayer and asked for guidance and inspiration both for himself and for Colleen. During the blessing the impression had come strongly to him that she was indeed pregnant and there would be difficult days ahead.

He called Malcolm Eccles the next morning and made the appointment for Colleen on her school lunch hour. Malcolm called him that afternoon. "The physical exam was pretty clear," he said, "but we're doing the lab test, too. She's a really nice girl. I don't need to know any details, George, but if there's anything I can do, let me know. My nurse will call you tomorrow."

George hung up the phone, then called Colleen and made an appointment for the next night. He was pretty sure what the test results would be, and in either case, they needed to talk again. The afternoon call from the nurse was what he expected.

That evening, he began softly. "Well, Colleen, I know this isn't what you want to hear. You're two months pregnant, and now we have to deal with that reality."

To his surprise Colleen looked relieved. "I knew I was pregnant," she said. "It's kind of a relief to know for sure. Don't worry about me. I'm going to be okay, but what do we do now? I know I'm going to have to tell my mother."

The bishop asked, "Do you want me to go with you when you talk to your mother?"

"Thanks, but no. Mom and I have a close relationship, and I'd feel better telling her by myself. She already knows something's wrong."

"I understand," he replied, "but tell your mother that we've talked and that if the two of you would like me to explain it to the younger children, I'd be pleased to come over. Now, what about Alex and his family? Do you want me to come with you then?"

She hesitated. "I don't think so. Alex said if I was really pregnant, he'd tell his folks. I just don't know what their reaction will be."

"Colleen," he urged, "if you need *any* help dealing with your family or Alex and his family, please let me know. After you've talked with them, we need to get together and work out your plans for the future. If you and Alex plan to marry, there are some very difficult decisions you will have to make. And if you don't, there will be another set, just as difficult."

Bishop Pratt did not hear from Colleen for more than a week. Then late one afternoon at work, he heard her resolute voice on the telephone, asking if they could visit that evening. When he arrived at the meetinghouse, Mariah and Colleen were already in the parking lot, the car motor running to keep the heater going. George unlocked the church and ushered them into the office, switching on the heater in the small room.

When they were seated, he said directly: "Mariah, I can tell that you know about Colleen's situation. How are you feeling about things right now?"

Mariah, strained but composed, looked straight at George and said: "Bishop, it was a terrible shock to me. I'm angry. I'm angry at Alex. I'm angry at myself. I'm angry at Fred for leaving Colleen without a father during her teen years. I'm angry at God. It's not enough bad luck that she should have to deal with a divorce the way the oldest child has to but that just one sexual experience should result in pregnancy." She took a deep breath. "You need to know this, but my own anger isn't very important. What's important is that I'm not angry at Colleen. I love her and I'll do anything in the world that I can to help her now."

"What about Alex's parents?" George asked.

Colleen said flatly: "Alex told his parents so we went over and discussed the situation with Alex, his mother, and his father. Alex said that he was responsible, but they"—her voice wavered but she went resolutely on—"they said that it's the girl's responsibility to keep things under control. Alex doesn't want to get married, and they support him in that decision."

Mariah said dryly: "If you ask me, the parents don't want Alex to get married, and Alex is going along with *them*. But that's neither here nor there. They offered to pay for an abortion, but Colleen refused. So here we are."

"You're going to have the baby?" George asked gently.

"Yes," said Colleen, "and Alex is not going to be a part of it. At first I kept hoping that Alex would see how we could make it work. It hurt so much when I realized that there was no chance of that. But when I saw how weak and indecisive he was, I realized I couldn't marry him, even if he changed his mind. I'd just have two children on my hands."

George was struck by admiration for her maturity, even as he felt a pang that life was requiring such maturity of her. "Colleen, you know the Church position on abortion," he said gently. "Are you ready to accept that position for you?"

"Of course I am," she replied steadily. "Abortion is *not* an option. What I did was wrong, but killing my baby couldn't possibly make it right. No, I'm going to have the baby."

"I'm proud of you, Colleen," said Bishop Pratt. "I just wanted to make sure that's really how you felt."

"It's how I feel," she said firmly. "But what I don't know"— her voice became uncertain—"is what happens next. Mom and I have talked. I know that the Church has a good adoption program, but I'm not sure I'll feel very good about placing my baby for adoption. That might be just another way of getting rid of it. I know from Mom that you don't have to have a husband around to be a good mother."

"That's got to be your decision, too," Bishop Pratt agreed. "And fortunately, you'll have several months in which to come to a decision. The Church makes a judgment about the righteousness or unrighteousness of conceiving a child, depending on the circumstances, and on aborting or not aborting, also depending on circumstances. When marriage is not possible, the official Church policy is to prefer adoption as a situation that's usually better for the baby, but it makes no final judgment. Either decision can be a righteous one. What do you think, Mariah?"

Mariah took Colleen's hand. "I'm really proud that Colleen feels so much love and responsibility for the baby already, but I don't think she knows how hard it is to be a single parent. I've told her that I think the best thing for her and the baby is placement; but if she decides to keep the baby, I'll support her in every way I can."

"What about the younger children?"

Mariah nodded. "We've already talked with them. Jesse and Sarah are very excited about the baby—they're just eleven and ten so they're not aware of the social consequences. Amy is halfway between thinking it's very romantic and being horrified and embarrassed. I'm a little worried about her. Raymond's fifteen, and he's just so angry and humiliated that he can hardly talk. He wants to punch Alex out. And he knows what the kids at school are going to say. But primarily, he just wants to protect Colleen. It's drawn our family closer together, if that's what you're asking. Colleen isn't going to have to waste any of her energy fighting battles at home."

Colleen asked, "Bishop, what's your opinion?"

George Pratt answered carefully: "Colleen, I think that how you make the decision is more important than the decision itself. I know you'll make it a matter of intense prayer because that's the kind of person you are. I want you to know that I'll pray, too. If you want priesthood blessings at any point, I'm here for you, and so are your home teachers. I think your motives are really important. If you keep the baby to punish yourself for having made a mistake—because you feel you have to raise the baby to expiate your sin—that's a mistake. If you keep the baby because you want someone to love or because you hope Alex will change his mind, that will be a mistake. If you place the baby for adoption because you want to be free of an embarrassing reminder or because you'll feel noble and sacrificial, those are also mistakes. You're an individual. The baby is an individual. You live in a family of individuals and in a ward of individuals. This decision affects all of them, but it affects the baby the most, and you next, so those interests are paramount. Are you following what I'm saying so far?"

Colleen nodded. Her eyes were wide. She looked frightened and very young. George went on even more gently, speaking out of his own pain. "My heart aches for you. I think of our circumstances when Phyllis and I married. I think of Will, just a couple of years younger than Alex, just a year younger than you. My first impulse is to say that what's best for the baby is a loving couple who desperately want a child because they can give the baby a home with a mother and father. They will love the child as much as you would. You're seventeen. Someday you'll fall in love, marry, and have other children. You're too young to be a parent.

"But that's my first impulse. My second realization is that

your life will never be the same from this point on, whether you keep the baby or place the baby. Whatever decision you make, you're going to have to live with the consequences for the rest of your life. Other people can help you with the decision and support you as you live with the consequences, but only you can make the decision and live through the consequences. I'd like you to counsel with the LDS Social Services people so that you have a clear picture of what adoption would entail and get an idea about what kind of adoptive parents are available—and also do some reading about the experiences of adoptive parents and children."

"I'd like to do that," said Colleen, "but right now it seems very secondary. What do I tell my friends and the people in the ward?"

George hesitated. "You know, there's a foster home program so that you could go live with an LDS family in another state while you're having the baby."

Colleen shook her head decisively. "Mom and I already talked about that and decided against it. I definitely don't want to go away. I need my mom. I need my family."

Mariah interjected: "And I absolutely insist that she graduate from high school. Getting an education is going to be tough enough without dropping out in her senior year."

"Colleen, that may not be easy," said the bishop. "I think everyone will be supportive and helpful. I want to believe that everyone in the ward will rally round, but there's bound to be some talk. I"—he hesitated—"you have to be prepared for people who feel they have to express disgust and condemnation in case anyone thinks your situation is romantic and glamorous. I just don't know how all the people will react."

Colleen's eyes flashed. "I don't care what people say. If they're so narrow-minded and judgmental, I don't want them as friends anyway."

George sighed. "You're thinking mostly of the other girls in the ward, aren't you? I'm thinking of their parents." He thought for a moment, then said slowly: "Colleen, I feel we have good, loving people in the ward who are really trying to be Christians. If they were told the situation, I honestly feel that most of them wouldn't condemn you but would try to support you."

Colleen's emotional endurance was almost gone, and George could see that. Mariah interposed firmly: "I think that needs to be Colleen's decision, too, but I don't think she can or needs to decide right now who to tell and how to tell them. And it's really not necessary, unless she becomes ill, to make that decision for another few weeks."

George agreed. "I admire the strength and maturity both of you are bringing to this situation.

"Let me talk for a moment about one very important issue. Colleen, you know you have broken a most serious law, and I know you feel deeply sad and repentant. But always remember that for the repentant person, the Savior's atonement is absolutely complete and his love is infinite. No matter what others may think, the Savior's compassion and love will always be available to you. And he has promised that his forgiveness is forever. We are told that 'though your sins be as scarlet, they shall be as white as snow.' Rely on him and he will strengthen and comfort you."

Colleen and Mariah could only nod, as tears filled their eyes and they felt the confirming Spirit of the Lord with them at that moment.

Then the bishop said, "Before we leave, Mariah, would you like a blessing? I hadn't realized how this situation would bring back a lot of issues from the divorce."

Tears sprang to her eyes and she blinked them back. "Thanks, Bishop," she said. "I went to Gene Thompson, our home teacher, for a blessing the same day Colleen told me. I'm sure that's what's kept me together during these last few days."

George stood in the doorway of his office and watched the two women walk down the hallway, Mariah's arm around Colleen, their heads together, talking softly.

The next Sunday was the first Sunday in February. Anthony Rovetti tenderly blessed their new daughter, Diana. Colleen was the first one on her feet when Jim Butler turned the time over to the members for testimony-bearing. George realized he was holding his breath as one of the deacons brought Colleen the microphone. From where he was sitting, he could see her holding Mariah's hand with one hand while her other, white-knuckled, clutched the microphone.

"Brothers and sisters," she began steadily. "I have something to tell all of you. This is the hardest thing I have ever done in my life. I have prayed for the Spirit of the Lord to strengthen me. I hope you will understand me. I'm expecting a baby."

She paused. George could see the congregation go rigid with shock. Some people turned unbelievingly to their neighbors, their faces questioning, Did I hear what I thought I heard? George's eyes sought Phyllis's and he read the sorrow on her face, but no surprise.

Colleen continued firmly. "I am not married. I will not be married. Please don't ask me about the father or how it happened. I have already dealt with that with my family and the bishop. I know what I have done is wrong. I hope you can appreciate my sadness and my repentance and what I've already gone through. I could have gone away from home to have my baby, but I really want to be here with my family and friends. I feel I am still a good person. Last year in English, we read *The Scarlet Letter*. Please, don't make me feel that I must wear a scarlet letter for the rest of my life."

George's eyes swept the congregation. Tina Quinn and Haley Hall, both members of Colleen's Laurel class, were weeping. Marjean Suzuki, the Laurel teacher, had buried her face in Dean's shoulder. Thirteen-year-old Amy Dalton, sitting beside Mariah, had her arm around eleven-year-old Sarah. Gene and Meredith Thompson must somehow have guessed what was going to happen. They were sitting on the same row as the Daltons, with ten-year-old Jesse between them. Gene had a firm hand on fifteen-year-old Raymond's knee. All of the children were watching Colleen as she continued.

"I haven't yet decided whether to keep the baby or give it up for adoption," she continued. "Please don't ask me about that either. Either decision is hard. I would like you to accept my confession and repentance and help me in the six or seven months that are ahead. I truly do have a testimony of the gospel. I can't begin to tell you how much I love my mother and my brothers and sisters for their marvelous support. I could not have come this far without the help of Bishop Pratt. He has been wonderful to me. I pray that the Lord will bless me and you, in the name of Jesus Christ, amen."

Almost immediately, Haley Hall stood up, sobbing almost uncontrollably. "I want Colleen to know how much I love her. She's a wonderful person with great faith. This is a terrible thing that has happened, but it doesn't make her a bad person. Please help her. And Colleen, I want you to know that I'll always be your friend."

Sister Kershaw, a woman in her seventies who bore her testimony every fast meeting, was already on her feet when Haley sat down: "Brothers and sisters, I can't tell you how tender my heart feels at this moment. Over fifty years ago, my sister faced the same situation that Colleen is in. She wanted to stay home and have the baby, but my parents were so afraid of gossip and criticism that they made her go to another city and have the baby alone. She kept the baby for a while but finally had to give it up so she could support herself. Our family was never the same. That sister never came back into the family circle. Oh, how I hope that never happens to Colleen, whom we have all known and loved. She is part of our ward family, and our circle of love should hold her tight."

Kay Rovetti rose, cradling her newborn daughter in her arms, and spoke softly into the microphone: "We've only been in the ward for about three months and I don't know Colleen very well, but I want to remind everyone here that Colleen, like every other pregnant woman in America today, had the option of choosing not to give birth to the child she has conceived. Colleen, I feel that your decision to have your baby is a brave one. You are choosing the way of life, not the way of death. I pray the Lord will strengthen you for that righteous decision."

Terry Harvey was next. "I know Colleen pretty well as a diligent student in my classes over at the high school, but that's not what I want to talk about. Probably none of you know that I'm adopted. It's not something I talk about very much—not because I'm ashamed of it but because it's just not relevant in most circumstances. I wish I knew more about my birth parents, but I know my mother was pretty young, younger even than Colleen. I've always been grateful to her for giving me life. I wish I could find her someday and introduce her to Marsha and our boys. I'd just like to express my support to Colleen and her family during this difficult time, and I'm one who wants to help out in any way I can."

The expressions of support and love came from all parts of the congregation. George felt the tension easing from his shoulders. His faith in his congregation was not misplaced. He could see other reactions in the congregation, too—the protective looks of some parents toward their own young daughters, the embarrassment of some teenagers that the subject was being talked about at all, Marjean Suzuki's obvious self-recrimination, the distaste on the faces of a few older members. But the warmth and support went on.

Darrel Hodges rose and said: "I know Colleen doesn't want to talk about how it happened, but I think we should remember that another person was involved in this baby; and I want to say something to the young men in this room. I want you to remember the look on Anthony Rovetti's face after he got through giving Diana that beautiful blessing and held her up for us to see. You saw a real man, behaving like a real man, and experiencing the joy of true manhood. Don't do anything that will cut yourself off from having that kind of experience." Every teenage boy in the audience straightened, and George realized they had just heard the most memorable lesson on chastity that they were likely to receive in their lives. Darrel never talked about his own brief and wild marriage in his teens. What dreams for children had he given up along with that marriage?

So many people wanted to talk that the meeting went overtime. Finally, George leaned over to Jim. "I want to say something, and then we'd better end," he suggested. Jim nodded. George rose and walked to the pulpit.

"Brothers and sisters," he said, "I have prayed fervently for an outpouring of the Spirit this morning, and I know you have felt that cleansing, bonding spirit of love among us. We are of one heart today. This experience is our ward family's experience. Let us not let any gossip about Colleen cross our lips. Colleen will need our support, not just today, but in the months to come. Don't treat her as a person with a handicap or a disease. Interact with her normally as you have always done. Let her make up her own mind about the baby. I know the Lord will bless her in that decision. I know each of you would like to speak, but we must close."

Following the closing song and prayer, people crowded around Colleen and her family. In the arms of Jocelyn Smith, Mariah finally allowed her tears to flow. Colleen stepped out to meet Marjean, reaching to embrace her. George gave his thirteen-year-old daughter Susan a special hug as he left the stand, feeling a renewed commitment, not only to Colleen but to all of the youth in the ward as they faced their temptations.

Discussion

All of us commit sins or transgressions. As John said, "If we say that we have no sin, we deceive ourselves, and the truth is not in us" (1 John 1:8). It would be required in the millennial world that people would completely repent and be pure before the Lord. John further promised that if we confess our sins "he is faithful and just to forgive us our sins, and to cleanse us from all unrighteousness" (1 John 1:9). There is a process of repentance that the Lord has outlined—that we confess our sins and forsake them.

Colleen Dalton and Alex Eastman have both committed a grievous sin in violating the law of chastity. As a result, they will become parents. Alex, however, is denying the responsibility of parenthood, something he is biologically free to do because the burden of pregnancy is borne exclusively by Colleen. Although Colleen has the legal option of requiring him to recognize and support the costs of the pregnancy, the real issue is Colleen's repentance. When and if Alex repents is a matter between him and God, and Colleen is wise not to invest her energy in trying to control his behavior.

Her own situation is complex enough. Colleen must repent for her sexual transgression—and it is important to note that this repentance would be required whether she was pregnant or not. Unchastity is the transgression, not "getting caught." She confesses her sin to the bishop and has already forsaken her transgression. Thus, she is truly repentant before the Lord. Next is the issue of the Lord's forgiveness. He has indicated that he is prepared, even eager, to forgive the repentant and sorrowful transgressor. Finally, there is the question of the forgiveness of Colleen's family, friends, and ward members.

There is no question that Colleen is sorrowful for what has occurred, but her godly sorrow developed when she considered the consequences of this pregnancy. It is understandable, though wrong, that she did not confess her act of fornication but waited until she was fairly sure she was pregnant. Denial and hope are powerful human emotions. But in the case of sexual transgression, the Lord has indicated that lust and unmarried intercourse constitute the sin. To have been truly consistent with the counsel of the Lord, Colleen should have gone to the bishop immediately after she and Alex had committed fornication.

But the Lord's mercy and willingness to forgive all people in all circumstances, save murderers and sons of perdition, encourage Colleen to hope for forgiveness. The bishop has the right to act for the Church as far as Colleen's membership being jeopardized is concerned. He correctly appraises Colleen's repentance and has the right to assure her that she is forgiven as far as the Church is concerned. If she were considering the idea of an abortion, it would have been his responsibility to counsel her in serious terms about the consequences of this action, since the pregnancy is not apparently life-threatening and did not result from rape or incest. Under such circumstances, if Colleen had decided to seek an abortion, her membership may have been imperiled.

After her visit with Bishop Pratt, Colleen courageously confesses her situation to her mother. Fortunately (unlike many youth in the same predicament), she was confident of the love and forgiveness of her mother.

Her decision to tell the people in the ward in a public meeting, rather than going away to have the baby or telling a few people privately and letting the word spread, has the precedent of tradition. Public confession for transgressions of various kinds was not uncommon in the nineteenth-century Church, probably based on the counsel given in the Doctrine and Covenants: "And if thy brother or sister offend many, he or she shall be chastened before many" (D&C 42:90). In contemporary policy or practice, however, nothing requires Colleen to confess before the ward. Her courage and desire for honesty lead her to choose this method of bringing her circumstances to the ward's attention; and her trust in the ward members' charity is fulfilled. In a true millennial spirit, the other members give Colleen their complete forgiveness.

Some might feel that forgiveness is not quite appropriate on the part of ward members. Has Colleen really wronged them? She has certainly not injured them in the way that her actions have injured herself. However, such a view overlooks the network of mutual responsibility and care that exists in a ward. In any community bound together by shared covenants, standards, and expectations, commitments and responsibilities are also mutually shared. When one member violates that commitment and breaks the community standard of behavior, an injury has been done to the whole body. Colleen has acknowledged both the shared bond and the shared standard of behavior in asking for forgiveness; the ward acknowledges both the bond and their own violated expectations in extending forgiveness. For the other young people, perhaps the most important lesson is an increased feeling of responsibility for their behavior, not only to themselves and to their families but also to the entire ward.

The bishop acts appropriately in helping Colleen work

through this difficult personal situation. He listens and understands without condemning. He not only gives Colleen empathy, emotional support, and the spiritual strengthening of a blessing, but also helps her with the practical matters of a confidential medical examination and offers to go with her to talk to her mother, her family, and Alex's family.

Mariah's feelings are naturally mixed. In addition to her love for Colleen and pride in her daughter's maturity, she sorrows over the difficult circumstances facing her, experiences again some negative feelings left over from her divorce, and realizes that she has emotional and spiritual work to do on her own if she is to be a support to Colleen and to provide appropriate leadership in her home. In all cases, both Mariah and the bishop honor Colleen's agency.

Not much is said about Alex. His decision not to remain involved with Colleen removes him from the relationship. Because Alex is not a member of the Church, the bishop has no jurisdiction over him. It may appear that he is getting off scot-free in the situation. Certainly our culture tends to blame the young woman more than the man in situations of unwed pregnancy. But the violation of the moral law is certainly as much Alex's responsibility as Colleen's; and he must, in the eternal economy of things, deal with his transgression.

However, Alex's repentance or the lack of it is not Colleen's responsibility. Instead, the relevant situation is that she, her family, the bishop, and the other ward members must also come to the point of forgiving him, if they are to be truly consistent with the teachings of the Lord. The Savior tells us, "pray for them which despitefully use you" (Matthew 5:44). Alex and his parents have "despitefully used" Colleen and Mariah, and the Christian response must be for Colleen and Mariah to pray that they may forgive Alex and his parents.

Should Colleen keep her baby or place it for adoption? This is a very difficult question. In my own family, we have seen the blessings of both decisions. In one case, the mother's choice to keep the child was a courageous act of love. In another case, great joy came into our family when a baby was received through adoption. But as Colleen, the bishop, and Mariah understand, the final decision is Colleen's, for she will bear the heaviest burden of consequences. Others must be ready to forgive, love, and support, without in any way glamorizing her situation, condoning the sin, or pretending that the situation does not call for repentance. Determining whether Colleen's repentance is acceptable is not, however, within the stewardship of ward members. Only the bishop has that responsibility.

The transgression in this scene involves intense emotions. Colleen's repentance is unusually public. However, the processes of repentance and forgiveness are universal regardless of the transgression. Everyone sins. Everyone must be allowed the opportunity to repent. And everyone must forgive others. How often? Even seventy times seven. Will people sin in the Millennium? Not through the influence of Satan; however, we are told that the individual "that knoweth to do good and doeth it not, to him it is sin" (James 4:17). It is possible that people may still lack strength to translate their knowledge into action, even in the Millennium; but I feel great hope and joy in the idea that repentance and forgiveness may be millennial processes as well as mortal ones.

12

Managing Interpersonal Conflicts

And if thy brother or sister offend thee, thou shalt take him or her between him or her and thee alone; and if he or she confess thou shalt be reconciled (D&C 42:88).

Therefore if thou bring thy gift to the altar, and there rememberest that thy brother hath ought against thee;
Leave there thy gift before the altar, and go thy way; first be reconciled to thy brother, and then come and offer thy gift (Matthew 5:23–24).

The Principle

Almost every leader in the Church or any other human organization has been faced with the uncomfortable situation of being caught in the middle when others are having disagreements or conflicts. These conflicted persons come to the leader for help, each usually wanting the leader to side with him and to take some action that will benefit him and diminish the other. What constitutes effective leadership when the leader is a third party to the interpersonal conflicts of others?

First, it is important for the leader to understand the problem. This means listening to both parties with an open ear and an open mind—not beginning with any favoritism or bias toward one party or the other. Second, it is also important that the leader not allow these persons in conflict to transfer the problem to the leader by such comments as, "What are you going to do about it?"

Third, the leader's role is to help the two in conflict to work through *their* problem and find a livable compromise. Sometimes just listening and reviewing correct principles with one or both parties may be enough. Sometimes the leader can help by getting the two combatants together on neutral territory, by encouraging them to articulate their own positions and understand each other's feelings through reflective listening, and then by helping them propose solutions and agree on a plan of action. It seldom happens that both parties have equal power in the situation; age, gender, callings, or Church experience frequently tilt the balance in one direction or another. The leader can, by asking questions and providing an outside view, assure that the solution really is a mutually satisfactory one that guarantees the dignity of both parties.

Another option in some cases is that the leader can be a traveling envoy—visiting each party, helping them get an insight into the situation, and preparing them to take their own actions as they resolve the issue between them. This is a difficult approach, since there is only a fine line between asking questions and taking messages—and virtually no line at all between carrying messages and getting caught in the middle.

It is very difficult to follow the Savior's commandment to love our enemies and do good to those who despitefully use us. Not only should we be loving individuals in our own right but we should unilaterally seek reconciliation if we remember that someone has reason to have hard feelings about us. Furthermore, if someone has offended us, it is our responsibility to go to that person and discuss the matter with the intent of becoming reconciled.

It is both easy and ordinary to develop negative, even bitter, feelings toward others. It is also common for us to reciprocate, even retaliate. We love those who love us and treat curtly or disdainfully those who, in our judgment, have committed an offense against us. Jesus called this the old law: an eye for an eye and a tooth for a tooth, which is what reciprocal behavior entails. If we are to live millennially, we must overcome this human propensity and learn to love our enemies—and that includes those whom we think have enmity toward us, or we toward them.

The Plainville Second Ward, even though trying to live on a higher plane, must still deal with the inevitable though unfortunate problem of hurt feelings. Such situations arise simply because of living and working together. Following is a situation in the ward that shows this pattern: someone is offended, but the Relief

Society president exercises leadership by helping the two persons
involved to resolve the conflict.

Plainville Second Ward:
Interpersonal Conflict

The phone rang on Tuesday afternoon, just as Jocelyn Smith,
the Second Ward Relief Society president, walked into her house
from her seven-to-three shift at the county hospital. As she
shrugged out of her coat, she scooped up the phone with the ease
of long practice. An urgent and somewhat angry voice said: "Jocelyn, this is Vivian Hale. I need to see you as soon as possible.
When could we get together?"

Calmly, Jocelyn said: "I just got back from the hospital, but
I'll be going out visiting this evening. If you like, I could drop by
your house about 7:30, okay? Fine. See you then."

She hung up her coat, turned up the furnace, and checked the
mail before her eighteen-year-old twin sons drove up in the
pickup. Between reading a letter from her daughter Ellen about
baby Shauna's bronchitis, making dinner, deciding with her husband, Russell, whether to sign up for the travel-lecture series at
the county museum, and getting Stuart and Sterling fed and off to
wrestling practice, there wasn't much time to wonder what problems Vivian might be having

Leaving Russell cheerfully cleaning up the kitchen with long
pauses while he watched the Trailblazers dodge the Phoenix Suns,
she uncomplainingly put on her coat and went out to visit La-
Verne Kershaw, who had come down with the flu. She found the
old woman sneezing but feisty, then drove over to Vivian and
Glen Hale's home, knocked on the door, and was admitted by Vivian, who was still obviously upset.

"Whatever is the matter, Vivian?" Jocelyn asked at once, even
before she gave Vivian her coat. "I can tell that you're really in
turmoil."

Vivian blurted out: "You've got to change my visiting teaching assignments. I absolutely will not visit Barbara Wilson any
more."

"Let's sit down," suggested Jocelyn, moving ahead of her into
the living room. "Tell me, what's caused this feeling?"

"Alice McIntyre called me. She said that Barbara Wilson had told her I had said—well, never mind, but it was terrible. Barbara's such an awful gossip, and everyone knows it, but I can't stand her spreading stories about me around the ward."

"Alice wouldn't have told you unless she felt it was important for you to know," Jocelyn observed, "so it must affect your family somehow. I think you'd better tell me what Barbara was supposed to have said about you. Or was it about your family?"

Vivian shot her an uncomfortable glance. "Well, Alice said that Barbara said that I said the play the activities committee is putting on is pretty elementary and that Donna and Janice are too advanced to be in it, and that I then went on to say that most of the ward programs weren't very high quality. She also said that I was complaining that there are favorites in the ward who get to do all the important things. Well, Jocelyn, I never said any of these things."

Jocelyn probed gently. "Of course not, but it doesn't seem likely that Barbara deliberately lied about *all* of this, does it? Is there any way she could have gotten a mistaken impression?"

Vivian responded, "Oh, sure. You know how Barbara is. During that ward birthday party two weeks ago, I was helping to clean up in the kitchen. A bunch of us were there, and so was Barbara. You were out by the serving tables making food baskets to send out to some of the people who were sick, weren't you?"

Jocelyn nodded.

"Well, we were all talking about this and that. I said my girls were very busy with the school orchestra, and I wasn't sure they'd have time to try out for the ward play. Lily Butler said she hoped it would be better than last year. She'd written last year's script and said she'd never felt so inept in her life. We were all teasing her about taking two trips to Atlanta to do research on writing Southern dialect. Then David Chun came through carrying something and said it was going to be tough to get the right romantic leads since Dennis Shumway was on his mission and Traci Pixton was in college. Somebody—I think it was Marsha Harvey—said those two had had the leads for three years in a row and she thought they were maybe interested in each other. Then Ada said, 'Well, if they are, I hope he writes her longer letters than *we* get!' and everybody laughed."

Vivian shrugged, still vexed. "Nobody was accusing anybody of anything or even complaining. We were all working together and laughing and just making conversation. Barbara wasn't part of it, but she was listening. She distorts everything and then blabs to anyone who will listen to her. I just don't want to go visiting in her home and pretend that everything is just fine when I know I feel very resentful toward her. So will you please assign me a new sister to visit?"

Jocelyn Smith was troubled. She knew that Vivian was being no more than truthful in describing Barbara Wilson's tendency to gossip. But Barbara was also one of the most generous women in the ward and would help anyone in need. What kind of a relationship could Vivian and Barbara ever hope to have if Vivian simply avoided the woman instead of dealing somehow with her feelings?

Slowly, she said, "Vivian, I understand why you're upset. Before we make a change, I feel that I need to think about this—to pray and get a better sense of what to do than I have right now. Would you mind waiting for a few days? I promise that I'll get back to you before next Wednesday, and we'll discuss it again."

Somewhat reluctantly Vivian agreed. Over the next few days, Jocelyn prayed sincerely and thought often about the situation. She considered briefly calling Alice to get her version of the transmitted report, but Vivian's version sounded so exactly like the banter over work during a ward project that she accepted the report without question. Besides that, she had known Alice for fifteen years. Alice was the last woman in the world to tattle on someone or retell gossip; quite obviously she had told Vivian for the precise reason Vivian had reported: she thought Vivian should know.

Jocelyn read again the scriptures that described dealing with hurt feelings, injuries, and even enmities. She kept coming back to Doctrine and Covenants 42:88: "And if thy brother or sister offend thee, thou shalt take him or her between him or her and thee alone; and if he or she confess thou shalt be reconciled."

She felt strongly that Vivian needed to try to follow these instructions. Otherwise the thought of Barbara Wilson would be a dark spot on her heart for a long time. Would they ever work willingly together? Would it even become something of a feud? She decided to try to get Vivian to deal directly with Barbara about the feelings she had and her perceptions about the reported remarks.

She called Vivian Saturday morning and arranged to run over in a few minutes. Vivian was much less agitated but still demanded as soon as Jocelyn came in, "Are you going to take Barbara off my beat?"

Again, Jocelyn asked patiently, "Why don't we sit down for a few minutes? Yes, I'm willing to do that; but I've thought and studied and prayed about your situation. I feel strongly in my mind and heart that there is something you should do before we make any changes in assignments. I know this will sound difficult, but hear me out. You know that Bishop Pratt has asked us to try to live the highest laws of the gospel. Can we read together what seems to be the law for dealing with offenses?"

Willingly Vivian brought out her triple combination, and together they read the relevant verse in section 42. "Okay, okay," Vivian said. "I get the point. If someone offends us, we need to go directly to that person and try to work things out ourselves. But I don't want to. I wouldn't know what to say. I'd be so upset, I think I'd either get mad or cry or both."

Jocelyn had thought Vivian might say this. "So it isn't that you don't *want* to follow the Savior's instructions in this matter, but that you don't think you're capable of doing it correctly?" she queried.

Vivian nodded glumly.

"Let me rehearse with you what to say and do," Jocelyn offered. "If you get to the point of feeling comfortable, would you be willing to go?"

Somewhat reluctantly, Vivian agreed, and Jocelyn began to ask her how she'd begin, coaching and switching to a little role-playing by pretending to be Barbara.

"I don't know," Vivian muttered, still not totally convinced. "It seems to go okay with you, but you're not Barbara. That could be a whole different experience." She sighed and squared her shoulders. "But you're right. I know this is what I'm supposed to do and that this is the right way to try and solve the problem. I wouldn't feel good now if I didn't give it my best shot."

"That's the spirit," encouraged Jocelyn. "And I promise, if things don't work out, I'll change your assignment."

"I'm going now, before I lose my nerve," Vivian announced. "Glen," she called downstairs, where the power saw was whining, "I've got to go out for about half an hour. Can you keep an eye on Val and Reed? They're doing calisthenics in our bedroom, and I don't want them jumping on the bed. Nick's at his Sunday School party."

"Sure, honey," Glen called back.

"Wish me luck," said Vivian to Jocelyn.

Jocelyn walked outside with her, feeling proud of the woman's courage.

But it was a nervous Vivian Hale who rang the Wilson door-bell ten minutes later. Barbara answered the door, her hands covered with bread dough. "Come on in and sit down," she invited. "I'll just finish kneading this while we talk. What's it about?"

Vivian sat down at the table and took a deep breath. "Barbara, I heard from another woman in the ward something that you said *I* said. I felt very offended, and at first I was just going to try and avoid you; but I didn't feel that that was the way the Savior would want me to behave. I thought it would be better if I came and talked with you."

Barbara stared at her, her round face a picture of astonishment, and sank into a chair. "Vivian, you're really upset! I don't know what you heard, but I assure you I never said anything that was meant to hurt you or offend you. Who was it? What did she say?"

It was a natural question, and Jocelyn had included it in the role-playing. Vivian felt more at ease as she answered: "Barbara, I don't think it's too important who the person was, and I recognize that she was partly at fault for passing on something she had heard. It would have been better if she had said nothing at all or if she had come and talked with you. But this is what she told me." Vivian then summarized the information.

Barbara, agitated, began to pick the dough off her hands. "Vivian, I'll admit that I've told some people about the conversation in the kitchen after the birthday dinner and maybe I read between the lines a little about why people said what they said. And I probably said you were there, but I honestly didn't say *you* had said all of those things. Now, someone may have misunderstood and thought I was just talking about you, but I certainly was not try-ing to put all of those things on you. I wish people wouldn't go around turning innocent things into big dramas." She stopped and gasped, "What am I saying? That's just what I did!"

Vivian had to smile. She reached over and patted Barbara's floury hand. "Barbara, I really believe you when you say you had no intention of saying anything that would hurt me. I think this is a good lesson for both of us about how passing information might wind up hurting someone without meaning to."

Tears sprang to Barbara's eyes. "Vivian, I'm so glad you came and talked with me. I would have felt terrible if you'd stopped being my friend over such a stupid thing. I'll never do this again, I promise."

Vivian hugged her, flour and all. "Barbara, we *are* friends. This incident is closed—and I mean closed."

She drove back home with a light heart and promptly called Jocelyn. "Oh, Jocelyn," she exclaimed, "things worked out even better than in our role-playing. I think we both learned so much about the problems gossip can create. I was so scared to confront her, but it was a great experience to deal directly with a problem like that rather than running away from it."

Jocelyn said, with real relief: "Oh, Vivian, thank you so much for calling. I've been praying ever since you left, and I'm so happy for you." She laughed and added: "You know, Vivian, it may not be possible for Barbara to become perfect all at once. If she makes a mistake again, you'll know that she doesn't intend to hurt anyone, and you'll know how to talk to her about it. Will you be able to forgive her again if it's necessary?"

"The way I feel now," said Vivian exuberantly, "I could forgive anyone."

"Well," smiled Jocelyn, "if we can all feel that way, it just may be possible for us to help one another reach the celestial kingdom."

Discussion

The difficulty between Vivian Hale and Barbara Wilson is a problem that many have either seen or experienced. Gossip, in one form or another, usually gets back to the persons involved.

Vivian's reactions are human. Her feelings are hurt, and under such circumstances, the usual pattern is to either strike back or withdraw. Vivian has thought the matter over and has decided to withdraw. She calls the Relief Society president and demands a change of assignments. She will not visit Barbara again and she has no intention of trying to become reconciled.

Jocelyn's leadership is important. She listens to Vivian without judgment and without taking sides. In a gentle way, she tries to find out exactly what happened as Vivian understands it. Vivian has a remarkably detailed memory of the casual group conversation, but it clearly seems to have been a pleasant and somewhat random interchange with no malice on anyone's part. At this point, Jocelyn could also talk to some of the other people involved in the incident if she felt the need to gather more information. However, the report of the incident rings true, so she asks for time to think and pray about the situation. She does not want to make a hasty decision.

After prayerful consideration, she goes back to Vivian and recommends the approach of the scriptures. To Vivian's credit, after some coaching and support, she is willing to try. Although Vivian feels awkward and uncomfortable, she not only tells Barbara why she has felt offended by her actions but also communicates that she wants to work the matter through to a reconciliation. Barbara feels wrongly accused and immediately wants to know who has provided Vivian with the information. Thanks to the role-playing, Vivian avoids getting into a discussion of personalities and keeps the conversation focused on the information.

The scene shows some important factors in reconciliation. Barbara is willing to admit that she sometimes "talks too much" and tacitly concedes that she injected some drama into a fairly ordinary conversation to make it more interesting in her report, but she insists that she never intended to hurt anyone's feelings. Vivian willingly accepts Barbara's explanation, even though she knows Alice's dry report is more likely to be accurate than Barbara's imaginative one; she keeps focused on her end—reconciliation—rather than details of accuracy. Thus, she makes it easier for Barbara to promise to try to avoid future problems. The scene ends with the two women's reconciliation, both intellectual and emotional. However, Jocelyn's counsel was wise; despite Barbara's good intentions, she may easily slip into the old pattern again, and Vivian still may be called upon to forgive her again.

Jocelyn's leadership role in this case is as a mediator; she happens to be brought into the conflict because she is the Relief Society president; however, many others who may have no formal position may also act to reduce conflict. When Jesus said "blessed are the peacemakers," surely he had such individuals in mind (Matthew 5:9).

To be a mediator or peacemaker, it is important not to take sides. Parents must often help their children resolve conflicts, but often their goal is simply to end the conflict rather than help the children resolve their differences. Parents may be too tired or too impatient to go through the reconciliation process and may just yell, "Will you two knock it off? I'm sick and tired of your constant bickering!" Such an approach may bring silence, but it does not always bring peace. Although it may be the only recourse a parent feels he has under stress, at another moment when the mother or father is in personal control one of them might try effective peacemaking, following these principles of conflict management.

Yet difficult as it is to help children resolve conflict, the problem for adults is even more gigantic. Our injured pride, our sense of fairness, our disdain for our antagonist, and our fear of potential conflict may all combine to make us avoid confrontation and reconciliation. I know from my personal experience that initiating the procedure of working out a grievance or a difference takes a great deal of humility and courage. But knowing the Lord's counsel in this area, when we find ourselves in conflict with another, we should initiate the reconciliation process ourselves and not wait for a third party to come to our aid.

13

Developing Teenagers

Angels speak by the power of the Holy Ghost;
wherefore, they speak the words of Christ.
Wherefore, I said unto you, feast upon the words of
Christ; for behold, the words of Christ will tell you
all things what ye should do. (2 Nephi 32:3.)

The Principle

In the restored Church, a major assignment for many leaders is
to work with the teenagers in the branch or ward. For many,
working with "the youth" is a terrible task, one to be endured as
heroically as possible and one to escape as quickly as possible.

There are certainly valid reasons why many adults find
teenagers a difficult group to manage. Often they are unruly, talk
too much, are disrespectful to adults, don't want to sit and listen,
ask too many questions, and don't seem to want to be in church.
Yet these same adults know that these hard-to-handle teenagers
will be the leaders in the Church tomorrow (if they don't become
disaffected) and will also turn out to be highly effective missionaries and later husbands, wives, and parents when their turns come.
The question all youth leaders wrestle with is: How do you capture and sustain the interest of these young people so that they
catch the vision of the gospel and find satisfaction in their Church
service?

Although teenagers are restless, have generally short attention
spans, and possess low thresholds for boredom, pure entertain-
ment is not the answer. These teenagers are bright and insightful.
They know when they are not really being challenged. They resent
it when their insights and their contributions are not really re-

spected, when their perspectives are not sought, and when their concerns receive scant consideration. They resist strong impositions of authority that demand conformity and obedience.

In my experience, the most successful alternative is to find ways of involving these youth in meaningful activities that push them to learn and grow and that give them opportunities for significant spiritual experiences. The core of the restored Church is a testimony of Jesus Christ held in the mind and hearts of the members. All parents and adult leaders deeply want to weave testimony into the fabric of young people's lives. Because it seems to be a universal principle that "sacrifice brings forth the blessings of heaven," then service is the way that one truly understands the message of the gospel. As we follow the Savior's path, we gain the Savior's perspective. His redemptive and sacrificial love becomes real for us as we also sacrifice for others. In activities of significant discipleship, we gain a deeper conviction of the correctness of his principles.

In the millennial period, how will young people come to know the Savior? It will be easier then, because Satan will be bound and the evil influences that now abound will be absent. However, as we prepare for the time of the Millennium, we must help our young people develop testimonies in an atmosphere of opposition between good and evil, between good and better, and between better and best. We need to let them work, make sacrifices, make choices, make mistakes where necessary, study the gospel for themselves, and learn for themselves.

The following scene from the Plainville Second Ward shows how Bishop Pratt, after seeking inspiration, devised a plan for implanting a testimony of the Savior in the hearts of the young people in his ward.

Plainville Second Ward: The Teenagers

The group Bishop Pratt worried about the most in getting the ward to implement his millennial program was the teenagers. They were all good kids and, except for a few, were active and faithful in fulfilling their assignments. He knew this and was grateful. But obviously, being active and being faithful about assignments wasn't enough. All winter long, Colleen Dalton's courageous presence was a reminder that it would take more than that. He had no complaints about their teachers. Their leaders were tops. But still, George spent a lot of time looking at the teenagers, spent more time talking to them in the halls, and spent more time remembering the pressures and stresses of his own teenage years as he grew up in Plainville.

He recalled how important it was for him to be popular and accepted at Mountain View High. When he first hesitantly entered those crowded halls, he saw a group of athletes standing together in the main hall, laughing and talking and occasionally teasing one of the girls who were part of the "in" group. If anyone had offered him a place in that circle, a letterman's sweater, and a pretty girl laughing at his jokes in exchange for his soul, he probably wouldn't have hesitated.

By his junior year when he was a reserve halfback on the football team, he was standing in that circle; but he found that this yearned-for status brought with it certain dilemmas. He had always been active in Plainville's little branch and had a developing testimony of the gospel. The branch met in a rented hall. There were just a few active families and a handful of young people his age. At school none of the other Mormons was part of that magical popular group that he admired so much and in which he was now included to some degree. He felt confused, embarrassed, and full of conflict when kids from church wanted him to eat lunch with them or go to a church activity, especially when the lettermen were also partying. He tried to keep the two groups separate, to have church friends and school friends.

In the school group, he found himself in dangerous territory from time to time. A number of the fellows and girls smoked. They didn't pressure him when he refused, but his excuses sounded lame to his own ears. At one party, he made an even stupider excuse when someone passed around a bottle of liquor. Then Rebecca, a pretty sophomore who had moved up from California, stunned him by inviting him to a girl's choice dance. He borrowed the family car and felt quite suave and eloquent when she laughed at his comments, danced so smoothly that he didn't step on her once, and obviously enjoyed being with him. When they drove up to her house, she smiled and said: "I had a wonderful time, George. Why don't you come in for a 7-Up?"

"Why, sure," he agreed eagerly. He was feeling brave enough even to meet her parents. But inside, everything was quiet. Her parents had gone to bed. Somehow he found himself sitting on the couch kissing a very enticing Rebecca and experiencing powerful desires he had never known he had. He pulled away and, mumbling something about having to get up early the next day, almost ran out the door. He was afraid she would laugh at him the next time she saw him, but although she continued to treat him with interest, he never dated her—too fearful of his own emotions. Had he ever talked about these problems with his own parents? Not a chance.

He looked thoughtfully at his own teenagers—Will, a thoroughly decent kid, Susan with her strong mind. What did they need? What could he give them? Certainly things weren't going to be any easier for them. They had the same, even more, temptations. Movies, TV, and magazines contained material that was unknown when he was in high school except in smutty, dog-eared, worn materials boys secretly slipped to each other. Until there was actually snow on the ground, boys and girls alike wore shorts and tank tops. Society's moral code seemed to accept physical intimacy of all types as the accepted relationship between men and women who were not married. How could he get the group of teenagers in the ward to reject the culture of their school peers and band together, adhering to a set of standards that would be radically different from the world?

It was March. He had been bishop for ten months and had gone through the teen interview cycle for three quarters. He knew that kids wanted answers they could understand and respect. They wouldn't accept the law, no matter who laid it down, unless it made sense to them. Why is premarital sex wrong if people really love each other, and they're careful not to get pregnant? What's wrong with French kissing? Why can't you make out? Why is hard rock "bad"? He'd had enough of these questions thrown at him. He wished he'd been better at fielding them. Had his inadequate defense made it easier for Colleen Dalton to think that being in love would somehow make things right?

He also knew that these young men and women came from good homes, were moved at times by the Spirit, and would bear their testimonies at a youth testimony meeting. It was literally as though they had an angel on one shoulder and a devil on the other, each trying to gain control. Could they commit themselves to their spiritual sides more completely than he had done when he was that age?

What had made the difference in his own life? He'd always wanted to go on a mission and it had been a steady goal in his family. Although he probably would have backed out if he'd had a good excuse when he actually turned nineteen, there was no good excuse and he found himself in the New England Mission. He had always been active in the Church and had borne his testimony a few times before his mission, but it was a frightening experience to be among people who rejected him and his message. One minister had called him a "teacher of the devil's doctrine" and had told him to go back home and stop deceiving the people. In his anxiety and desperation, he had begun to study the scriptures as he had never done before. As he read the message of Alma to Corianton, its significance burned into his mind and heart for the first time.

Alma 42 was like a personal revelation, and he saw clearly for the first time the absolute necessity of the atonement of Christ. He was filled with gratitude as he realized how the need for a Savior had been foreseen from the beginning. When the plan of free agency was chosen, God knew that human beings would be unable to obey all of the laws of God. The law of justice would demand that human beings pay the penalty for their own sins, since each sin had a penalty attached. The law of mercy would allow the Savior, sinless and not under the demands of the law of justice, to suffer the penalty for erring humans if they would repent of their sins and accept his atonement. It was this testimony of the atonement of the Savior that Bishop Pratt knew was the foundation of this commitment. If this was true for him, then perhaps the key would be to help these young people in their teenage years to come to a full understanding of Christ, to accept him as the Savior and want to be like him.

As he went about his duties, he found himself pondering that question. How could he get anyone to understand and accept the Savior and his atonement? Everything he knew about this process indicated that an individual had to have a desire to know, had to study and pray about the matter, and had to be free from grievous sin. Bishop Pratt prayed diligently, asking the Lord to inspire him so he would know what to do for these young people. After one session of prayer, late at night, he suddenly awoke, for there had come into his mind the clear program that he should follow.

As the head of the priests and the Laurels, he as the bishop would teach a series of lessons to the sixteen-, seventeen- and eighteen-year-olds on the meaning of the life of the Savior. They would then be asked to prepare these same lessons and teach them to the fourteen- and fifteen-year-olds. It would then be the responsibility of this age group to teach the lessons to the twelve- and thirteen-year-olds, and they, in turn, would go into the Primary and teach the same lessons to the eleven-year-olds who were preparing to graduate from Primary. Their advisors—both men and women—would help them prepare the lessons, but the young people would do the actual teaching.

In his heart, the bishop knew that he had to get the young people to study things out in their own minds, to have the message of the Savior's mission clear enough in their understanding that they could teach this to others. He knew that if they would study and pray and teach with the Spirit, they could have a personal testimony of the Savior of the world.

He called up Jeff Burns. "Find out when the next joint planning meeting for the Young Women and the Young Men will be held, will you, Jeff?" he asked. "Find out if I can preempt the meeting."

"I know the Young Women officers and teachers are meeting on Tuesday for a planning session," Jeff responded promptly. "Brenda's the secretary. But from what she said, I don't think the Young Men presidency is doing the same."

"Maybe we'd better set up a separate meeting," the bishop said thoughtfully. "Ask if I could come half an hour earlier or half an hour later and get the young men in on it."

Jeff had it arranged by the next day. The Young Women's presidency was more than pleased to postpone their planning session in favor of the bishop's meeting, and the Young Men officers and teachers agreed to attend.

Bishop Pratt felt a strong, steady glow of warmth come over him as he looked into the faces of these people who worked so hard on behalf of the youth. When he described his plan, they supported him with enthusiasm. On Sunday, they arranged a combined meeting of the five priests and four Laurels; again Bishop Pratt explained his plan and asked them for their support. He could see their willingness, but also a certain amount of skepticism.

Seventeen-year-old Stuart Smith raised his hand and asked, "Why us and not the regular adult teachers? You'd think they'd know a lot more about Jesus Christ than we would."

Bishop Pratt answered: "I've been impressed that you will be blessed with deeper insights into the gospel through the process of teaching. I also think that it's going to have more impact on the teachers and Mia Maids if you teach them than if the adults teach them." He paused, his eyes resting on the eager face of his own son, seventeen-year-old Will. "If we're going to live like a millennial ward, then all of the youth need to be committed to the Savior, and the Spirit has indicated to me that this is the best way to commit our young people to the Savior."

Colleen Dalton nodded. "I know how much we all need the Savior as a reality in our lives. I wish someone I respect as much as Ellen Smith or Traci Pixton had taught me about the Savior when I was fifteen."

Seventeen-year-old Brian Bateman was staring silently at his shoes. The bishop wondered what he was thinking. Other heads nodded, but no one, to his mild surprise, made a wisecrack. They worked out a teaching schedule that covered the next four weeks. First, Bishop Pratt, with the assistance of the advisors, would teach a sample lesson. The group of nine young people would work on a sequence of four lessons together: the preexistence, Christ's mortal mission, his crucifixion and resurrection, and the significance of the sacrament. They would prepare all of the lessons together, but two of them would be chosen to actually present the lesson. This way everyone would be involved in preparing the lessons, and most of them would also have an opportunity to teach. When Bishop Pratt left, the advisors were talking eagerly with the young people about the idea of teaching the lessons in family home evening for practice as well.

The next week, Bishop Pratt gave the first lesson: the council in the preexistence, the selection of Jesus as the Savior, the war in heaven, and the difference between the plan of the Father, as supported by Jesus, and that of Lucifer. He bore a strong testimony about the high price that had been paid for agency and challenged the young people to prize it and use it wisely. The next week was April conference, but the young people planned to meet on both Tuesdays and also on Sunday night.

When George casually asked Will, "How's it going?" Will responded enthusiastically: "I think this is really a good idea. The Atonement always seemed kind of dry and ordinary in seminary, but this is really interesting. Ross Martinez was telling us Tuesday how much the idea of Jesus volunteering for his mission meant to him when he learned about it." He added gloomily: "I'll bet those teachers are going to give us a hard time, though. They've got an attitude problem."

George grinned to himself. From running into Loraine Snow he knew that the young people had been meeting after school, too, looking up more references and outlining the lesson. At the next to the last meeting, they drew straws to see who would teach. Sterling Smith and Donna Hale were chosen and went through a practice session, with the other priests and Laurels acting as the class. It sounded good, and they fasted and prayed in preparation for the lesson; but they were still nervous when they went into the actual class. Astonishingly enough, there were no problems. The novelty captured the attention of the teachers and the Mia Maids, Sterling and Donna were both popular in the ward, and the fourteen- and fifteen-year-olds knew that they were going to be teaching the same lesson, so they listened attentively, participated willingly in the discussion, and asked reasonable questions.

It took planning and coordination, but the sequence of four lessons went off as planned, then the teachers and Mia Maids began the same sequence. The deacons and Beehives were especially creative, staging a mock war for the ten- and eleven-year-olds that portrayed the fight between Satan and his one-third and the other hosts in the preexistence. As each age group finished its responsibility, they held a special joint evaluation and testimony meeting. Will had co-taught with Haley the lesson on the sacrament, and there had been a special, hushed reverence in his voice as he blessed the sacrament on Sunday that brought stinging tears to George's eyes as he listened.

The advisors were moved as they reported the testimonies borne by the young people. Gordon Potter, the teachers quorum advisor, summed it up for the ward's fourteen-year-olds: "I looked at kids like Dixon Reynolds and Toni Scott that I didn't think had an idea in their heads besides skateboarding and false fingernails and I'll swear I saw the stripling warriors of Helaman."

The interaction between classes had helped each group to know the younger group better. The bishop then had each set of advisors talk with their age group about how to set a good example and be a positive influence on the younger kids in the ward. They all agreed that they needed to set a good example. The fourteen-year-olds mentioned shyly how "neat" it was when the older kids said hi to them at school. They brainstormed topics to discuss and asked for a fireside on being friends as boys and girls, "without all this dating game phoniness," as fifteen-year-old Janice Hale put it. Kitty Millett, the most popular seminary teacher, led a rousing discussion about friendship. Colleen Dalton, five months pregnant, was there, participating unostentatiously and sensibly with the class. George wondered if there was any end to her courage. Next, the priests requested a discussion on dating, physical affection, and responsibility. Doug Pixton, a doctor in the local clinic with a famous wry wit, conducted a frank and hilarious discussion. Colleen didn't come to that one.

It was easy for the young people to understand the concept of worthiness. Through the experience of learning about Jesus and preparing themselves through fasting and prayer to teach by the Spirit, they knew what that Spirit felt like. It was something they all wanted more of. In their discussions both Kitty and Doug had focused on being sensitive to the Spirit, treating others in a Christlike way, and not offending the Holy Ghost. Gratefully George heard these young people answering their own questions about making out and French kissing by saying things like, "I can see feeling very close to someone—talking and holding hands—and still having the Spirit, but it doesn't seem likely to me that I could keep the Spirit and do those other things."

"I don't want to wonder, when I'm kneeling at the sacrament table, if I'm worthy to be there," summed up Brian Bateman earnestly. The bishop remembered the withdrawn boy, staring at his shoes during the class's first discussion, and felt a faint faraway shiver. Brian had come back from some unknown edge of danger.

"And I don't want to wonder, when I take the sacrament, whether I'm doing it with clean hands," added Tina Quinn.

Bishop Pratt had no illusion that the series of lessons had solved the problem, but it was a beginning: stronger personal faith, a deeper understanding of the Savior's atonement, and a stronger bond of social responsibility for each other. The foundation was laid.

Discussion

Preparing young people for a life of devotion and commitment to the gospel of Jesus Christ is a major challenge to leaders in the Church today. There are so many enticing attractions that vie for the attention of youth. Bishop Pratt, in reviewing his own experiences in high school, recalled his immense desire to be popular and included by the "in group." Yet when the most socially desirable group has standards and values contrary to Church teachings, it often puts the LDS teenager in a difficult dilemma trying to decide how to balance Church standards and peer group at the same time.

George Pratt also knew that his first conscious striving after spiritual things occurred during his mission. When a young man or woman serves an honest mission and dedicates his or her life to the Lord and the service of others, deep conversion takes place. How could he replicate, even partially, the missionary experience in the ward with teenagers before they were called on a mission, especially since some of them, realistically speaking, would probably not serve missions?

He gave the matter much thought and prayer, knowing that the Lord rebuked Oliver Cowdery for "suppos[ing] that I would give it unto you, when you took no thought save it was to ask me" (D&C 9:7). Then the inspired plan came to him that required both study and action of the teenagers. George knew that "faith without works is dead" (James 2:26) and that one must be a doer of the word, and not a hearer only (see James 1:22). Furthermore, only doing "the will of the Lord" will teach an individual the correctness of the doctrine. Rather than trying to entertain the teenagers with fun and games, Bishop Pratt felt strongly that he should involve the teenagers seriously in both studying the life of Christ and in teaching the plan to others. His plan, discussed and approved by the advisors and officers who had to implement it, taught each age group a model lesson, then turned them loose to study and prepare a series of four lessons on the Savior to be presented to the next younger age group. The sequence of preparation and presentation thus lasted for three months, drawing in younger age groups, retaining the attention of the older group, and resulting in positive effects.

Obviously, such a program is not the only way to immerse teenagers in the core concepts of the gospel. The bishop might have used service projects, or a junior missionary program where the young people would team up with the full-time missionaries. But this program, confirmed by the Spirit, seemed most appropriate for the young people in his ward. The issue presented here is clear—how will those who select a millennial path help young people find that path and follow it?

In 1976, I accepted an assignment to teach in a graduate program for the Air Force in Europe. One of the locations was in Athens. Bonnie came with me and so did our three youngest children—then a college-age daughter and two teenage boys. We immediately located the small LDS branch in Athens and enjoyed our attendance very much. The membership consisted of a single Greek family, a few U.S. military families, and a few American families, like ours, that were attached to the military.

At first we were disappointed that there were so few teenagers—only ten or twelve all together. Our daughter promptly became involved in Relief Society, but we feared that our sons would lack the development they would have received in our large, well-organized ward at home. We were surprised and delighted to find that our sons loved this new situation. Every young person introduced himself or herself to our family and welcomed the boys into the ward. Our sons were invited to visit the same international school as most of the other young people, but it was their Church meetings—priesthood and Sunday School—where they spent the most time together.

"Meetings here are sure different," commented one of our boys. "These kids want to be in church. They talk about how to represent the Church to all of their nonmember friends."

Bonnie and I were grateful when the boys were invited to a youth pizza party by the other youngsters, but even more grateful when they returned with a glowing report. All of the young people took the bus to a popular pizza parlor where they ate pizza, played games, told stories, and "fooled around." "You wouldn't believe it," they said. "There weren't any grown-ups there, just the kids. But all of the kids were there, right down to the thirteen-year-olds. The older ones seemed to want the younger ones there and arranged the tables so we could all sit together. One of the older boys said he'd offer the blessing on the food."

This action astounded our sons. It would have never entered their heads to pray in a Provo pizza parlor, but they were chastened by the ease with which these teenagers behaved as Mormons should. In the games and talk, everyone participated. The older ones wanted to hear what the younger ones had to say. Each felt a real part of the group. They wanted to be together, and they felt responsible for each other. That was sixteen years ago, and our sons still speak, almost with reverence, of a millennial-like experience with a group of teenagers in Athens.

While this experience is not the same as the scene in the chapter, I became convinced that young people will respond to others of different ages if given a chance. They will willingly and lovingly become their brothers' and sisters' keepers. I believe that they basically want to be good themselves and want to help others develop a testimony, go on missions, and marry in the temple. Although practical considerations make the current age groupings convenient teaching units, it also makes it hard for the young people to learn from each other except as family members or friends of the family. In the Millennium, perhaps the Church will have a similar structure for its youth; but if so, it will certainly be true that we will find other ways for young people to be deeply committed to helping all others like them in the ward.

14

Competition: Win/Win Versus Win/Lose

Love your enemies, bless them that curse you,
do good to them that hate you, and pray for them
which despitefully use you, and persecute you
(Matthew 5:44).

The Principle

In almost every industrialized country, a culture of competition has developed. It influences almost every aspect of life. Children compete in families to see who will get dressed first or get their work done fastest. Students compete for grades in schools. Athletes compete for a position on the team so they can compete with other teams. Businesses compete with each other for market share and profits. Even in the Church, we sometimes see missionaries competing to see who will get the most baptisms, athletic teams competing between wards, and quorums competing in some stakes to see who has the greatest attendance at stake priesthood meetings.

In contrast, it seems that during the Millennium, where everyone presumably will be committed to the values of loving his or her neighbor and doing good to those who are seen as the "enemy" or the competition, the spirit of competition will no longer be a primary motivational force. How will leaders deal with the matter of competition? It will be important for leaders to have new visions about managing relationships with others who may be seen as competitors. A win/win orientation must replace the old win/lose notions. This means that all leaders will strive to see that, as they interact with "the competition," the goal will be to have everyone win, and not some win while others lose. Everyone wins when each group is competing only against its own past performance. Everyone wins when he or she can do more for the other group or have a better home/visiting teaching record this month than the month before.

During the Millennium, pure competition will probably be replaced by actions based on love and service. But as we enter the millennial path, leaders must start now to develop new attitudes while old competitive activities still exist. The scene below from the Plainville Second Ward is about ward basketball. From my years of experience, probably nothing presents competition in the Church in a worse light than the athletic program. See how the coach of the basketball team tries to get his team to shift from a win/lose orientation to one in which they all try to win as they honestly attempt to love the "enemy."

Plainville Second Ward: Ward Basketball

Gary Hart sat in his favorite easy chair, but he was not reading the newspaper, watching TV, or working the crossword puzzle. Normally these were his favorite relaxations after the kids had gone to bed and Laura was busy with her own projects. Gary was thinking about the basketball game schedule he had just received from the stake.

Since he had been the ward coach for the past two years, Gary had a rather clear and unromantic view about the range of wild, unexpected actions that were bound to occur at these games. Church basketball was often more like a tag team wrestling match than a ball game. Players fouled each other and claimed innocence, yelled at the referees, and sulked on the bench. The crowds of members acted more like crazy people than Saints. Gary wondered how in this world it would be possible to follow the bishop's vision about a Zion-like ward in the area of ward basketball. He just could not see his team, particularly in the heat of the contest, loving the "enemy," doing good to those who despitefully used them, blessing them that cursed them, or turning the other cheek.

He began to think through his alternatives. One, he could resign. He could tell Bishop Pratt that he would even serve on the Boy Scout committee if he would take him out of this impossible situation. Two, he might tell the bishop to cancel basketball. After all, there probably wouldn't be any basketball in the Millennium; people would be too busy doing temple work. Three, he could tell the players to just stand around and be nice and let the other team always win. But he knew they wouldn't stand for that. Finally, he considered the toughest alternative—to play as hard as possible but to behave entirely as a team of Saints should.

If he accepted this last possibility, what would this mean to the ward team? He thought through the list: accepting every ref's decision gracefully and cheerfully; avoiding deliberate fouls; complimenting other players on good plays; playing together as a team, with no one player trying to grab the glory; meeting team commitments by showing up on time for all practices and games; cheerfully moving off the floor so everyone got a chance to participate; admitting mistakes; being glad when a teammate made a good play; never blaming or complaining if someone else made a mistake or a costly error; and getting the ward spectators to cheer the good plays of both teams; not yell at the referees, and be gracious as winners and as losers. He groaned.

It seemed like an impossible task. The men who played on the team were all good men. Most were Church active. Two inactive senior Aaronic men and one nonmember were key players. Gary was not sure they would even understand what he was trying to create—a good basketball team that lived the gospel fully on the playing floor. Did he?

But after weighing all the alternatives, Gary knew in his heart that the only acceptable thing for him to do was to try. He would never know if his millennial team was possible if he didn't give it his best shot. With some deep feelings of trepidation and worry, he called all of the team members and told them of the first team meeting. It was right after Christmas and they had a month before the first game. He also had it announced in sacrament meeting that anyone who wanted to play on the ward basketball team should come to the first meeting at his home.

To his surprise, twelve men were present. Eight had been on the team before and four were new players. After an opening prayer, Gary told those present about wrestling with the dilemma of creating a millennial team and of all the alternatives he had considered. He then opened it up for a discussion among the players. Did they think it was possible to build a good basketball team that lived complete gospel standards?

The discussion was lively, sometimes heated. The men were

concerned about making a mistake, slipping from their good intentions, dealing with a dirty team from another ward, handling refs that were seen as incompetent or biased, and responding to a hostile crowd. But nobody questioned whether it was a good idea. In fact, Terry Harvey said: "I'd love to see this work. I have a terrible time coaching the basketball team at high school and trying to teach them about sportsmanship when they see something else happening in the stake games. I'd like my own boys to grow up seeing a different view of Church sports."

Finally, it was Les Lynch, the nonmember, that clinched the decision. He had been quiet through much of the discussion but broke into the talk with this comment: "I'm really impressed with the high ideals expressed by Gary, and his hope about what might be possible. I've played with you Mormons for two years now, and I must admit I've often been puzzled over the behavior of players and fans. You're such good people ordinarily; but when it comes to sports, many of you change personalities almost completely. I'd like to try playing basketball the way true Christians ought to play, so I support the coach 100 percent."

There was a moment of silence after that. Some felt a bit ashamed that it was a member of another faith who was showing them the high road. One by one, they all agreed that they would all honestly try to have a season that no one had ever even tried to experience before. They thought of making up a list of rules to guide their behavior, but Terry said: "You can't make up enough rules to cover every situation. Let's have one guiding principle. I read President Kimball's biography, and he loved basketball. I suggest that we all think in our minds whenever any situation comes up, 'How would President Kimball act if he were here?' and then act accordingly."

"Who's President Kimball?" asked Les.

"I'll loan you the book," laughed Terry.

But Gordon Potter interjected, "Why don't we ask ourselves, 'What would Jesus do?'"

Darrel Hodges squinted down his nose. "I dunno," he commented. "I just barely can see President Kimball on the floor, but I can't picture the Savior as a basketball player at all."

"Hey, no big deal," said Gary, smiling. "Take your pick. Use either the Savior or President Kimball as a guide for your conduct during the season. But now we get to the tough part. What do we do when our fine goals break down under the stress of reality?"

They agreed that if any member saw a teammate behaving un-becomingly that they should kindly and privately talk to the team-mate and not criticize behind his back or just ignore the behavior. They also agreed to have a locker-room meeting after every game to assess how they had behaved and to see what they needed to do to improve.

At first, practices were awkward. Players were so concerned about behaving just right that they were afraid to play with any in-tensity. They said "Pardon me" or "Excuse me" for any contact at all. They backed away from trying to rebound, and they kept pass-ing the ball around; no one wanted to shoot and be thought of as the "hot dog."

Gary finally called the players together on the floor. "Men, something is wrong. Our goal is to be a good team that plays with gospel standards. Right now, we are obeying the standards, but we're not a good team. You have got to use all of your skills. Shoot when you have a shot, hustle after the ball, be intense but with good humor; and the opposing team will see that we are try-ing to win but to win with honor."

After that the quality of the play increased markedly, and the players began to enjoy the new spirit they felt in the contest.

As the first real game arrived, every team player was a bit ap-prehensive. Would they really be able to live up to their commit-ment in a league contest? In the team prayer, Lyle Nelson, a sharp-shooting guard, prayed deeply and sincerely that they would play their best and remember how they had agreed to behave.

Gary had put a notice in the ward bulletin inviting all ward members to come and watch the team play but was clear about the standards: "As a team we are committed to observing all of the highest ideals this ward has embraced. We want our fans to be-have as a millennial group would act and show the other team a brand of Christian sportsmanship they will never forget."

At the start of the game, each of the team members of the Second Ward went over to his opposing counterpart, shook hands, looked the other square in the eye, and essentially said: "I hope you have a good game. I'm playing to win, but I want more to play as a real Latter-day Saint (or Christian) should play. Good luck."

There was a puzzled look in the eyes of many of the opposing team players; some even snickered, for they had never heard any-one make a statement like that. The other team controlled the tip-off, and the game began. Everything went smoothly for a time. The score was tied at six, twelve, and fifteen all. Then, Lyle Nelson got free and drove hard for a lay-up. The opposing guard, who had been left behind, tried to catch up, ran into Lyle from behind as he was going up for the basket, and knocked him sprawling on the floor. It looked like a deliberate, dirty foul. In the stands, Kerri Nelson uttered a faint shriek. All of the members of the Second Ward team could feel their anger rising.

Quickly those nearest Lyle helped him to his feet. "You okay, buddy?" Les asked, concerned.

"You could say I was floored," Lyle gasped, irrepressible even with the wind knocked out of him. He walked over to the player who had fouled him. The young man was standing alone, looking both defiant and sad. Lyle reached out, shook his hand, and said loudly, so all could hear: "That was a good try to keep me from scoring. I know you weren't trying to hurt me but just to help your team. Keep up the good work." He smiled, patted the other boy on the arm and said to the referee, "Do I get a foul shot?"

He made the two free throws and then left the game for a break. From then on, the whole quality of the game was different. The play of the other team changed subtly. Instead of the rough, aggressive defense they had been playing, they now began to play cleanly, trying not to foul. When Lyle returned to the game, the fans from the other ward clapped and cheered, and a couple of the opposing players patted him on the back. "Glad you're okay," one of them said.

It was a marvelous game. Every man seemed to play to his best level, and it was a long basket by the guard who had fouled Lyle, with just a few seconds to play, that won the game for the other team. Members of both teams came together and shook hands and congratulated each other. The fellow who had fouled Lyle came over to him and spontaneously threw an arm around his neck. "I'm really sorry I hit you like I did. I've got to be honest. I *was* trying to stop you, and I didn't really care whether I hurt you. When I saw how hard you hit the ground, I felt really bad and I half-expected the teams might get into a fight. I couldn't believe it when you came over and said what you did. Nobody has ever acted like that toward me in any ball game I've ever played. It may sound a little corny, but I'm going to try and act like you did if anything like that happens to me."

Lyle didn't even try to speak. He just put his arm around the other player and hugged him. Members from both wards were mingling with each other and congratulating each other on the fine game from both teams. In the locker room, Gary Hart faced his players. "My dear brothers," he said with emotion in his voice, "I'm so proud of you I can hardly speak. I know we all would have liked to win the game, but the score doesn't reflect who the real winners were tonight. This game was the test, and I know now that it is possible to play good basketball and still live up to our own standards. And I think you all can feel that we'll win our share of games before the season is over."

In the team critique after everyone had showered and dressed, they all expressed their deep satisfaction with the way they had played the game and the positive outcome on the other team and the fans. They had won many games in the past; but as the team members left to go to their homes this time, there was more brotherhood and unity than any of them had ever experienced before.

The rest of the season was not without its interesting incidents. In the fourth game, a referee called a foul on Tom Reynolds at a critical moment in the game. He turned to the referee and protested: "What are you talking about? I never even touched him."

With that, the referee called a technical that nearly cost them the game, but they were able to pull the game out at the end and win. In the team session afterward, they talked about the protest. Tom was still feeling sore about the call and protested, "Can't you even stand up for yourself? I know I didn't foul that player. It was a bad call. Even the Savior stood up to the money changers in the temple."

"Hey, Tom," Gary responded. "No argument on the call. All of us agree it was a bad call, but the refs aren't like the money changers. The money changers were deliberately desecrating the temple, and the referees are just doing their job as best they can. Sometimes they're going to make mistakes."

"Figure the odds," offered Jerry Bowen. "This time the mistake went against us; but if you think about it, we've also had mistakes made in our favor, so it balances out."

They all agreed that, in the future, they would accept the calls of the referees and thank them for their efforts after each ball game.

At another home game, Carol Scott brought her two college-age brothers to watch Chris play. Caught up in the game, they both loyally resented what they felt was a bad call against Chris. "Boo!" they yelled, jumping to their feet. "Open your eyes, ref," roared Jason. "You might see a good game."

Carol tugged on Clint's sleeve. "Sit down, you hotheads," she ordered. "We don't do that."

Confused, they saw that they were the only ones standing or saying anything and reluctantly sat down. "What's the matter," Clint protested. "Don't you stand up for your team?" Fourteen-year-old Toni explained promptly, "Sure we do. It's just that our ward members are good sports all the time and we don't call names."

It was a marvelous season. Every member of the team got considerable playing time in every game. They wound up second in their league and were invited to the regional tournament, where they moved to the semifinals before losing by three points. They received the trophy for being the best sportsmen in the tournament. In the final team meeting, the players talked about the season and what they had learned. They laughed at some of the funny experiences and were sobered as others talked about the season as really a spiritual experience for them.

Almost at the end of the meeting, Les Lynch stood up. He cleared his throat and spoke carefully. "From time to time a number of you in the past have tried to interest me in the Church. I always had my doubts. You were all good guys, but I didn't see that your membership really made any difference in how you lived your lives. This season I saw the difference. You really are able to live up to different standards. If you're willing, I'd like to learn about the Church and to find out what this idea of a Millennium is all about."

That night, as Gary prepared for bed, he marveled to Laura: "Never in my wildest dreams did I ever imagine the joy and satisfaction I feel now about being a coach of a ward team. I used to think it was a really tough assignment, but I wouldn't trade how I feel and what we accomplished with the help of the Lord for any other position in the ward."

Laura smiled and kissed her husband, full of pride and contentment.

Discussion

While opponents in ward basketball may not be a real "enemy," still the elements of being abused, despitefully used, and scorned are often present in a ball game. Such incidents represent a test of one's willingness to "turn the other cheek" and to try and love those who are competitors and, in a sense, enemies.

Gary Hart may be correct in his guess that the Millennium will not feature competitive sports. But if it does, the teams surely will play like the Plainville Second Ward team.

How realistic is this scenario? The Christlike behavior of the Second Ward team had a very positive effect on the opposition in their first game, but people will not always be influenced for good as they experience Christlike actions toward them. However, there is the famous example of the Anti-Nephi-Lehies in the Book of Mormon. The converted Lamanites who had made an oath not to shed more blood knelt and waited while the enemy came upon them and killed them without any resistance until the attackers themselves sickened of the slaughter.

The team does some important things in trying to play Christian basketball. They talk over the whole situation in advance and anticipate some of the conditions they might face. Also, they agree that following each game they will take time to critique their own play to see how they performed and to honestly try to help each other play in a manner consistent with their agreed-on standards.

An interesting consequence of the team's new behavior is that ward members, right down to the teenagers, quickly internalize the new rules and can explain them—and the difference in play means that there are many opportunities for such explanations.

Outside of ward basketball, who are one's enemies? Some are identified kinds of collective enemies—Communists, drug dealers, and criminals. However, even these "enemies" can change, and we saw the attitudes toward communism change almost overnight with the amazing breakdown of Communist governments in the eastern-bloc countries.

Perceived enemies vary at different stages in our lives. For some high school and college students, the "enemy" is a rival school or team. In business it could be a competitor. Some in management see the labor union as the enemy. In any situation involving a scarce resource—a job, a position on the football team or drill team, a scholarship—the competition may be seen as an "enemy." Some see anyone who disagrees with them or tries to control them in any way as an enemy. This would include parents, teachers, bishops, police, or others in authority.

Ordinarily we fight our enemies. We try to avoid them, stop them, hurt them, punish them, or make them avoid us. However, the fundamental challenge raised by the Savior in his Sermon on the Mount is that, regardless who is seen as an "enemy," we should treat them very differently than these normal responses would dictate. If we are to travel along a millennial path, we must love our enemies and treat them as we would want to be treated ourselves.

15

Adversity

For all those who will not endure chastening,
but deny me, cannot be sanctified (D&C 101:5).

The Principle

Everyone who holds a leadership position in the Church will sooner or later confront the challenge of adversity. Either they will experience adversity themselves or people will come to them, struggling with deep trials and sorrows, and ask for guidance and support. Adversity, personal trials, and tribulation come in many forms—death, accidents, illness, financial reversals, alienation from a child or other loved ones, loneliness, depression, and sometimes the sinful or hurtful actions of others.

Leaders need to be able to cope with personal adversity and to help others deal with their adversities. Often these situations are complicated by the fact that the suffering is unfair, unmerited, and even incomprehensible. How does a leader help a parent who has lost a baby through sudden infant death syndrome, or a person who has been disfigured in an accident she didn't cause? What do you say to someone who must live with a chronic illness or who has lost everything financially because of the greed of someone he trusted?

It is helpful to know that there are stages common to people who must deal with trials. The first reaction is shock, which brings with it a merciful kind of numbness. It is also very common for the person to deny what has happened, struggling to comprehend the magnitude of the disaster. The next most common stage is anger. It is normal to blame the Lord or doubt that he is just or loving. Sometimes someone will become "stuck" in this stage for a long time and become bitter. A wise and sensitive leader can acknowledge the individual's pain, provide emotional support through these stages, and help him or her move toward acceptance of the inevitable. A final stage is reconciliation—a feeling of peace about the situation and even a sense of growth. Even the Savior "learned obedience" from the things that he suffered (see Hebrews 5:8).

The scriptures tell us that whom the Lord loves he also chastens (D&C 95:1). If we think of chastening as a punishment, then it is hard to understand why some who are apparently truly innocent should be punished. But there is a significant difference between *chastening* and *chastisement.* To be chastised is to be rebuked because of some offense, but to be chastened is to go through a process of being purified or refined. At times, because the Lord loves us, he may both chastise and chasten us. If one is being chastised, the leader's role is to help the person put his or her life in order. However, if a person is being chastened, the leader must help the person understand the purifying and refining role of adversity in one's life.

In either case, the leader must be with the person going through adversity—being supportive, accepting, and nonjudgmental. The leader accepts and reflects back the feelings of the one with the trials but does not necessarily agree with them or take them on. For instance, if a suffering parent rails against God, the bishop doesn't need to agree but instead validates the feeling by reflective listening, saying something like: "You feel very angry at God right now. You don't understand why this had to happen." Then instead of feeding the anger, the leader will try to share a different perspective or hold up the hope of coming to terms in a different way with the emotional turmoil.

In the scene that follows, it is that tower of strength, George Pratt, who faces a time of terrible adversity and it is Phyllis who provides the leadership that helps him through.

Plainville Second Ward: Tragedy

It was Saturday night, the end of a beautiful October day. The Pratt family had spent the day working in the yard together, raking up leaves and pulling up the last of the dying petunias. Darrel

Hodges had driven Colleen Dalton and baby Howard by to say hello, and Colleen reported that her summer of heavy classes at the community college meant she was eligible to apply for a work-study program as an accountant. Vivian Hale had honked as she had taken her station wagon full of Val and Reed and their friends to celebrate after their last Little League game. Will had gone to a movie with the Smith twins and Tina Quinn. The rest of the family had watched a movie on the VCR and then gone to bed. About midnight George and Phyllis surfaced toward consciousness, aware that someone was ringing the doorbell. Phyllis, who woke up faster, was already putting on her robe. "Go back to sleep, George," she said, "I'll see who it is."

She turned on the hall light and moved to the front door with a deep feeling of apprehension. She knew something was terribly wrong. Standing on the porch was a policeman with a serious and apprehensive look. Phyllis said slowly, "Something has happened to our son, hasn't it?"

The officer nodded and asked, "May I come in?" Phyllis opened the door and the officer stepped into the vestibule. "Please sit down, ma'am." He took her arm and guided her to the sofa. "It is my painful duty to tell you that your son, Will Pratt, was killed in an automobile accident about an hour ago."

From the bedroom, George heard the two soft voices, then he heard Phyllis moan. He, too, had that tight, heavy feeling inside that told him that something had happened to their oldest son. As he got up from bed he prayed, "Oh, please Lord, don't let anything be seriously wrong with Will." But when he entered the front room and saw Phyllis crying softly and the officer standing silently by, he knew the worst.

He stared at Phyllis. "Will is dead, isn't he?" It was a statement, not a question. Phyllis could only nod.

He moved toward her and sank down beside her. He didn't seem able to breathe. "What about Tina and the twins?" He sat clinging to Phyllis as if she were the only reality, trying to take in the officer's explanation.

When the young people were driving down the river road toward the Roma Pizzeria, a drunk driver crossed the median at a high speed and smashed head-on into the car. Will was sitting in the passenger seat, and Sterling Smith was driving. Both of them were killed. Tina and Stuart were listed in serious condition at the hospital but were expected to live.

"Can we see our son?" George asked. His tongue seemed thick.

The policeman spoke slowly. "The two boys in the front seat were pretty badly injured. The coroner thinks you shouldn't see them until the mortician—until later." George nodded, his face a blank.

When the officer had gone, Phyllis said: "George, we've got to think. Jocelyn and Russell have lost a son, too; but they'll be at the hospital with Stuart. Peter and Lynnette will be there with Tina. We need to go to them. But there are the other children, too. When should we tell them? How can we tell them?" Her voice rose to an anguished wail and she buried her face in her hands, sobbing. George mechanically put his arm around her, staring across the living room.

In a few minutes, Phyllis pulled herself together and said: "I think we ought to get them up now and tell them, not wait until morning. This is something that we must all face as a family."

George agreed. He could see that Phyllis was thinking more clearly than he. All he could feel was the shattering sense of loss and hurt that whirled inside his mind, roaring, drowning every coherent thought under the wild insistence: "This can't be. It must be a nightmare. Surely we will wake up and find it isn't true."

Phyllis took over. She woke up fourteen-year-old Susan first and had her make cocoa while she roused ten-year-old Tommy and six-year-old Ben from their heavy sleep. She brought them together into the living room, where George was still sitting, and quietly told them: "Something terrible has happened, something that will hurt our family and the whole ward. Will and Sterling Smith were killed in an accident tonight, and Stuart and Tina are badly hurt." While they absorbed the impact, she and George cradled them and told them the details that they knew. All three children were crying.

Tommy shouted, "I hope they send that drunk to the electric chair."

In his misery, George found himself agreeing, but Phyllis said, even as tears flowed down her cheeks: "Tommy, we can't judge that other person. We don't know what caused him to drink and drive. But we cannot allow ourselves to hate him. We must try to forgive and leave any judgment to Heavenly Father."

Phyllis went to the phone. "I'm calling Blaine and Jim," she said over her shoulder. "They need to know. The Smiths and the Quinns need someone with them, but we have to be with our own children. I think I should call Pamela Hardy and Becky Sorensen, too. Jocelyn can't be expected to deal with Sterling's death and Stuart's injuries and still do what the Relief Society president would normally do. The counselors will just have to take over."

They clung together, weeping and praying. Lights flashed against the facade of the house. It was Dean Suzuki pulling into the driveway to be with them. Eventually Tommy and Ben drifted off to sleep again. Jim Butler came by from the hospital an hour or so later, reporting that Tina had a broken collarbone and a concussion. "It's a good thing they were wearing seatbelts," he added. "The car rolled—," he glanced at George's set face and fell silent.

For the next few days, the whole family went through the motions of living. The phone rang constantly, and people from the ward and community almost lined up at the front door to bring food and condolences. Jim and Blaine helped plan the funerals and make the arrangements. Phyllis went to the hospital, where she and Jocelyn clung together, weeping. Stuart was in agony, less from his broken leg and broken ribs than from the loss of his twin. Somehow the decision was made for a joint service.

George moved through the days numbly, acquiescing when Phyllis asked him a question. Nights were the worst. He prayed constantly for a sense of peace, but peace would not come. He found himself having imaginary dialogues with the Lord: "Why did this happen to us? I've tried to do everything you've asked of me. What more do you want? Why take my son? Couldn't you have spared him and taken me? He was so young with his whole life ahead of him. I just don't understand." It was shatteringly painful but still somehow comforting when Will's friends came by with awkward hugs, uncontrolled tears, and stammered words of sorrow.

At the funeral, the meetinghouse was packed with members and friends. John Stratford, the stake president, spoke movingly about the fine and worthy lives of these young men, explaining the mission of the Savior and the promise of the Atonement. Linda Potter sang. Dwight Hall spoke as their priests quorum advisor, his voice breaking. The funeral was lovely and inspiring, but Bishop Pratt felt nothing. He found himself shaking hands mechanically with his own brother and saying, "Thank you for coming." He felt dead inside. Words came from far away and took an immense effort.

He went back to work with a sense of relief at the familiar routine. At Church he attended all of his meetings, conducted affairs, and handled the usual business matters. When Stuart, balancing on crutches, bore his testimony at the beginning of December that he had two missions to prepare for, his twin's and his own, George wept with the rest of the congregation; but the tears brought him no relief. When Tina went back to college, he accompanied Phyllis to give her a poster for her dorm room, but he could not seem to follow the conversation. At odd moments, he found himself paralyzed by grief, his whole being drowned in the awareness of the loss of his son.

Finally, Phyllis confronted him directly with his behavior about six weeks after the accident. They had gone to bed, and George had tried to sleep; but as always, he slipped into memories of the past and bitter feelings when he knew the future would never be the same.

He thought he was lying motionless, but suddenly Phyllis sat up and turned on the light. "George, I know how deeply hurt you have been because of Will's death, but I have lived with a George Pratt for the past several weeks whom I have never known before. Where is the faith that has always been so sustaining to all of us? What happened to your feeling of confidence that, if we trusted in the Lord, all would be well with us? What has happened to you?"

The questions released something in George. He struggled up, leaning back against the headboard, the words spilling out—his feelings of being abandoned by the Lord, that life was not fair, and that he felt he deserved more because of all of his service in the past. Now he was filled with fears and doubts. He felt empty inside, with little to give to anyone. Perhaps he should ask to be released.

Phyllis took his hand. "George, we were all devastated when Will was killed. None of us will ever get over it completely. I prayed and prayed and asked for understanding and peace. A scripture kept coming to my mind: 'Thus saith the Lord, whom I love I also chasten.' I kept thinking that to be chastened meant to be punished, and it made no sense that our son or our family should be punished. But I went to the dictionary and read that one meaning of chastened is to be purified, to be refined, to cause to be more humble or subdued. Then, I read every reference in the scriptures about the Lord chastening his people. It became very clear to me that the Lord is going to put all of us through the refiner's fire. If we cannot endure chastening, it is not possible for us to achieve all of the eternal goals we want as a family. I don't think God arranged for that driver to get drunk and kill our son just to see how we'd take it. It was an accident, a statistic, bad luck, bad timing. But whatever the cause, we have to deal with the fact that it happened. Will's loss is a great test for us. Do we really believe that his spirit is now in paradise? Is the resurrection a reality or a myth?"

George sat unspeaking, feeling drained and exhausted.

Phyllis shook him by the arm, insisting that he look at her. "George, we must meet this test of our faith. You are the priesthood leader in our home. We need your strength and your example. I do, the children do, and the members of the ward do. You've always felt that you received a special calling to help this ward prepare to live as would be required in the Millennium. Did you expect that because you're the bishop you'd be free from your own test? I have received my own witness that our son is safe and at peace. I feel the Savior's love for me, and I know that he loves you. He's with us in this. He feels our grief and grieves with us, but he wants us to accept his love, instead of shoving it aside to drown in sorrow. Please exercise your faith and your priesthood, and regain the spirit of your callings as a husband, father, and bishop."

Phyllis stopped. She wondered if she had said too much—or not enough.

George took Phyllis's face between his hands and kissed her tenderly. "Phyllis," he began wonderingly, "even as you spoke, I felt the darkness lift from my soul. There was light in my life again. For the first time since Will's death, I feel like really praying."

Discussion

Adversity will come to all, if we think of adversity as the test of faith the Lord gives those he loves. The Pratt family was not immune from trials, even though George was the bishop. Bishops are humans going through mortal experiences. They will at times feel fear and doubt. They cannot and should not be expected to provide all of the leadership all of the time. The wife in any healthy marriage provides some of the leadership, blessing the whole family, including the husband, because of her inspired direction. Sometimes even a child takes that role.

The Lord told Joseph Smith that there would be benefits derived from adversity. He said, after describing the trials Joseph would go through, "All these things shall give thee experience, and shall be for thy good" (D&C 122:7). In the normal course of events, George Pratt will be a better bishop after going through his personal Gethsemane. He will be able to understand better the feelings of others who face similar situations and able to offer greater love, support, and understanding.

All of the scenes about Plainville Second Ward have some basis in fact but are usually combinations of several incidents. This chapter is different. I wrote it shortly after I had spoken at the funeral of my nephew, Kirk Dyer, of Portland, Oregon. Kirk was eighteen and had just graduated from high school when he was killed in a car accident. To some extent, this chapter is based on the emotional experiences of my youngest brother, Bob, and his wife, Yvette.

As a parent, I cannot imagine a deeper trial than to lose a child. Yet adversity frequently comes to my loved ones and people around me. A child drowns. A mother suddenly dies of cancer, leaving a family of young children. An effective and energetic businessman suddenly runs into reverses he cannot control and, a few months later, faces bankruptcy court. A beloved seven-year-old develops cystic fibrosis, and the family deals with the knowledge that she will not survive her teen years. A troubled fifteen-year-old runs away from home, and the parents discover that he has been taking drugs for two years. The number and types of trials people face are almost endless. We have been told that this mortal probation is the time of our testing, to see how we will use our agency and how we will meet the tests that come to us.

My whole life experience tells me that all will be tried. In the depths of those trials, it is natural for us to plead to Heavenly Father as Christ did that the bitter cup may be taken away. Seldom is it. But it is true that the bitterness can be taken away. I hope that we can find the strength to respond, as the Savior did, "Nevertheless, not my will but thine" (Luke 22:42). Of all the challenges facing the Saints, in whatever position or situation they find themselves, I believe that there is no greater act of service or love than to help another face adversity. The words of Alma sound the challenge to all who would call themselves "Saints":

> And now, as ye are desirous to come into the fold of God, and to be called his people, and are willing to bear one another's burdens, that they may be light;
>
> Yea, and are willing to mourn with those that mourn; yea, and comfort those that stand in need of comfort, and to stand as witnesses of God at all times and in all things, and in all places that ye may be in, even until death, that ye may be redeemed of God, and be numbered with those of the first resurrection, that ye may have eternal life. . . . (Mosiah 18:8–9.)

16

Putting Your Hand to the Plough

And Jesus said unto him, No man, having put
his hand to the plough, and looking back, is fit for
the kingdom of God (Luke 9:62).

The Principle

The story of the Plainville Second Ward is just a story. However, the principles the ward members try to live are real. They are the revealed will of the Lord to his people. If the Latter-day Saints are to be prepared to live during the Millennium, they must be willing and able to live by every word that proceeds from the mouth of God.

Are the principles so hard to put into practice in the world in which we find ourselves now? Certainly the standards, values, morals, ethics, and norms of acceptable behavior that members of the Church in almost every country of the world experience in the society around them are not consistent with millennial standards. Father Lehi saw in his vision that some would partake of the fruit representing the love of God and then would become ashamed and, because of the scoffing of those around them, would fall away into forbidden paths and be lost (1 Nephi 8:25–28).

Both Lehi and Nephi, who had the same vision, indicated that the only true path is to lay hold of the iron rod, which is the word of God, and cling to it tightly until the goal is reached. Fortunately, the plan of the gospel provides every person with support—teachers, Church leaders, friends, quorum brotherhood for the men, and Relief Society sisterhood for the women. These people will almost always be willing to provide love and help if we will open ourselves to them.

It has been the theme of this book that the great influence for change toward more Christlike living must come from leaders at all levels. They must all share a common vision. They must develop new skills to handle old problems. The leaders will be the role models. They will show the way—not just talk about it.

The members of the Plainville Second Ward are not yet perfect. This story is not how they will live during the Millennium. It is a conceptualization of what it might take for a group of members in one ward to put themselves on a millennial path. That path means living in the world but not being of the world. We are still expected to follow Church programs and procedures that may not be necessary during the Millennium. For example, we still pay tithing, but at some point we must be able to live the law of consecration and be willing to give all that we have to the Lord—not just one-tenth.

There were some risks in entering on a millennial path. In the scripture at the beginning of this chapter, the Lord indicates that if we truly put our hand to the gospel plough, and then turn back, we are not fit for the kingdom of God. There is also the parable of the person who, having been rid of an evil spirit, returned to a wayward path and found himself repossessed by seven devils (see Matthew 12:43–45). Fortunately, there is always the principle of repentance. No matter how often we err, we may still repent and be forgiven.

What does it take to begin a journey along the millennial path? It will take vision, courage, support, and a plan. If we are truly in the last days, the Saturday night of time, then perhaps it is time for those with vision and courage to start a millennial journey in their homes, in a quorum or a Relief Society, even a ward.

And what is the state of the Plainville Second Ward? Read now the results of their ward conference.

Plainville Second Ward: Ward Conference

It has been almost two years since Bishop Pratt introduced the millennial program to the Plainville Second Ward in May. At the annual ward conference in April, the bishop announced that he wanted every president of every ward unit to give a progress report on its journey toward a Zion community.

Sacrament meeting was extended to two hours, so that the entire ward could hear the reports. Brian Bateman, a priest who had just turned eighteen, reported on the work in the Aaronic Priesthood. "I can't believe the change that has come over all of us, both fellows and girls, in our ward this past year and a half," he began. "We all feel like we lost our best friends when Will and Sterling died, but we all feel like we have a lot to live up to, too. I've talked with a lot of our young people, and they are of one mind that the major impact has been our understanding of the Savior and his atonement and what that means to each of us individually. I believe that almost all of us have reached the point where, before making any important decision, we ask ourselves, 'What would the Savior want me to do?' This has led all of us who are priests to plan on going on a mission. We feel we understand the importance of temple marriage and that is a major goal for all of us. Finally, we have been able to feel that all of the Aaronic-age youth are part of one big family. We're concerned about each other, and we've tried to help each other, to talk together, and support each other. It has been the most influential year in my life."

Next came the Sunday School. Kent Simonson gave the report. He told the ward that the greatest change in the Sunday School was how the Sunday School presidency worked with the teachers to improve the teaching. With Ron Hardy's permission, he briefly described Ron's transformation as a teacher, then said: "In every class we've worked with the teachers to help them review their teaching and to plan ways to improve. Sometimes it has meant that the presidency has interviewed the class members to get their suggestions that have been passed on to the teachers. The teachers themselves have met together and shared what has been successful and have helped each other devise better teaching methods. Our teachers have attended a wonderful teacher development class taught by Kitty Millett that is always filled, for she has incorporated into the class all the things we have learned about successful teaching in our own ward. The spirit of cooperation prevails in the Sunday School. People who used to shy away from genealogy now come to our class. The McDougalls will work with them individually to learn about genealogy or family history, starting from the exact point where they are. Everyone in the Sunday

School is dedicated to helping everyone in the ward learn more about the gospel and its application in our lives."

Next was Dean Suzuki, elders quorum president, essentially speaking for the Melchizedek Priesthood, since the ward had so few high priests. His voice was almost awe-struck as he said: "If anyone had told me that we could have built this quorum into a group of real brothers, never having to rely on just a few old stalwarts to do all of the assignments, never having to plead for volunteers, and completing every assignment on time with deep quorum unity, I would not have believed it. I can honestly say that we have interviewed every quorum member personally. We know their concerns and the state of their minds and hearts. We have tried, and I believe we have been successful, to develop a program to help every quorum member—whether it be in employment, increased brotherhood, or help in the family.

"I believe that we finally know how to do effective home teaching. Not only have we consistently been over 90 percent, but I'm convinced that the quality is remarkable. Our reports indicate that real changes have occurred in families because of good home teaching. And you all know what our second season of playing millennial basketball is shaping up to be."

Following Dean, Jocelyn Smith, her always-serene face marked by a new patience, summarized the progress in the Relief Society. In part of her report she observed: "I believe we've always had a close feeling of sisterhood in this ward. Our sisters have always been faithful and committed to the gospel of Jesus Christ. But this year I feel we have moved to a level of spirituality we have never known before. There have been so many wonderful experiences this year that have had significant effects on all of us. The experience of Colleen Dalton tugged our hearts, and we admired her and Mariah and the other children so much. I believe that there has been no spirit of judgment, but only a desire to serve and encourage. And what a joy it was to celebrate with her and Darrel as they became a new family with little Howard.

"I know how grateful Russell and I and our children are—," her voice faltered, "—for the unfailing kindness and support of the whole ward as we still struggle with Sterling's loss. Only my counselors know how I've leaned on them and what a strength they've been to me.

"As wives and mothers we have seen the effect of our ward activities in the lives of our husbands and our children, and it has been wonderful to us. In our testimony meetings, many of our sisters have expressed deep gratitude for the increased devotion of their husbands—how they have become the spiritual leaders in the home. We have had some great experiences with new converts to the Church. How we have learned to love the Bowens! And now Les and Mina Lynch are members. For the first time in my memory, the sisters did not complain about the time basketball took away from the family. In fact, we've been proud to support the team at the games.

"In Relief Society our reports have always looked good, but the reports just do not convey the growth in sisters personally, the growth of whole families, and the increased love of people toward one another. We have learned to understand and appreciate sisters who are different from each other—in age, experience, personal style—and have learned to accept and include everyone."

Lily Butler reported on the joy of working with children once the Primary began focusing on meeting the children's spiritual needs, and Nola Gardner, weeping, testified of the bonds of love that had developed among the Young Women during the past two years.

Then it was George's turn to address the ward. He stood before the congregation with tears in his eyes. In a trembling voice, he said: "Brothers and sisters, my report has been given by those who have spoken before me. You have heard about the state of the Plainville Second Ward. I knew that I had received personal inspiration about what this ward should strive to become. I did not know whether I was capable of approaching such a lofty goal—to begin to live as we surely must in the Millennium. Often I would lie in bed, unable to sleep, wondering if what I asked of the ward would be so grand in scope that if, instead of inspiring you, it would discourage you with what seemed like unreasonable expectations. When our son was killed, it was a terrible time for me. My faith was tested to the limit; and if it had not been for my wife, I'm not sure I would have passed through that greatest trial of my life.

"At every step, I've been wonderfully supported—by my family, the stake president, my counselors, the ward leaders, and, as far as I can determine, every member of the ward. To say that these two years have been thrilling to me would be an understatement. I've never felt closer to the Lord, never felt the Spirit so immediately directing me. We are not extraordinary people. We are just good Latter-day Saints. We are not perfect, but now I believe that we all feel that perfection is possible. Individuals and families have changed. I know that the Lord has blessed us and that he will continue to guide and direct us if we will stay in the path we have entered this year, holding fast to the iron rod.

"My biggest fear is that we will become complacent and, like the Book of Mormon people, live righteously for a time and then slip back into sinful ways. I pray that we will keep the goal of becoming a millennial ward high in our minds and hearts, and that we will be a leaven that will influence the Church wherever members of the Plainville Second Ward will go. This I ask, as I thank all of you. As your bishop, I leave my blessing with you, in the name of Jesus Christ, amen."

The final speaker was President Stratford. When he arose to address the ward, for some moments he looked around the audience without speaking. Finally, he said: "I just wanted to look at a group of people who have accomplished more than I ever imagined possible. When Bishop Pratt first came to me and described his personal inspiration, I was supportive, but I wondered if our people were ready yet to aspire to such a lofty goal. Here was a new bishop in a rather small, relatively new ward, out here in Oregon away from the center of the Church. As the bishop said, we are not any different from Church members in wards all around the world. However, my brothers and sisters, the Spirit clearly tells me that the time will soon come when wards and branches all over the Church will be filled with a millennial spirit, and people will prepare themselves for that great day when the Savior will come again in all his glory.

"You have experienced what I believe it takes to become a Zion community. You have learned to be of one heart and one mind, to dwell in righteousness, and to have no poor among you. First, it was necessary that there be a leader with a clear vision. Second, the leaders in the ward rallied around the bishop and learned of his vision, and each developed his or her own plan to implement that vision in his or her part of the ward. Where there is no vision, the people perish; and where there is no plan of action, a vision can also perish.

"No ward will achieve the millennial state you have identified unless each person says, 'I must do my part to accomplish the vision.' It cannot be left to just a few of the leaders. There have been some common sayings that express what I feel. It has been said, 'I am only one; but I am one and I will do what I can.' And again, 'It is better to light a candle than to curse the darkness.'

"How I love and admire the people of this ward. You have felt the hand of the Lord in your midst. I hope you appreciate the almost miraculous events that have occurred in the past twenty-three months. I promise you that if you will continue to live faithful to your commitment and testimonies of the Lord Jesus Christ, even greater things will occur in your ward, your families, and your personal lives. I say this in the name of Jesus Christ, amen."

Index